MOSAICS
IN
ROMAN BRITAIN
STORIES IN STONE

MOSAICS
IN
ROMAN BRITAIN
STORIES IN STONE

PATRICIA WITTS

First published in 2005 by Tempus Publishing
Reprinted 2007

Reprinted with updates in 2010 by
The History Press
The Mill, Brimscombe Port,
Stroud, Gloucestershire, GL5 2QG
www.thehistorypress.co.uk

British Library Cataloguing in Publication Data.
A catalogue record for this book is available from the British Library.

ISBN 978 0 7524 3421 6

Typesetting and origination by
Tempus Publishing
Printed and bound in Great Britain by
Marston Book Services Limited, Didcot

CONTENTS

LIST OF ILLUSTRATIONS

BLACK AND WHITE PLATES

ACKNOWLEDGEMENTS

The information and ideas in this book have their origins in my doctoral research. I am immensely grateful to my supervisors, Professor Martin Henig and Professor Peter Salway, for their invaluable support and guidance at that time.

Membership of ASPROM (the Association for the Study and Preservation of Roman Mosaics) and ARA (the Association for Roman Archaeology) has not only provided contacts with leading scholars and mosaic enthusiasts but also many friendships. My work has been enriched immeasurably by discussions over a number of years with ASPROM and ARA colleagues, in particular Anthony Beeson, Dr Stephen Cosh, Dr Janne Hill, Dr Janet Huskinson, Dr Ilona Jesnick, Peter Johnson, David Johnston, Professor Roger Ling, Dr David Neal, Grahame Soffe and Bryn Walters, to all of whom I offer warm thanks for sharing information and ideas.

It is also a pleasure to record my thanks to Dr David Smith. He has not only made an outstanding contribution to the study of Romano-British mosaics through his impressive published output but, on a personal level, has always been helpful and encouraging. Robert Field's enthusiasm for the geometric patterns that form the setting for the figured panels, and Elaine M. Goodwin's insights as a professional mosaicist, have widened my appreciation of ancient mosaic art.

For helping with this book by assisting me with access to mosaics and illustrations of them, and for permission to reproduce photographs, I wish to thank: Charles Browne; Mark Corney; Stephen Cosh; Roman Baths Museum, Bath and North East Somerset Council; Tom Tupper and Peter Allison, Bignor Roman Villa; Neville Carr and the Oglander Roman Trust, Brading Roman Villa; Gail Boyle and Les Good, Bristol City Museum; Philip Crummy, Colchester Archaeological Trust; Paul Sealey, Colchester Museum; Corinium Museum, Cotswold District Council; Peter Woodward, David Ashford and the Dorset Natural History and Archaeological Society at the Dorset County Museum; English Heritage; David Rudkin and the Sussex Archaeological Society, Fishbourne Roman Palace; Martin Foreman, Hull and East Riding Museum; National Monuments Record; The National Trust, Stourhead House;

Victoria Newton-Davies, Newport Museum & Art Gallery, and Newport City Council Museum & Heritage Service; North Lincolnshire Council; Mr John Wingfield Digby, Sherborne Castle Estates; Salisbury and South Wiltshire Museum; The Society of Antiquaries of London; David Bromwich, Somerset Studies Library; Somerset Archaeological and Natural History Society; Somerset County Museums Service; St Albans Museums; Winchester Museums Service. All photographs are by the author unless otherwise stated in the caption.

PREFACE

This is the book I wanted to have when I first started admiring Roman remains in sites and museums around Britain. As a childhood passion for archaeology later deepened and focused upon the mosaics, I was keen to know who the characters were in the tessellated scenes that I found so intriguing, what stories lay behind them, and how, if at all, they related to one another. The existing books on the subject, from short guides to scholarly tomes, were useful but always seemed to stop just at the point when they were getting interesting. I had an unsatisfied appetite for more information, was puzzled by contradictory interpretations of well-known mosaics, and was frustrated by the absence of detailed discussion of the lesser known ones.

I first started to research the subject when I undertook a three-year course of evening classes in British archaeology, after which I embarked upon a PhD examining the iconography of all the known figured mosaics of Roman Britain and the contexts in which they were laid. Since obtaining my doctorate, I have continued to research and write about aspects of mosaics as well as studying art history and delving further into the classical texts that relate the myths depicted in the mosaics. These approaches are often the least used but potentially the most rewarding in trying to enhance our understanding of the ideas behind the figured pavements.

Although this book confines itself to the figured mosaics of Roman Britain, I have travelled widely to study comparative material in other countries. Participation in international colloquia organised by AIEMA (l'Association internationale pour l'étude de la mosaïque antique) and ICCM (the International Committee for the Conservation of Mosaics) has provided the opportunity to learn about new discoveries and to have stimulating discussions with friends and colleagues abroad. Although regional styles of mosaic are clearly evident, the most striking conclusion to emerge from studying the Romano-British mosaics in their empire-wide context is the iconographic similarity between mosaics whose geographical spread is wide. The closest parallels, in terms of iconography if not in style of execution, frequently come not from the provinces nearest to

Britain but from North Africa and, in particular, the Middle East. It is against this background that I have sought to interpret the Romano-British material.

Despite the impressive number and quality of mosaics still surviving from Roman Britain or noted in antiquarian records, many of them are little known outside Britain. Even among British archaeologists, there is a tendency to concentrate on a few notable examples. No doubt this is in large part because detailed information is contained within diffuse and sometimes obscure sources. The impressive four-volume study *Roman Mosaics of Britain* by Dr David Neal and Dr Stephen Cosh will go a considerable way to redressing some of the practical problems by collating much of the source material in an accessible form. At the time of writing, Volume I to III have been published, with the final volume in an advanced state of preparation.

The gap I am hoping to fill with this book is to provide an in-depth study of a particular category of mosaics, namely those depicting figured scenes or characters. I have concentrated upon those that are easily accessible in museums and on sites, but it would give a distorted picture to consider these alone. The importance of some lost mosaics, particularly those found at Bramdean, Frampton and Pitney, warrants their inclusion. It would also be inappropriate to leave out some major mosaics currently held in store, such as those from Keynsham and Newton St Loe. Similarly, I have included the Withington Orpheus mosaic and the internationally important mosaic from Hinton St Mary, both now in the care of the British Museum, even though sadly only a small part of each is currently on display.

I have not attempted here to provide an exhaustive catalogue of every known Romano-British figured mosaic, although I am in the course of preparing such a work for separate publication. Rather, this book aims to look in detail at the most interesting examples and to discuss them in the context of their cultural background, especially the surviving body of writing from Greek and Latin authors. It considers the significance of the images to their contemporary viewers, notably the patrons who commissioned them.

The book does not presuppose any knowledge of the subject. It is designed to be read as a whole but has also been structured for reference, especially on sites and in museums where the enquiring reader might wish to know more than a label or brief guidebook can contain. Where the interpretation of a given mosaic is disputed, I have tried to set out the views of others as well as my own – and hope that the reader will be stimulated to reach his or her own conclusions. I have also borne in mind the descriptions and comments found in guidebooks and popular works on Roman archaeology, and have tried to address these where appropriate.

In deference to the format preferred by Tempus, I have eschewed footnotes. This should make the text easier for the general reader to digest. I am, however, conscious of the needs of specialists. The section on Further Reading has been compiled with a view to helping not only the interested general reader who would like to follow up a particular aspect, but also the specialist who wishes to delve further into the iconography of the Romano-British mosaics. When I first started to research the subject, I had no idea of the enormity of the task or the superabundance of references to be tracked down and digested. In the event, many turned out to have little bearing on the aspects in which I was interested. I hope that by selecting the works most relevant to iconography it will enable others to pursue the most fruitful avenues. The section also serves to draw attention to many valuable articles in lesser known publications, particularly the ASPROM journal, *Mosaic*.

It has been a delight to revisit museums and sites in the course of writing this book, and to meet some of the people who are currently the custodians of our tessellated heritage. Formal acknowledgements appear above, but here I would like to express my appreciation for the friendliness and help I have received. I hope this book will encourage readers to see the mosaics for themselves. If, in doing so, they gain as much pleasure and insight as I have done, it will have served its purpose.

Patricia Witts
Wraxall
August 2004
Updated April 2010

NOTE

As the majority of the Romano-British figured mosaics fall within the late third or fourth centuries AD, dates are not given in the text except where it is generally accepted that they fall outside this period.

For consistency, the Roman names of deities are used throughout. A list of the Greek deities with whom they were identified is provided at the end of the Glossary.

Descriptions of the location of a panel (e.g. top left) assume that the viewer is looking at the mosaic from the direction in which the central image is seen correctly.

1

INTRODUCTION

Everyone loves a story, the Romans as much as ourselves. The stories illustrated in their mosaic pavements graphically link us to their world in a way that literature, with its language barrier and nuances of interpretation, cannot. When we look at a figured scene, we are seeing exactly what the Roman viewer saw – give or take a crumbling tessera or two. Whether it will mean the same to us as it may have done to the Roman who walked across that floor, or gazed at it from a dining couch or from a bench in a bathroom, is more difficult to assess. We not only see with our eyes but also with the whole weight of our cultural conditioning. But if we familiarise ourselves with the myths that were as much a part of daily life, or perhaps even more so, to the Romans as popular television soap operas are to many people today, we can perhaps begin to edge towards an appreciation of their interests and concerns.

Narrative scenes, deities and characters from Greek and Roman myth were literally set in stone, along with personifications, episodes from the arena, and animals of many kinds. In the fourth century AD, Roman Britain was exceptionally rich in the number and variety of its decorated pavements. Although many of the scenes are commonly found in Roman art throughout the empire, some are highly unusual, incorporating distinctive imagery that may well have arrested the attention of the Roman viewer as much as it intrigues the modern museum-goer or site visitor.

Many of the mosaics are a visual expression of stories related in the works of ancient authors. The frequency of allusions to certain myths or characters shows the degree of familiarity the author was able to presume on the part of his contemporary audience. Whether or not the patron or designer of a mosaic owned or had read a given book, the literary works are evidence of the cultural background to which they belonged. The writings of Ovid, particularly *Metamorphoses*, and of Virgil, especially *The Aeneid*, remain popular today. Lesser-known compilations include Apollodorus' *Bibliotheca* and Hyginus' *Fabulae*, while the reader of Philostratus and Nonnos will find passages that call to mind scenes shown in the mosaics. These authors and many others were dealing with subjects that enjoyed extraordinary longevity.

As well as telling a story, mosaics were used to depict gods and goddesses in a non-narrative context. Some portray personifications or record popular pastimes. Many include animals. The degree of meaning attributed to the mosaics varies greatly between different scholars. For some, they are no more than pleasing decoration, while for others they embody allegorical or quasi-religious ideas concerning life and death.

The durable nature of a mosaic and the labour involved in creating it suggests that the decoration was not chosen on a whim. Were the images intended to convey a particular message or to impress visitors, or were the scenes and figures selected simply because they appealed to the patron and were in tune with his or her interests? However elaborate, attractive or fascinating, a floor is only a floor: the lowest status decorative surface because it is trodden underfoot and can easily be obscured by furniture and rugs. Can we expect such a surface to have been used as a medium for communicating religious ideas, as some have argued, or is it more likely that its decoration reflects a disparate collection of attractive scenes and motifs, as others contend? Perhaps we need to tread a middle path between the two extremes.

The majority of Romano-British mosaics, now thought to number in the region of 2,000, were decorated solely with patterns and motifs, but figured mosaics account for about 200 of them. Not all of the mosaics survive. About a third are sufficiently intact to enable the main subject to be determined with certainty, even if some of the surrounding details are damaged. Just under another third survive in part. The remainder are known only from drawings of varying degrees of accuracy or from photographs or written descriptions. Many of the surviving mosaics have been lifted and can be seen in museums. If not lost, the remainder are still *in situ*, some on display under cover buildings, but others buried underground.

The surviving remains vary in size from the small fragment found at Dinnington (Somerset) (only 6cm x 8cm), thought to be part of a head, to the 'Great Pavement' at Woodchester (Gloucestershire) (nearly 15m x 15m), depicting Orpheus with a splendid array of birds and beasts (*25*).

Their geographical spread extends from the Isle of Wight in the south to Yorkshire in the north, and from Devon in the west to Essex and Kent in the east. A number of examples have been found in South Wales but none in Scotland. Most figured mosaics are concentrated either in the south west, especially in the counties of Dorset, Gloucestershire, Hampshire, Somerset and Wiltshire, or in the area around the Humber estuary in the north-east.

The chronology ranges from the first to late fourth or possibly even early fifth centuries AD. Mosaics can be dated archaeologically if coins are found sealed beneath them or if sherds of Samian pottery, which is capable of being closely dated, were used in their construction. Alternatively, the date of a mosaic can be estimated by looking at the construction sequence of the building in which it was laid if an earlier part of that building has itself been dated archaeologically. Evidence of this sort is rare. Most mosaics have been dated stylistically by experts using comparisons with other mosaics that have been dated by independent means.

Putting the Romano-British mosaics into a precise chronological sequence is often controversial. Stylistic dating, while useful, is clearly not infallible. There is, however, broad agreement that the majority of the mosaics in Roman Britain were laid in two main phases: between approximately AD 150 and 200, mainly in towns, and between the late third and the fourth centuries, mostly in villas. The majority of the figured mosaics were created in the fourth century.

With a few exceptions, the figured mosaics were laid in domestic contexts, either villas or town houses. Some represent the only such mosaic to survive from the site, but other Roman homes were decorated with several elaborate pavements, and most also had plain floors in other rooms. When sufficient evidence is found to enable a mosaic to be considered in its architectural context, the location and orientation of the images can suggest the type of function the room was intended to serve. There are thematic links, too, with marine subjects often found in bath suites, and with subjects and motifs related to Bacchus, the god of wine, being a natural and popular choice for dining rooms.

HOW MOSAICS WERE MADE

We know virtually nothing about the people who created the mosaics. Several Romano-British mosaics have letters or devices that could be signatures of the mosaicist or designer, but the evidence is equivocal. Examples, both from Sussex but of different periods, include the letters 'TER' in one of the panels of the Seasons mosaic at Bignor (*1*), and the small bird perched on the leaf-scroll border of the Cupid on a dolphin mosaic at Fishbourne (*2*).

By the time mosaics were being laid in Roman Britain, the craft was many centuries old. Patterned floors using natural pebbles, a technique that continues to be practised today, were laid in Asia Minor from the eighth century BC. The earliest known figured floors are found in Greece and date from the late fifth to early fourth centuries BC. Tessellated pavements, the type found in Roman Britain, developed from the third century BC onwards and eventually spread throughout the Roman empire.

Tessellated pavements were constructed using small cubes, known as tesserae, placed together to create the shapes of figures, motifs and patterns. True mosaic is distinct from another type of flooring called *opus sectile* in which larger pieces, often of marble, were cut to shape. Mosaic decoration was not confined to floors but was also sometimes employed on walls and vaults. The collapse of buildings means that it rarely survives from such contexts. On the other hand, fallen debris has often covered a floor and thereby ensured its preservation. The durability of mosaic floors has made them one of our best surviving sources of evidence for interior decoration.

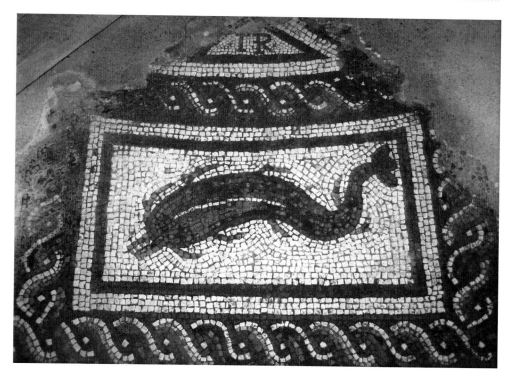

1 TER inscription, Seasons mosaic, Bignor. *Courtesy Bignor Roman Villa*

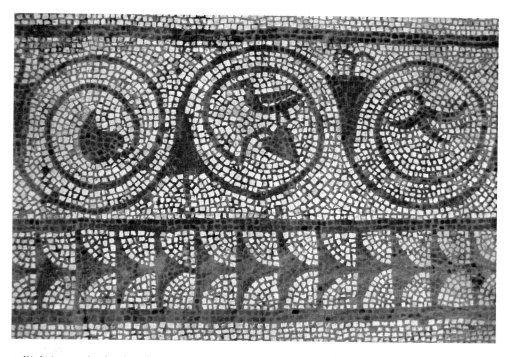

2 Bird 'signature' in border of Cupid on dolphin mosaic, Fishbourne. *Courtesy Sussex Archaeological Society*

The materials for the tesserae were mostly obtained from the natural stone available in the neighbourhood, supplemented by cut brick, tile and pottery. This gave a range of shades predominantly of blue/black, red, white and yellow. Marble and glass were occasionally employed. Sometimes tesserae were re-used from older pavements or cut from redundant *opus sectile* floors. In Roman Britain, they ranged in size from less than 0.5cm, as seen, for instance, in the gladiators panel at Bignor (*colour plate 22*), to 3-4cm in coarse outer borders. It is thought that stone was sawn into sticks from which individual tesserae could be chipped using a hammer and chisel in a similar way to the hammer-and-hardie technique used by modern mosaicists. This is borne out by a scene on a grave stele from Ostia depicting mosaicists preparing tesserae for use.

Vitruvius devoted a chapter to the laying of mosaics in his book, *De Architectura* (VII, i), written in the first century BC. He recommended paying careful attention to levelling the soil, spreading rubble over it mixed with lime, then, after the rubble had been rammed down, adding a layer of powdered pottery mixed with lime (*opus signinum*) to create a sound bedding. The tesserae were set in a top layer of fine mortar before being levelled and rubbed down. In practice, Vitruvius' standards were rarely met. Many Romano-British mosaics, particularly in the later period, were laid on the flimsiest of foundations.

Traces of guidelines have been found underneath some mosaics, either scored into or painted on the mortar bedding. It is also thought that designs could be pegged out using string. The question of whether mosaic panels were prefabricated is contentious as there is no clear evidence of how mosaicists operated. It seems likely that the figured details were made separately and that each figure was then laid as a whole, with the background tesserae being filled in around it. This could explain why some figures (such as Bacchus in the Grand Mosaic at Pitney, *6* and *colour plate 7*) were at an odd angle, and why others (such as the lion's tail at Verulamium, *74*) appear to be truncated.

Prefabrication could have employed either the indirect or the reverse method. With the former, the figure or motif would have been made on a tray or bed of sand. Fabric would then have been glued to its upper surface so that it could be moved and transported to site, in much the same way as mosaics are sometimes lifted today. After the panel had been positioned in its bedding, the fabric would have been removed. The reverse method envisages the tesserae being laid face down, perhaps onto a cartoon sketched on fabric. The panel would then be inverted for placing in the mosaic. Although the debate about the indirect versus reverse method has been a matter of controversy among scholars, it is worth bearing in mind that both techniques are practised today according to the preference of the mosaicist. The same may well have been true in Roman times.

Prefabrication envisages parts of the mosaic being made away from its ultimate location, or perhaps even acquired from a dealer, but does not necessarily imply the existence of a physical workshop away from the site. The work could, for instance, have been carried out on a table alongside the mosaic. Piles of loose tesserae found on some sites suggest that tesserae were often prepared, or at the very least stored, nearby.

It is thought that the borders were laid direct. Where mistakes are visible, they could be the result of incorrect setting-out or of the mosaic being laid from two or more different directions, probably but not necessarily by different craftsmen. Apparent 'mistakes' where one colour changes unexpectedly to another might be no more than a reflection of lack of supplies. The patterns used in the borders invariably included guilloche. Other common designs were meander, wave pattern and leaf scrolls, particularly acanthus.

Much research has been carried out, particularly in Britain, to identify similarities in motifs, composition, style and themes, in an attempt to build up a picture of how the mosaicist's craft operated. Dr David Smith's pioneering work proposed four 'schools' of mosaicists: the Corinian (based at Cirencester, Gloucestershire), the Durnovarian (based at Dorchester, Dorset), the Durobrivan (based at Water Newton, Cambridgeshire) and the Petuarian (based at Brough on Humber, Yorkshire). Further work by him and others has divided the Corinian mosaics into an 'Orpheus school' and a 'saltire school', added a Central Southern Group, and proposed further refinements.

There has also been a debate about terminology, with 'school' perhaps giving too rigorous an impression: *officinae*, workshops, traditions and groups are all words that have been adopted in this context. While we have no clear evidence for how closely and in what business relationship mosaicists worked with one another, or whether they operated from formal premises, perhaps in towns, the patterns of similarities discerned between various mosaics are notable.

The work on 'schools' hints at the geographical areas in which certain mosaicists worked, but the transmission of ideas was not limited to the influence of individual craftsmen. It is thought that pattern books were used from which a patron could perhaps choose a mosaic in a similar way to the modern consumer choosing wallpaper from a book of samples. Although no pattern book survives, they could have been made of perishable materials and the suggestion that they existed seems a naturally plausible one. They need not have contained entire designs but perhaps just individual elements. However, we might expect greater standardisation if such books had been in existence, whereas the reality is that figures are rarely identical: overall, they conform to Graeco-Roman iconography and, as such, would have been readily recognisable to their audience, but subtle differences set them apart from one another. Items such as illustrated manuscripts, textiles, decorated silverware and coins could all have been used as sources, and the roles of the patron and of the designer of the mosaic (who might or might not have been the same person as the mosaicist) may have been greater than we have appreciated. The whole topic would repay detailed study.

Many mosaics show evidence of ancient repairs, often in the form of patching rather than an attempt to restore the lost portion of the design. This is sometimes said to indicate that the building had remained in use after knowledge of the craft had been lost. Alternatively, the function of the room could have changed and the appearance of the mosaic was no longer a priority, or something that offends modern aesthetic sensibilities might not have been so important to a contemporary inhabitant of the Roman house.

THE HISTORY OF DISCOVERY

The first recorded discoveries of Roman mosaics in Britain date from the seventeenth century. A small panel in the Jewry Wall Museum, Leicester, showing Cyparissus with a stag, is the earliest find on display (*colour plate 5*). Recent discoveries include the well-preserved dolphins and cantharus mosaic from Bradford on Avon (Wiltshire) (*colour plate 1*), which was unearthed as part of a planned excavation in a school playing-field, and a dolphin and fish from Lopen (Somerset) in an extensive pavement found by chance when the landowner was creating a new driveway.

Figures can easily be overlooked or go unnoticed. For instance, in 2003 a small bird was recognised near the centre of the mosaic in room N11 at Fishbourne, some 40 years after the mosaic had been unearthed in one of the most widely publicised excavations of the twentieth century. Features in a drawing made in the seventeeth century of the now lost mosaic from Wellow (Somerset), subsequently described as 'unintelligible', were convincingly identified as Orpheus playing his lyre in 1994. Shapes recorded from a mosaic found at Micklegate Bar in York in 1814 which later perished were popularly described as 'joints of venison' for a number of years before it was tentatively but plausibly suggested in 1996 that they could have been busts of the seasons. Fresh insights, together with the unearthing of material filed in archives, are constantly expanding and refining our knowledge of existing mosaics, complementing newly unearthed floors and exciting rediscoveries. The Orpheus mosaic found in 1727 in Littlecote Park (Wiltshire), for instance, was feared lost until it was unexpectedly revealed for the second time 250 years later (*colour plate 2*).

The formal study of Romano-British mosaics was arguably started by John Aubrey (1626-97). His fascinating manuscript, *Monumenta Britannica*, in the Bodleian Library, Oxford, has a chapter devoted to the subject. The first published references to mosaics appeared in the eighteenth century in Bishop Gibson's editions of William Camden's *Britannia*. Private correspondence of this period involving the notable antiquaries of their day often provides further illumination, even of mosaics that still survive. For instance, letters written by William George, a steward on the Littlecote estate, contain descriptions of the now-restored Orpheus pavement and also give an account of the Achilles mosaic at nearby Rudge which has since been lost. Francis Drake's and George Stovin's letters to Dr Stukeley in 1747, and Stovin's personal journal in the Lincolnshire

Archives, are invaluable resources for the mosaics of Winterton (Lincolnshire) (*65* and *colour plate 12*). Although the site has been re-excavated using modern techniques, information in the letters helps us to build a more complete picture by relating the surviving remains to panels that have since been lost.

As antiquarian pursuits became increasingly popular, the *Gentleman's Magazine* covered new discoveries of mosaics while the Society of Antiquaries included illustrations of mosaics in the first two volumes of *Vetusta Monumenta*, respectively published in 1747 and 1789, and in its journal, *Archaeologia*. The latter is particularly important for recording the excavation of the mosaics of Bignor (Sussex) between 1811 and 1815, and of Great Witcombe (*3*) and Withington (both Gloucestershire) a few years later. *Archaeologia* also recorded the excavations at Silchester (Hampshire) at the turn of the nineteenth and twentieth centuries, and of the Keynsham villa (Somerset) between 1922 and 1924.

The compilation of county histories such as those by Collinson for Somerset in 1791 and Nichols for Leicestershire in 1795 was part of a growing interest in topographical studies. This had the useful effect of ensuring that information hitherto confined to private correspondence reached a wider audience, along with material collated from diverse earlier publications. Volumes of the *Victoria History of the Counties of England* have continued the process, along with the work of the Royal Commission on Historical Monuments (English Heritage), whose volume devoted to the Gloucestershire Cotswolds is particularly important for the number of mosaics it covers.

Although early illustrations of Romano-British mosaics vary considerably in quality and accuracy, some of those who executed these rare sketches and paintings claimed no artistic skills, and we are fortunate to have any record at all. By the end of the eighteenth and beginning of the nineteenth centuries, William

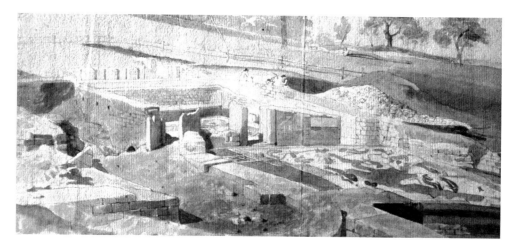

3 Excavations in progress at Great Witcombe. *Courtesy Society of Antiquaries*

Fowler (1761-1832), an architect and builder of Winterton in Lincolnshire, and Samuel Lysons (1763-1819), a barrister originally from Gloucestershire who went on to hold prestigious positions in London, were both producing high quality hand-coloured prints. Despite their well-known rivalry, they have between them enhanced our appreciation of many mosaics since lost or surviving only in a deteriorated state.

Major discoveries of mosaics were made throughout the nineteenth century. Samuel Hasell's excavations at Pitney (Somerset) were published by Sir Richard Colt Hoare of Stourhead in 1831. Hoare also extended his patronage to the talented schoolmaster and artist, John Lickman, whose many paintings of mosaics are still coming to light. Professor Buckman and C.H. Newmarch studied the mosaics at Cirencester (Gloucestershire) for their account in 1850. The mosaics of Aldborough (Yorkshire) were published by Henry Ecroyd Smith in 1852. William Bathurst's description of the temple site with mosaics at Lydney Park (Gloucestershire) appeared posthumously in 1879, while in 1881 John Price and F.G. Hilton Price published the excavations of the villa of Brading (Isle of Wight) with its exceptionally important mosaics. These accounts were all well illustrated.

The invention of photography paradoxically led to a decline in the standards of recording mosaics. Photographs were usually oblique and often did not include the whole mosaic. As Dr David Neal and Dr Stephen Cosh have explained in the introduction to the first volume of their corpus of Romano-British mosaics, the photographic process frequently does not pick up details and colour contrasts in the way that a painting can. On the other hand, any painting, however carefully executed and however experienced the artist, takes us a step away from the original mosaic, and even the most skilful paintings rarely replicate every single tessera.

Among the many important finds of the twentieth century are the mosaics discovered at Brantingham (Yorkshire), Fishbourne (Sussex), Low Ham (Somerset), Lullingstone (Kent), Rudston (Yorkshire) and Verulamium (Hertfordshire). Although they are all pavements that can be seen today, photographs taken at the time of excavation of these and other mosaics are far from superfluous. They record the original condition of the mosaic before it is inevitably changed by lifting, conservation and sometimes even partial loss. The fate of some other mosaics is heartbreaking. One of the pavements from Bramdean (Hampshire) was used for hardcore in the construction of a new road in Winchester, while the High Wycombe villa (Buckinghamshire), with its poorly recorded mosaics, gave way to a municipal swimming pool.

In the 1960s, an internationally renowned mosaic was discovered at Hinton St Mary (Dorset), and there were significant developments in mosaic studies as a whole. Professor Jocelyn Toynbee enhanced the profile of the subject by treating mosaics alongside painting, sculpture and other media as objects worthy of serious art-historical attention. In one of the chapters in *Art in Britain under the Romans*, she brought together and briefly discussed most of the mythological pavements then known.

At the same time, Dr David Smith was embarking on his seminal theory, expounded and refined in a number of scholarly papers, that schools of mosaicists could be discerned in Roman Britain. He also catalogued depictions of mythological figures and scenes. Ironically, although the study of Romano-British mosaics has since gone from strength to strength, accessibility to them has not always improved. For instance, the Hinton St Mary mosaic – an important primary artefact – has been relegated to the obscurity of a storeroom, save only for the central roundel which remains on display in the British Museum.

The first effort to produce a comprehensive account of Romano-British mosaics since Aubrey was made by Thomas Morgan in 1886. He did not profess to record every single floor, but provided details of 180 of the principal examples, many of them figured. Despite a number of errors, this early attempt to provide something approaching a British corpus and to discuss the mosaics in the context of Roman literature and mythology, and of mosaics from other countries, has perhaps not been as well regarded as it deserves. The corpus currently in course of publication by Dr David Neal and Stephen Cosh, an ambitious and magnificently produced work aiming to record every known Romano-British mosaic, is destined to become a standard reference tool. Its great strengths lie in the details spotted by the authors' perceptive and practised eyes in the process of painting the pavements, and in their stylistic analysis of designs and motifs.

Mosaics have now been studied and enjoyed as archaeological finds for a longer period than they were in use as floor decoration in Roman Britain. Their great fascination lies not just in their innate attractiveness as some of the best surviving remains of Roman art, nor in exploring how and by whom they were made, but in considering what stories they illustrated, what figures and concepts they portrayed, and above all what they meant to those who designed, made, commissioned and enjoyed them.

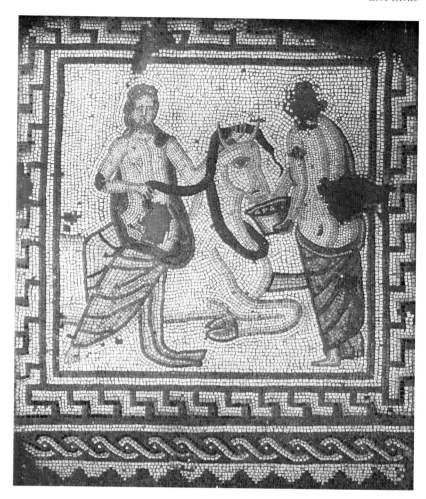

4 Europa
and the bull,
Keynsham.
Photograph:
© *Charles
Browne*

back at the shore as, with her garments fluttering in the breeze, she clung onto
her mount.

The mosaic in the apse of the Lullingstone villa (Kent) shows the sequel to
the scene depicted at Keynsham (*colour plate 3*). The bull speeds across the water,
his front hooves in the air and his rear hooves dipped in the sea. Europa is
diaphanously dressed and holds a veil that billows in the breeze as she is carried
swiftly away. Her left foot trails in the water.

The main protagonists are flanked by a pair of winged Cupids. One holds onto
the bull's tail with both hands while the other precedes the group and turns with
one arm outstretched and the other holding an upright torch with a small red
flame. They have been interpreted as respectively restraining and encouraging
Jupiter's wiles, but the leading Cupid is perhaps better seen as holding a marriage
torch to herald the union, while the other is playfully towed along as the bull
speeds on his way.

The Lullingstone scene is strikingly similar to the description of a painting of Europa and the bull given by the third-century AD writer Achilles Tatius (*The Adventures of Leucippe and Clitophon* I,1,13). He refers to the bull being led by Love in the guise of a small boy holding a torch who turns smilingly towards the bull as if he was amused that, for the sake of love, Jupiter had turned himself into such a creature.

Above the scene at Lullingstone is a Latin inscription reading:

INVIDA SI TA[VRI] VIDISSET IVNO NATATVS
IVSTIVS AEOLIAS ISSET ADVSQVE DOMOS
'If jealous Juno had seen the swimming of the bull
more justly would she have gone to the halls of Aeolus.'

This alludes to the opening episode of Virgil's *Aeneid* (I, 12-123). Juno, the wife of Jupiter and staunch supporter of the Greeks in the Trojan war, was aghast to hear that descendants of the Trojans were fated to father a warrior nation that would destroy Carthage, a city she loved. To forestall Aeneas and his band of Trojans who had set sail after the fall of Troy, she went to Aeolia, the home of winds and storm-clouds. Juno appealed to Aeolus, the ruler of the winds, to whip up a storm that would sink the Trojan ships. The Lullingstone inscription is a neat quip about marital jealousy, indicating that Juno would have had greater justification in seeking help from Aeolus if the intention had been to thwart her errant husband's affair.

The inscription is not only significant in showing an acquaintance with the works of Virgil. It has been demonstrated that the metre of the couplet and the use of a mythological exemplum indicates that the author was also familiar with the poetry of Ovid. In other words, the Lullingstone mosaic is evidence for the level of classical learning and education enjoyed by the patron who commissioned the mosaic – and also, presumably, by his guests and visitors.

Another layer of significance has been suggested by the identification of the encoded names of Avitus (the villa owner?) and Jesus hidden in the inscription, which would thus provide evidence of Christianity. The renowned Lullingstone wall-paintings showing Christian orantes and a wreath with a Chi-Rho flanked by the letters alpha and omega clearly attest to a Christian presence at a slightly later stage of the villa's history. The proposed Christian cryptogram in the inscription must, however, be open to doubt, especially as there is no consistent pattern in the counting of the letters to obtain the words identified.

The room decorated with the Europa mosaic at Lullingstone is widely accepted as one of the clearest examples from Roman Britain of the type of dining room where the diners reclined on a semicircular couch. The couch would have been placed on the broad outer border of plain tessellation around the edge of the apse, allowing the diners to view the Europa scene as they enjoyed their meal. It has even been suggested that the slightly elongated draftsmanship of the figures was a deliberate attempt to ensure a correct perspective from couch height. The direction of the lines in the outer border show how the mosaicist(s) initially laid the large red tesserae in a semicircle following the shape of the Europa panel, but then abandoned formality to place the tesserae in lines running in random directions as they approached the wall of the apse.

Among his other conquests, Jupiter was notorious for carrying off Ganymede, a prince of Troy, to become cup-bearer to the gods. This myth may have gained its particular popularity because it gave legitimacy to the love of an adult male for a young boy. The scene of abduction is shown at the Bignor villa (Sussex) (*57* and *colour plate 4*). Having fallen in love with the young prince, Jupiter chose to transform himself into a majestic eagle, and in this guise snatched up the object of his desire.

The rape of Ganymede was the first mosaic to be discovered at Bignor in 1811 and is beautifully rendered. Ganymede is shown naked save for a Phrygian cap, cuffed boots and a voluminous red cloak. He holds a pedum in his left hand, indicating his upbringing as a shepherd, and is held securely in the eagle's claws as they ascend aloft. Both figures gaze back at the direction from which they have come, and Ganymede extends his right arm as if in farewell.

The mosaic decorates the inner part of a room in the centre of the north wing. The outer part of the room has a hexagonal pool surrounded by a series of panels showing semi-clad dancing females attired in baggy, cuffed trousers (*57*). These figures are maenads, the female followers of Bacchus, the god of wine, and thus allude to Ganymede's new role as cup-bearer. They are usually described as holding tambourines, but the shape of the objects and the way some of them are held suggests they might be shallow dishes or paterae.

This room is generally regarded as a triclinium although some consider that it functioned as an entrance hall or atrium. The broad outer border of plain tessellation around the Ganymede panel is a suitable location for dining couches, here rectangular rather than the semicircular stibadium envisaged at Lullingstone. The convivial subject matter of the mosaics is highly appropriate for a dining room, while the pool, perhaps with a gently plashing fountain, might have been surrounded by real-life dancers performing after-dinner entertainment above their tessellated counterparts. Unlike the Lullingstone images, however, the figures of Ganymede and the eagle face towards the entrance to the room, and the perspective of the maenads' legs is foreshortened rather than lengthened.

Jupiter took the form of another bird, the swan, when he seduced Leda. Most representations of this popular scene have an erotic flavour. The mosaic at Littlecote Park (Wiltshire), however, shows a white bird, usually interpreted as Jupiter in the guise of a swan, decorously accompanying his female companion (*30* and *colour plate 2*).

Jupiter's transformations were not limited to living creatures. When an oracle warned Danaë's father that he would be killed by his daughter's son, he shut her in a tower to ensure that she did not have any lovers. Such stringent precautions were no deterrent to Jupiter, who infiltrated himself in the form of a shower of gold. As Ovid points out (*Amores* III, viii, 29-30), this tale illustrates the potency of gold.

This scene was probably the subject of a damaged panel in a mosaic at Frampton (Dorset). The Frampton site has variously been described as a villa or a religious complex. Three figured mosaics were found in the late eighteenth century, all long since buried or lost. The mosaic in room A was recorded in a watercolour made in 1794 by James Engleheart (*colour plate 6*) and in an engraving made by Samuel Lysons a few years later (5). A square panel on the right showed a bearded male head in the top left. The head recalls Jupiter looking down from on high as he does in a scene with Danaë in one of the panels in a mosaic depicting the Loves of Jupiter from Italica in Spain, now in the Casa de la Condesa de Lebrija in Seville. The Spanish mosaic shows Danaë seated in a chair, her robes held out to accommodate the shower of gold falling from the sky. The lines in the bottom

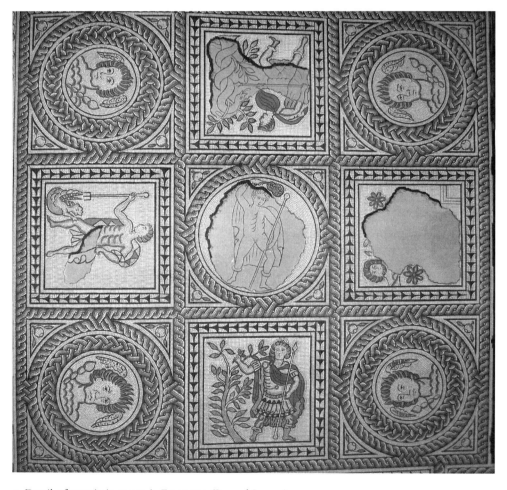

5 Detail of mosaic in room A, Frampton (Samuel Lysons)

right of the Frampton panel recall Danaë's seat or couch, with the golden shower being evoked by the petal- and leaf-shapes in the centre.

It has been suggested that this panel showed Achilles on Scyros, a story that will be discussed in the next chapter. A bearded head traditionally appears in such scenes, but there is no trace of Achilles in the Frampton panel, nor is it easy to reconcile the petal- and leaf-shapes with the Achilles myth. An alternative proposal is Hercules in the garden of the Hesperides. This idea, although attractive, seems unlikely because Hercules was an active participant when he visited the Hesperides to pluck the golden apples from their tree, and would not have been portrayed as an onlooker. Another suggestion is Medea contemplating the murder of her children, with the bearded figure representing either the children's father or their tutor. Again, it is difficult to fit the petal- and leaf-shapes into this interpretation. Their prominence indicates that they were significant to the scene.

When Engleheart painted his watercolour, the lowest part of the panel apparently survived but was devoid of detail. Other scenes in this mosaic had feet and tree trunks abutting the edge of the panels, making it likely that if the fragmentary panel had depicted standing or seated figures or a tree, some trace would have remained. Although it is impossible to interpret such a damaged panel with certainty, the elements are all consistent with the popular story of how Jupiter succeeded in seducing Danaë. She could have been shown, as she often is, in a reclining pose with her feet off the ground.

Neptune

Neptune was another divine philanderer. His most commonly depicted conquest was Amymone. She was sent by her father in search of water because Neptune, angered that their country, Argos, had been awarded to Juno and not to himself, had retaliated by inflicting a drought on the land. While on her quest, Amymone encountered a satyr who tried to rape her. She was rescued by Neptune and succumbed to his advances. Neptune lifted his curse and water flowed once more.

The encounter between Neptune and Amymone was one of the myths depicted in a lost pavement at the Pitney villa (Somerset). Hoare, who published an account and plates of it, described this pavement as the 'Grand Mosaic' (*6* and *colour plate 7*). It is known from illustrations made by its excavator, Samuel Hasell, in or around 1829, and from lithographs and other illustrations based on Hasell's work. A series of trapezoidal panels, with male and female figures shown alternately, surrounded Bacchus in the central octagon.

The bearded figure of Neptune was shown naked, striding towards Amymone with his red cloak billowing behind him. He had crab's claws on his head and carried a small trident in his left hand. Amymone was shown seated upon a pile of rocks, her right arm crossed over her body to rest on an upturned urn from which drops of water cascaded. Neptune and Amymone are numbered 2 and 3 in Hasell's watercolour (*6*).

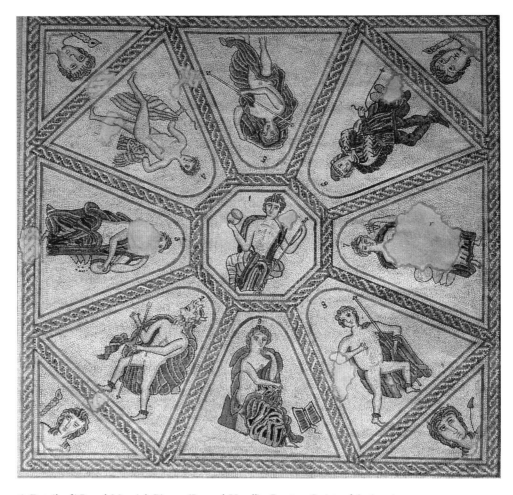

6 Detail of 'Grand Mosaic', Pitney (Samuel Hasell). *Courtesy Society of Antiquaries*

The room containing this mosaic is thought to have been a triclinium, with couches placed on the broad borders around the Cupid-seasons in the inner part of the room.

Bacchus

The love story of Bacchus and Ariadne was a popular theme in Roman art. Ariadne, the granddaughter of Europa, gave Theseus a thread to enable him to retrace his steps and escape from the Cretan labyrinth after he had slain her monstrous half-brother, the Minotaur. Having accomplished the deed, he set sail carrying Ariadne with him, but cruelly abandoned her on the island of Naxos. As she languished on the shore despairing of her fate, she was found by Bacchus who made her his wife.

The scene of Bacchus discovering Ariadne was depicted in a mosaic, long since lost and known only from an eighteenth-century sketch, from East Coker (Somerset).

A probable representation of Bacchus and Ariadne, along with members of their retinue, decorates the Seasons mosaic in the triclinium in the west wing of the Chedworth villa (Gloucestershire) (7). The floor in the northern part of the room (on the right in figure 7) is badly preserved and the centrepiece has been lost. The design is similar to the Grand Mosaic at Pitney and consisted of an octagon surrounded by trapezoidal panels, with a triangular panel in each corner of the enclosing square. The triangle nearest to the modern viewing platform contains one of the best known and most frequently reproduced images from a Romano-British mosaic, the diminutive figure of Winter, who will be discussed along with his seasonal companions later in this book. For present purposes, the discussion focuses on the couples in the trapezoidal panels, three of whom are reasonably complete with parts of two others just visible. Figure 7 shows a drawing made by George E. Fox in 1886, when slightly more of the mosaic survived than can be seen today.

In the panel above Winter, a female is seen from the rear, her naked back provocatively exposed above the folds of drapery winding around her legs. Her male companion stands with his right leg outstretched. He is naked save for an animal-skin cloak with jagged ends. He seems to be blocking the path

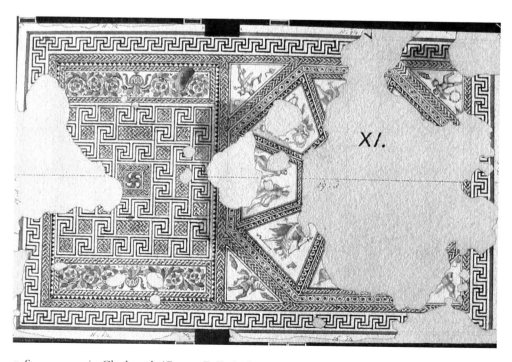

7 Seasons mosaic, Chedworth (George E. Fox). *Courtesy Society of Antiquaries*

of the female, who teeters unsteadily on crossed legs and thrusts her left arm out as if in alarm. However, in a tracing made by Fox, her right hand is shown burrowing under her partner's cloak to rest on his shoulder. If this is a scene of capture, the female is perhaps not an unwilling participant. Their attributes are a pedum below the satyr's right foot, a syrinx in the bottom right of the panel, and a thyrsus rising vertically above it: these identify the figures as a satyr and maenad, the attendants of Bacchus. The fronds of foliage faintly discernible in the background of the mosaic itself are probably stylised vines.

Next to Spring on the far side of the mosaic, a damaged panel shows a satyr in profile, wearing a spiky headdress (reeds?) and an animal-skin cloak. A maenad enveloped in a billowing veil wraps her right arm around his shoulders while he grasps her left wrist. They gaze at one another lovingly (*8*). In the bottom right of the panel is a tambourine, and the end of a thyrsus is shown horizontally in the bottom left, again identifying the figures as Bacchic characters.

Contrasting with the frenzy and passion of the characters in these compartments is the serenity of the seated couple in the panel between them. The female wears a semicircular diadem and the male appears to wear a stylised crown. He holds an upright thyrsus in one hand and a tambourine or cup in the other. The shape of his striped cloak creates the impression of a throne. Although they are often described as another satyr and maenad, their majestic poses and headdresses, coupled with their focal point in the room facing the area occupied by diners, suggests that these figures are not mere attendants but are Bacchus and Ariadne themselves.

The geometric mosaic in the southern part of the room (on the left in figure 7) and the border around the whole is replete with swastika-meander, a popular decorative motif, but here a particularly appropriate reference to Ariadne as it is a stylised version of a labyrinth. The accomplished acanthus scrolls flowing from pedestalled bowls on the western and eastern sides of this part of the room, also commonly found elsewhere and potent symbols of growth, here underline

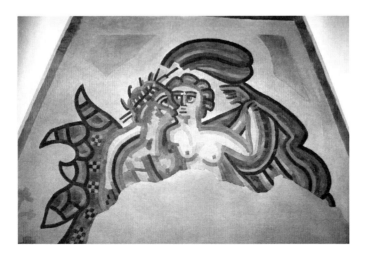

8 Satyr and maenad, Seasons mosaic, Chedworth (George E. Fox). *Courtesy Society of Antiquaries*

Bacchus' role as a fertility god. His characteristic drinking vessel, the cantharus, is recalled by the leaves that emerge from the bowls, turning the overall shape into a cantharus-like form.

Apollo

One of the amorous exploits of Apollo was his pursuit of Daphne, a nymph who cried out to Mother Earth to save her from the god's advances and was changed into a bay tree, a kind of laurel.

It is probable that this episode is depicted in the Seasons mosaic at the Brading villa (Isle of Wight) (*9* and *16*), although interpretation of the figures in question is controversial. A damaged panel (lower right in figure *16*) shows a semi-clad woman fleeing from or alarmed by a male of whom only the naked legs survive. A number of candidates have been suggested: Neptune with Amymone or Amphitrite, Daphne and Apollo, a satyr and a maenad or, most recently, Achilles on Scyros.

If the male were Neptune, we would expect the end of his trident to be shown in the lower part of the panel. Similarly, it is likely that a satyr would have a thyrsus, as is the case in the Chedworth mosaic. Both characters are usually portrayed wearing cloaks, a large billowing garment in the case of Neptune and an animal skin in the case of a satyr, but no trace of a cloak is visible behind the legs of the Brading figure.

The pose of the male is consistent with the identification of Achilles, who is often shown with one leg pointing towards the female and the other turned towards the viewer. Apollo, however, is also depicted in this pose. Although the alarmed gesture of the Brading female is suitable for one of the daughters of King Lycomedes at the moment when she sees Achilles throw off his woman's disguise (as discussed in the next chapter), it is also appropriate for Daphne fleeing from Apollo.

Portrayals of Daphne frequently show her surrounded by laurel, or with leaves sprouting from her finger tips, but this is not invariably so. The allusion to laurel can be made by a wreath worn by Apollo, so its absence from the preserved portion of the Brading scene is not conclusive.

The one telling difference between depictions of Apollo and Achilles is that the latter is always shown with drapery crossing his thigh: sometimes it is voluminous, sometimes a mere wisp, but there is always some drapery to remind us that Achilles has just flung off his female disguise. The complete absence of any clothing is, on the other hand, entirely appropriate for Apollo whose role as sun god ensures that he is never cold.

Another of Apollo's loves was Cyparissus, a beautiful young man whose favourite companion was a magnificent and tame stag. One day Cyparissus unwittingly killed the stag with his javelin. Inconsolable in his grief, he resolved to die and was changed into the cypress tree.

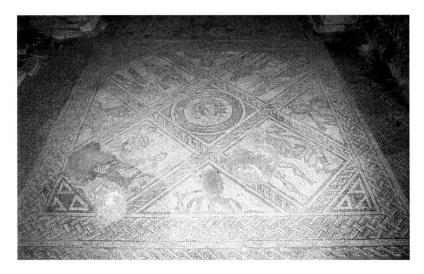

9 Seasons mosaic, Brading (part). *Courtesy Oglander Roman Trust*

Cyparissus is shown in a small panel from All Saints Church in Leicester, now in the Jewry Wall Museum (*colour plate 5*). It was found in the seventeenth century and is one of the earliest Romano-British mosaics to have been discovered. Cyparissus fondles the stag with his right hand, while Cupid prepares to fire an arrow. The white tesserae around Cyparissus' legs have been extended too far and make it look as if the stag has been cut in half, with its hind quarters on the extreme right of the panel. A small bush or clump of grass lies beneath. The vertical brown feature extending below Cyparissus' right elbow could be part of his cloak, but might have been intended to represent a tree trunk, perhaps to locate the scene in its wooded setting or as a reference to the cypress tree. The peculiarities of the draftsmanship are not necessarily a reflection of the abilities of the Roman craftsman: the mosaic has evidently been substantially repaired over the centuries since it was found.

Venus

Not all love stories involving deities were confined to the loves of the gods: goddesses, especially Venus, could also be the protagonists. Venus appeared in mosaics in rooms A and B at the site of Frampton (Dorset). Room B, whose function is disputed, consisted of a rectangular antechamber entered from the corridor, which led to an inner square room with an apse. Most of its images will be discussed below, as will the depiction of Venus in the mosaic in room A, but the first to be considered is the panel shown at the lower left of the square part of the mosaic (*10*).

A naked male lay prostrate on a pile of drapery. He was approached by a fully clothed female who placed one hand to her chest while the other held a downturned torch. These figures have been identified as either Venus mourning her dying lover Adonis, who had been gored by a wild boar, or the moon goddess Selene making one of her nightly visits to Endymion, her lover who had been granted eternal sleep and thus remained young forever.

Venus' love for Adonis and Selene's love for Endymion were both well known and it is not always easy to tell such scenes apart. There are no attributes to identify the Frampton figures with certainty and scholarly opinion is divided. The goddess was fully clothed, suggesting Selene rather than Venus who was normally more scantily clad. On the other hand, she lacked the crescent-shaped headdress usually worn by Selene, and there was no trace of the dog that usually accompanies Endymion. Most significantly, a sleeping figure characteristically has an arm curved behind the head. As this was not the case in the Frampton mosaic, the scene was one of death, not sleep, a conclusion reinforced by the downturned torch which symbolised death. It is therefore probable that the Frampton couple represented Venus with the dying Adonis.

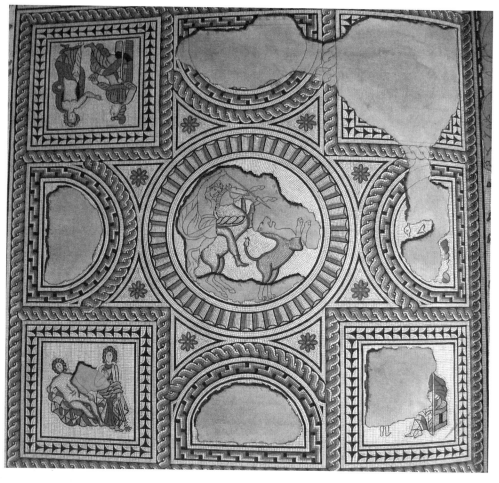

10 Detail of mosaic in room B, Frampton (Samuel Lysons)

THE JUDGEMENT OF PARIS —
THE PLEASURES AND PENALTIES OF LOVE

When Jupiter appointed Paris to judge which of the three goddesses, Juno, Minerva or Venus, was the most beautiful, they each offered him a reward if he found in their favour. Juno offered earthly power and wealth, Minerva offered military victory and skill in crafts, but Venus, who offered 'love' in the form of the beautiful Helen, was declared the winner. According to Homer, the judgement of Paris highlighted the pleasures and penalties of love (*Iliad* XXIV, 25-30), while for Athenaeus, it was a trial of pleasure against virtue (*Deipnosophistae* XII, 510c).

The beauty contest had been initiated by Eris (Strife). She appeared at the wedding feast of Peleus and Thetis, who were later to become Achilles' parents, and threw a golden apple into the group of wedding guests, who included the three goddesses, inscribed 'for the fairest'.

Although Paris resolved the contest between the goddesses, his love for Helen was the ostensible cause of the Trojan war. The victory of the Greeks in that war led to Aeneas' flight from Troy, and ultimately to the foundation of the Roman race. The judgement was therefore pivotal to other stories and to the legendary history of Rome. It illustrated both the supremacy of love and the extreme results to which it can lead. There are many allusions to it in ancient literature, and it was widely depicted in Roman art. Two probable examples featured in Romano-British mosaics.

In the panel shown at the top left of the square part of the mosaic in room B at Frampton, a semi-clad standing female addressed a seated male shepherd (*10*). His attire of Phrygian cap, tunic and trousers, was characteristic of Paris who, although a prince of Troy, was reared by a shepherd and tended flocks in the more tranquil times before he embarked on his romance with Helen.

Samuel Lysons, the excavator of the site at the end of the eighteenth century, was the first to recognise the figures as Paris and Venus. This identification is still accepted by many but some have suggested instead that the scene showed Paris with Oenone (whom he deserted for Helen) or Attis with a nymph. Depictions of Paris and Oenone are rare. The Frampton female is shown as if assertively addressing the male, making it much more likely that she is the goddess Venus than Paris' wife or the nymph who was sometimes shown with Attis. Lysons' original identification seems preferable.

Another seated shepherd was shown in the Grand Mosaic at Pitney (*6* and *colour plate 7*). He faced a female who held a syrinx but if, as I have suggested elsewhere, he was placed in the wrong position when the mosaic was laid, the original intention may have been to pair the shepherd with the naked female who held a sceptre in one hand and a voluminous cloak in the other. She had the boldness and allure of Venus, while the shepherd's contemplative pose, with one hand rubbing his chin, suggests that he was Paris in the throes of making his fateful decision. These figures are numbered 5 and 6 on Hasell's watercolour.

A clear allusion to the judgement of Paris is embodied in the golden apple held by Venus in the mosaic from the Rudston villa (Yorkshire) (*73*).

EROS AND ANTEROS – REQUITED LOVE

While Cupid (Eros) gained notoriety for inflaming passions that were not always reciprocated, his brother Anteros was the god of requited love. Eros and Anteros are thought to be the subject of the central panel on the second-century mosaic of the wrestling Cupids from Middleborough, Colchester (Essex), now in Colchester Castle Museum (*colour plate 8*). The lower parts of two naked wrestling figures survive. The one on the left is certainly winged but the one on the right is too damaged to tell.

Mosaics of wrestling Cupids from other provinces have been variously identified as generic Cupid figures or the specific characters of Eros and Anteros. What makes the latter identification likely for the Middleborough mosaic are the allusions the mosaic contains to the Cupids' mother, Venus. It has been plausibly suggested that the bird to the right of the wrestlers represents Venus herself in the guise of a dove, her sacred bird: it is hard to find another reason why a bird would be included in such a scene. The four lunettes each have a mythical marine creature, recalling the birth of Venus from the sea. Clockwise from above the central scene, these creatures are a goat, a horse, a bull and a badly damaged marine feline. The central panel is set in a saltire design, two arms of which each show a large lotus bud, a flower associated with Venus.

The acanthus scroll in the outer border is decorated with two different types of ivy leaf and lotus bud and has a small bird in the centre of each side. The excavator, Philip Crummy, has analysed the distribution of these motifs and concluded that there are errors in the presumed design, as the motifs are not repeated in a standard pattern. He suggests that the mosaicist laying this part of the pavement did not understand the scheme, indicating that he had not been involved in its conception. This reinforces the theory that the people who laid the mosaics were different from those who designed them, although it is also worth bearing in mind that the Romans seemed to be less troubled than modern patrons by what we would regard as 'errors'.

PHAEDRA AND HIPPOLYTUS – SPURNED LOVE

Ancient mythology is full of tales of unrequited love which could lead to tragic consequences, such as Phaedra's passion for Hippolytus. Phaedra was the wife of Theseus and sister of Ariadne. She tried to seduce Hippolytus, her stepson. When her efforts failed, she alleged that it was he who lusted after her, either because she was afraid that the truth would come out or because she was piqued at being rebuffed. Despite Hippolytus' innocence, his father cast him out of the city. As he drove his chariot along the shore into exile, a roaring monster reared up from the sea, frightened his horses, and threw his chariot down steep rocks, tearing his body apart.

Phaedra and Hippolytus were one of the couples in the Grand Mosaic of Pitney (*6* and *colour plate 7*). Phaedra was shown sitting deep in thought with her left hand held to her chin. A writing tablet lay near her feet, dropped from her right hand, or simply included in the scene to indicate its subject: the diptych featured in two different versions of the story, either representing a note from Phaedra to Hippolytus telling him of her love, or containing her false accusation. It is notable that Hippolytus, whom she faced, was the only male in the mosaic to be turning his body away from his companion. Naked save for a cloak, he held his right hand to his breast as if in alarm as he moved rapidly away. These figures are numbered 8 and 9 on Hasell's watercolour.

ATTIS AND SAGARITIS — INFIDELITY

Unlike infidelity on the part of gods and goddesses, which many deities practised with impunity, being unfaithful to a deity could prove disastrous.

One of the more colourful characteristics of the cult of the goddess Cybele was that her attendants were eunuchs. Ovid tells the story of how Attis, her most prominent devotee, came to castrate himself. Cybele made Attis promise to remain chaste but he found himself unable to resist the charms of the water nymph Sagaritis. In revenge, Cybele drove Attis mad and, in his madness, he cut off his manhood (*Fasti* IV, 223-244).

Comparison with a wall-painting from Pompeii has enabled the shepherd shown in the Seasons mosaic at Brading (*9* and *16*) to be identified as Attis. He is placed in the panel diagonally opposite the probable figures of Apollo and Daphne discussed above. He wears Phrygian attire and holds a pedum in his left hand and a syrinx in his right hand. His dress and attributes are appropriate for Attis, while his companion has reeds in her hair and rests her left elbow on an overturned vase, indicating that she is a water nymph. She has been identified as Sagaritis, but this is not necessarily the case. Sagaritis is rarely if ever shown in Graeco-Roman art. Instead, the nymph may allude to an important episode in Attis' early life. He was abandoned among reeds after his birth and, in a reference to this, he is frequently shown against a backdrop of reeds.

The identification of the Brading couple is contentious as some scholars see merely a pairing of an ordinary shepherd and nymph, while others suggest that they are Paris and Oenone. The appearance of the male figure matches that of Paris as much as Attis, but on the rare occasions when Oenone is portrayed she is not shown as a water nymph but simply as Paris' consort. Without the nymph on the Brading mosaic, it would be difficult to tell which of a number of shepherds the male figure was intended to represent. Her presence, with her prominent headdress of reeds, suggests that he is Attis.

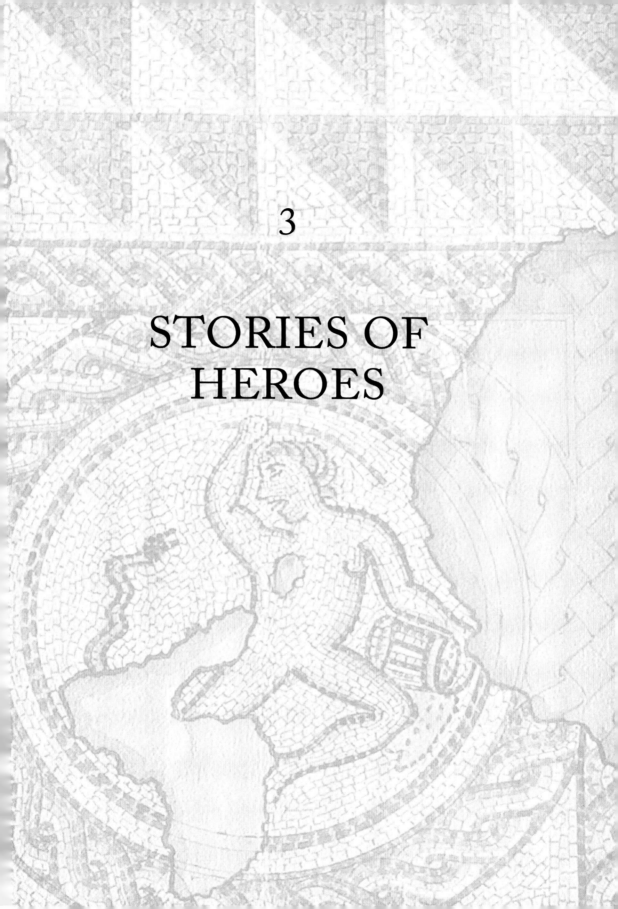

3

STORIES OF
HEROES

Along with love stories, tales from the adventures of famous mythological heroes were another favoured theme in Roman art. The heroes portrayed in Romano-British mosaics were, as in pavements from other provinces, primarily Achilles, Aeneas, Bellerophon, Cadmus, Hercules, Perseus and Theseus.

Achilles

In many ways Achilles seems an unheroic hero: he dressed up in women's clothes, sulked during the Trojan war when Agamemnon deprived him of Briseis (his favourite slave and lover) and even, in some legends, practised necrophilia on the body of Penthesilea, the Amazon whom he simultaneously killed and fell in love with. Of his various exploits, the interlude spent in women's dress at the court of King Lycomedes on the island of Scyros was exceptionally popular in Roman art, perhaps because it appealed to the Roman predilection for things not being entirely what they seemed.

Achilles' mother, Thetis, had been alarmed by a prophecy, and feared that if Achilles participated in the Trojan war he would be killed. To avert this potential disaster, she devised a stratagem to keep him away from the conflict by taking him, while he was a young boy, to Scyros to grow up among the king's daughters disguised as a girl. The prophecy eventually came true for, despite his mother's precautions, Achilles joined the Greeks at Troy, where he was eventually slain by Paris.

A number of accounts relate how this came about. Wily Ulysses had got wind of Achilles' whereabouts and travelled to Scyros with a view to unmasking him and securing his help in the war. Posing as a pedlar, Ulysses included a shield and a spear along with women's trinkets as he set out his wares. He arranged for a trumpet to be sounded suddenly, as if an enemy were at hand, whereupon Achilles threw off his female attire and showed his true manly nature by seizing the weapons.

One of the panels in the hexagonal mosaic from room W at the Keynsham villa, currently in store, shows Achilles at the moment of unmasking (*11*). He is on the left, rising from a chair as he casts off his clothes. On the right, a woman fleeing in surprise or alarm is one of the daughters of King Lycomedes, perhaps Deidameia with whom he had a romantic liaison. The bearded figure with a sceptre peering over a wall is thought to be King Lycomedes himself: although

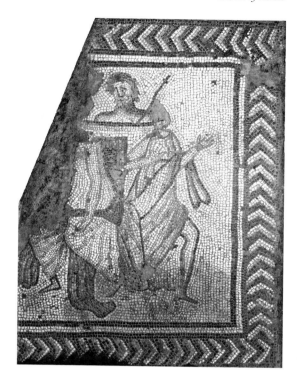

11 Achilles on Scyros, Keynsham.
Photograph: © Charles Browne

Ulysses is more central to the story of the unmasking, the Keynsham figure lacks Ulysses' distinctive helmet.

A similar scene, closer to examples in mosaics from other countries, was found in a mosaic at the villa of Rudge (Wiltshire), now known only from an antiquarian engraving. The lower parts of two figures were shown in a damaged medallion: a woman on the left and the legs of a man on the right. The man's pose was characteristic of Achilles shown in mosaics and wall-paintings elsewhere, when he leapt to his feet while flinging off his disguise. An overturned wool-basket between his legs, its contents spilling as Achilles sprung into action leaving behind his womanly pursuits, identified the scene. This detail is included in many other representations of the subject.

According to one theory, Achilles could be the subject of the scenes in the medallions of the central panel from the Horkstow mosaic (Lincolnshire). Two of the medallions survive and are in the Hull and East Riding Museum. Together with parts of a third, now lost, they were recorded by Samuel Lysons (*12*) and William Fowler (*colour plate 11*) shortly after the mosaic was discovered at the end of the eighteenth century. At that time, and for many years since, the figures were regarded as Bacchic characters.

One of the surviving medallions shows a naked woman with her left leg bent beneath her body and her right leg stretched out in front. Her left arm is bent behind her head and she seems to grasp the wrist of her male adversary as

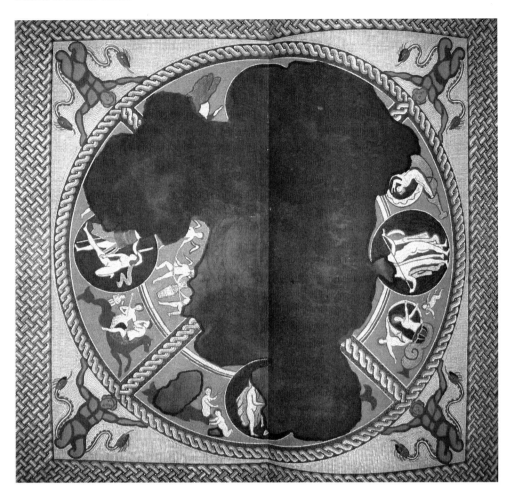

12 'Medallions mosaic', Horkstow (Samuel Lysons)

he clutches at her hair. The brown lines above and to the side of her head are thought to represent long hair and/or a veil. The male figure appears to wear a sleeveless tunic with jagged skirt, perhaps an animal skin. In the antiquarian illustrations, he had a vertical rod or staff and seemed to balance on only one leg, the other presumably being hidden behind the female's outstretched thigh.

It has been suggested that these figures are a warrior and doomed woman in a 'fatal pose', and that the male (perhaps Achilles) is in the act of killing the female (perhaps Penthesilea). Amazons are, however, usually represented with a distinctive pelta-shaped shield, which is lacking here. The identification of a death scene is persuasive, and the figures do not seem to be, as previously thought, a couple in a Bacchic ecstasy. The 'fatal pose' was adopted by a number of famous couples in Graeco-Roman art. In the absence of identifying attributes, the Horkstow couple remain enigmatic.

The other surviving medallion shows two standing figures, one on the left apparently facing the viewer and the other on the right turning away. The antiquarian illustrations show slightly more of the scene: the figure on the right appears to hold a tambourine and both figures held a linear object (perhaps a rod or thread?) horizontally at shoulder level. In the Achilles interpretation of the medallions, this object is regarded as a spear and the couple are identified as a pair of lovers, perhaps Achilles with Penthesilea, Deidameia, Briseis or even his close male friend Patroclus. There is, however, nothing to link the couple unequivocally with Achilles. The jagged edge and two-tone colour of the cloak falling behind the left hand figure suggest that it is intended to represent an animal skin typically worn by a Bacchic character.

The fragments of the now lost third medallion included a standing figure in profile. It has been suggested that this figure was Thetis and that the scene showed her dipping the baby Achilles in the River Styx in an attempt to make him invulnerable. The figure was, however, apparently male. Instead of the baby Achilles, it is more likely that the vertical shape below his outstretched hand was his left leg raised up in a pose adopted by many heroic males when addressing a female companion. A small oval object in front of his foot has been plausibly interpreted as the foot of this companion.

The cycle of scenes from the life of Achilles was portrayed in a variety of media, but it is difficult to relate the Horkstow medallions conclusively to any of these scenes. Their unusual iconography suggests that the mosaicist was working from a model he did not fully understand, and this in turn makes it difficult for us to comprehend what has been depicted. Particularly interesting and unusual features of this mosaic are the coloured background and the way in which the emotions expressed by the figures in the marine thiasos between the medallions appear to mirror the content of the medallions themselves. It has been convincingly shown, for instance, that the Nereid facing the 'fatal pose' medallion is depicted in a gesture of mourning. This type of insight is valuable as it helps to expand our appreciation of this complex mosaic. It may take us one step closer towards an understanding of it.

Aeneas

The famous love story of Dido and Aeneas, which was doomed to end in tragedy, is shown in a series of narrative panels in the unusual and internationally important mosaic from the villa at Low Ham (Somerset), now in the Somerset County Museum, Taunton (*13*). Its scenes are so close to the text of Books I and IV of Virgil's *Aeneid* that it is often suggested they might have been copied from the illustrations in an illuminated manuscript of this book.

After surviving the storm to which the inscription in the Lullingstone mosaic alludes, Aeneas landed on the shore of North Africa and reached Carthage, where he met Dido, its queen. He despatched one of his companions, Achates, back to the

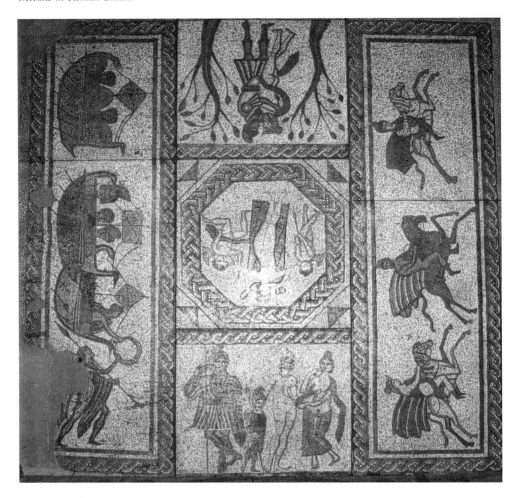

13 Dido and Aeneas, Low Ham. *Courtesy Somerset County Museums Service*

ships to fetch his son Ascanius and also to bring gifts for Dido, including a necklace shaped like a row of mulberries. Venus, the mother of Aeneas, sent Cupid in the guise of Ascanius to present the gifts and, at the same time, to inflame Dido with a passion for Aeneas. She was mindful of the special place that Carthage held in Juno's affections and was also wary of Juno's enmity towards the Trojans, so she wished to protect her son by ensuring that Dido was well disposed towards him.

In the battle of wills between the goddesses, Juno decided to outflank Venus and proposed that Aeneas should marry Dido. This, as Venus realised, would divert him from his destiny of travelling to Italy and founding the Roman race. Juno arranged for a storm to disturb Aeneas, Ascanius and Dido while they were out hunting, scattering their retinue and forcing Aeneas and Dido to take shelter together in a cave. This provided the perfect opportunity for them to consummate their union. Jupiter, however, was aghast that Aeneas might linger among his enemies without heeding his pre-ordained path, and declared that he should set sail without delay. He sent Mercury to address Aeneas, who was so shocked by this warning from on high that he immediately prepared to leave. He instructed his men to get ready to set sail while he pondered the best way of breaking the news to his erstwhile lover. Her intuition, meanwhile, alerted her to what was happening. She hotly accosted Aeneas and was not appeased by his protestation that divine intervention required him to desert her so that he could pursue his destiny. As Aeneas sailed away, she fell upon a sword in despair, entreating the Carthaginians to hate his descendants for ever more.

As displayed in the museum, the panel on the left of the Low Ham mosaic shows the Trojan ships sailing towards Carthage. A figure in the foremost ship hands a lavish necklace to Achates who stands at right angles, aligned as if moving towards the next scene. This panel embodies two strands of the story in one: the arrival and the gifts.

In the lowest of the three central panels, Aeneas stands leaning on his spear, looking sideways at the diaphanously clad Dido who regards him with a thoughtful demeanour. Between them Venus, resplendent in her body chain, puts her right arm around Cupid-Ascanius and holds Dido's left hand with her own. As Dido and Aeneas are taking a close interest in one another, Venus' wiles are evidently working.

The panel on the right depicts the hunt. Ascanius streaks ahead while Aeneas turns to look at Dido who brings up the rear.

In the uppermost central panel Dido, now naked, is shown embracing Aeneas, who is still clad in military gear. Their different attire was perhaps chosen to contrast Dido's vulnerability with Aeneas' implacable destiny.

The central panel sums up the story. Venus stands regally against the backdrop of a fringed cloth she holds up. She is flanked by a pair of winged Cupids: one lively on the right, holding a upraised torch, perhaps representing life (and Aeneas), and one subdued on the left, holding a downturned torch, standing for death (and Dido).

Amid this stirring story of passion and destiny, one small domestic detail might link the mosaic to its context. The floor was found in the bath suite of the villa and the central panel faced bathers as they emerged from the plunge pool. It has been suggested that the cloth behind Venus is a towel, and that she is shown as if herself emerging from a bath.

In a later episode related in Book VI of the *Aeneid*, Virgil tells how Aeneas visited the underworld. He was given instructions by the Sibyl of Cumae, who described a golden bough hidden in a tree. Because Proserpina, the goddess of the underworld, required this bough as a special offering, Aeneas would only be granted permission to descend to the nether regions if he was able to pluck the bough from the tree. It would come away easily if he was fated to be successful but, if his visit was not meant to be, nothing would shift it. He successfully broke off the golden bough and was privileged to be granted admission.

The scene with the golden bough has been identified in the central panel in the bottom row of the mosaic in room A at Frampton (5 and *colour plate 6*). Shown wearing full military dress as in the Low Ham mosaic, Aeneas carried a spear in one hand while breaking off the branch with the other. His Phrygian cap is just visible although it has been left uncoloured on some copies of Lysons' engravings.

Bellerophon

Bellerophon's adventures started when he fled from his native Corinth to the court of King Proetus after he had accidentally committed murder. When he spurned the advances of the king's wife, she, in an echo of the myth of Phaedra, accused Bellerophon of making advances to her. The king immediately sent Bellerophon to Iobates, his father-in-law and king of Lycia, with a letter asking Iobates to put Bellerophon to death. This gave Iobates something of a dilemma as it would have been bad form to kill a guest. As a compromise, he set Bellerophon the task of killing the Chimaera, not thinking that the mission would be accomplished successfully.

The Chimaera was a fire-breathing amalgamation of several animals. The monster was traditionally shown with the foreparts of a lion and a tail that ended in a serpent's head. It had a goat's head on its back. Bellerophon acquired the winged horse, Pegasus, and by riding this creature through the air he was able to swoop down upon the Chimaera and kill it with his spear. This popular scene enjoyed extraordinary longevity in Graeco-Roman art and appears in three surviving and one lost Romano-British mosaics.

The most complete example is at Lullingstone, where Bellerophon is shown in a cushion-shaped panel between busts of the seasons (*colour plate 3*). The hero is naked save for a red cloak and boots. He is depicted, mounted on Pegasus, in the act of thrusting his spear into the goat's head on the monster's back. Although the Chimaera is small in comparison with Pegasus, its fierce nature is underlined by the flames shooting from its mouth.

The Bellerophon panel at Lullingstone also contains four dolphins and two open shells. These were initially interpreted as referring to the hero's voyage across the sea to Lycia, but his travels to that country were not a significant part of the myth. It has since been suggested that the marine imagery is related to Pegasus, who had important connections with water. His name was taken from 'pegai', the Greek word for springs. He is said to have been born near the springs of Oceanus, and he himself had the ability to make water flow by striking a rock with his hoof.

The second surviving example comes from the mosaic found at Hinton St Mary (Dorset) (*14*), most of which is now in store in the British Museum. The larger part of this mosaic has a famous bust thought to represent Christ. Bellerophon appears in the damaged central roundel in the smaller part of the mosaic. Again mounted on Pegasus, and naked save for a cloak, he thrusts his spear towards the goat's head of a large but benign-looking Chimaera.

In 1991 another depiction of the scene was found near Croughton (Northamptonshire). Although this mosaic has been denigrated for the naivety of its draftsmanship, especially as Pegasus resembles a toy rocking horse, it is a particularly spirited and interesting rendering of the myth. Bellerophon wears, as well as a cloak, a belted tunic ornamented with an orbiculus above the right knee and a similar decorative patch on his right shoulder. His right foot is clad in a red shoe. The Chimaera turns its head aggressively upwards towards its attacker, breathing fire from its shaggy lion's head. This mosaic also incorporates small details not shown in the other depictions: four red crosses in a line curving either side of Bellerophon's head, and a sprinkling of dark tesserae below Pegasus' right foreleg. These have been interpreted as stars and water, respectively allusions to the apotheosis of Pegasus and to his ability to create springs.

The damaged medallion in the centre of the largest part of the mosaic in room B at Frampton was originally thought to depict a hunt (*10*). It has since been shown that this was another scene with Bellerophon and the Chimaera. The twisted feature by the rider's leg is part of Pegasus' wing, while the snake's head at the tip of the Chimaera's tail is discernible.

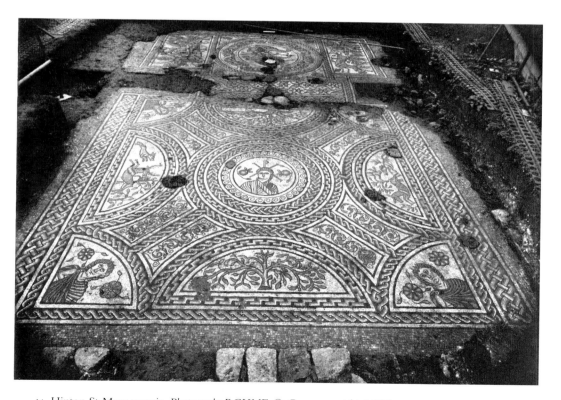

14 Hinton St Mary mosaic. *Photograph: RCHME, © Crown copyright. NMR*

Cadmus

Cadmus was the brother of Europa. He was despatched by their father to search for her after she had been abducted by Jupiter in the guise of a bull, as shown in the Keynsham and Lullingstone mosaics discussed above. During his travels, Cadmus sent his attendants to fetch some fresh water for a libation. Unfortunately the spring they found was guarded by the serpent of Mars, a fearsome creature that slew them all. When they did not return, Cadmus went to look for them and came across the scene of slaughter. Initially he tried throwing a boulder at the serpent, but it had no effect and eventually he skewered it to a tree with his spear.

A small chamber adjoining the room with the Grand Mosaic at Pitney (Somerset) had a mosaic, now lost, that depicted an episode from this story (*15*). It showed the serpent rearing up at Cadmus, who flailed at it with a stick. An overturned pail of water was featured on the right of the scene.

The central panel in the upper row of the mosaic in room A at Frampton depicted Cadmus in the act of spearing the serpent to the tree (*5* and *colour plate 6*). This panel was damaged by the time Samuel Lysons recorded it, but he was able to sketch in the missing parts from the earlier watercolour made by James Engleheart.

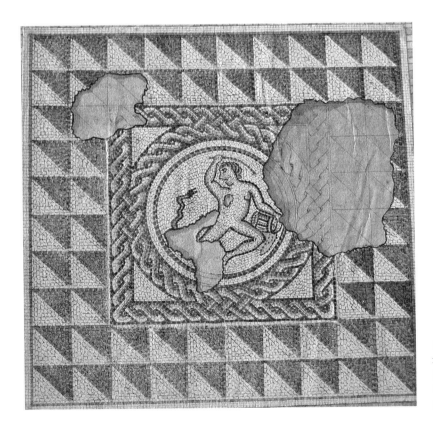

15 Cadmus mosaic, Pitney (Samuel Hasell). *Courtesy Society of Antiquaries*

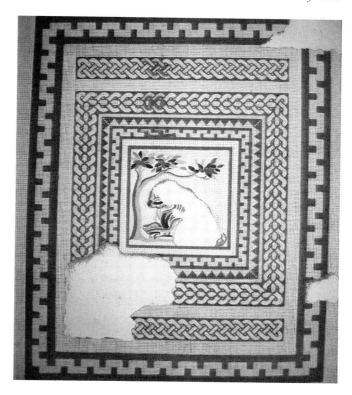

17 Lion mosaic, Aldborough
(H. Ecroyd Smith)

other provinces, the First Labour is sometimes represented by the lion alone. A mosaic at Aldborough (Yorkshire), now vestigial but more complete when discovered in 1832, is usually interpreted simply as a depiction of a lion (*17*). However, as representations of an isolated, supine animal are unusual, perhaps this was intended as a reference to Hercules and his First Labour.

Perseus

Despite his significance as slayer of the Gorgon Medusa, it was Perseus' role as the rescuer and lover of Andromeda that was popularly chosen for portrayal in classical art. Andromeda was the daughter of King Cepheus and Queen Cassiopeia of Ethiopia. Her mother boasted of being fairer than all the Nereids. On behalf of the slighted Nereids, Neptune sent a sea monster to avenge the insult by ravaging the country. An oracle decreed that Andromeda, although innocent, should pay the price of her mother's boastfulness, and she was chained to a rock to appease the monster. As Perseus was on his way home from slaying Medusa, he came across Andromeda and was in the process of asking her who she was and the reason for her plight when the monster appeared from the sea and alarmed both the princess and her horrified parents who looked on in distress. Pausing only to ensure that Cepheus and Cassiopeia would give him their daughter's hand in marriage if he were able to save her, Perseus despatched the sea monster with his sword and released Andromeda from her bonds.

A panel at the western end of the Seasons mosaic at the Brading villa shows Perseus and Andromeda after the crisis is over (at the top in figure *16*). They are seated antithetically as they gaze at the reflection of Medusa's head in a pool: the head would turn to stone anyone who looked at it directly. Close parallels for the Brading scene have been identified in Pompeian wall-paintings and on an oil-lamp thought to have been made in Italy in the first century AD and now in the collection of the Museum of Classical Archaeology, Cambridge. This suggests that the proprietor of the much later Romano-British villa had antiquarian tastes.

In this panel at Brading, the Medusa head is part of the narrative, but such heads were often given prominence in their own right. One is shown, for instance, in the centre of the eastern part of the Brading mosaic (lower middle in figure *16*), and fragments of curved lines in the central panel adjoining Perseus and Andromeda have been interpreted as another example. These, along with other Medusa mosaics, will be discussed in chapter 6.

Although sometimes described as a triclinium, the outer borders of the Brading room are too narrow to have held couches and it is more likely that the room served as an audience chamber. An adjoining room with a plain diamond pattern in the centre of its floor could have been used as the dining room. The outer border at the western end of the Seasons mosaic has the good luck motif of a swastika decorating a stylised gateway (at the top of figure *16*). It is thought that this might have marked the position of the villa proprietor's chair while he received visitors.

Theseus

As related in the previous chapter, Theseus played important roles in the stories of Ariadne, whom he abandoned, and Hippolytus, whom he expelled following the false accusation made by Phaedra. His most illustrious exploit was penetrating the Cretan labyrinth to slay the Minotaur, a monster with the body of a man and head of a bull. An annual tribute of seven young men and seven girls had been exacted from Athens, Theseus' city, to feed the monster, until Theseus brought an end to this barbarous practice.

According to the description of a buried and mostly lost mosaic of uncertain date from Oldcotes (Nottinghamshire), Theseus was shown in an attitude of attack in the centre of a labyrinth. Similar labyrinths with Theseus and the Minotaur are found in other provinces. Unpeopled labyrinths were also popular and would no doubt have reminded the viewer of Theseus' exploits. Examples have been found at Caerleon (Gwent), now in the Roman Legionary Museum, Caerleon, and at Harpham (Yorkshire). A replica of the latter is on display in the Hull and East Riding Museum.

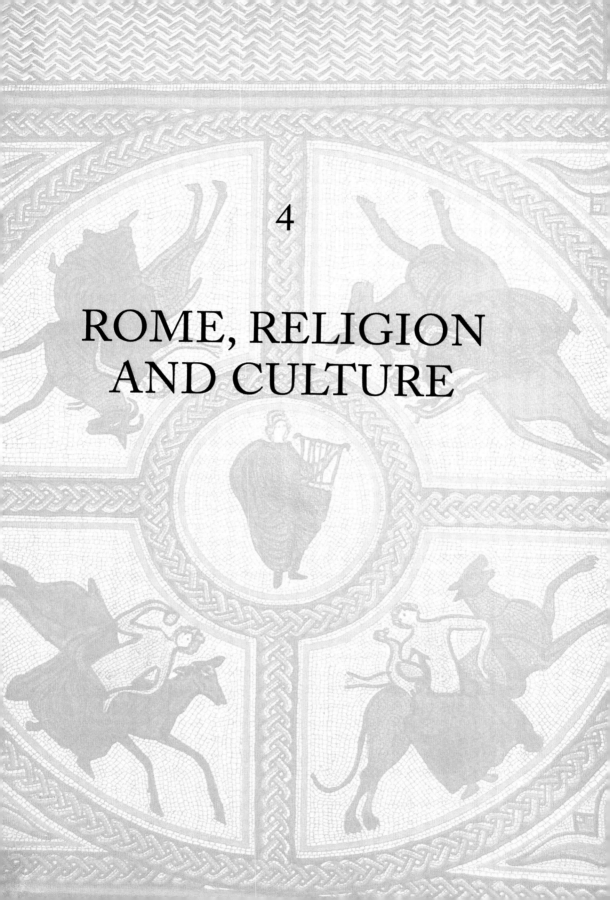

4

ROME, RELIGION AND CULTURE

As well as themes from classical mythology and literature, other subjects often depicted in mosaics related to the Roman empire, its religion and culture. They are all found in the mosaics of Roman Britain, where the image of Orpheus enjoyed especial popularity.

ALLUSIONS TO ROME

Aeneas, as the legendary founder of the Roman race and the hero of Virgil's *Aeneid*, was a pre-eminent symbol of the Roman empire. His appearance in the mosaics from Frampton (5 and *colour plate 6*) and Low Ham (*13*), and the allusion to his adventures in the inscription at Lullingstone (*colour plate 3*), did not just record episodes from his life, but would have reminded the viewer of the inception of Rome itself.

Another important foundation myth was the legend of Romulus and Remus. When Rhea Silvia was pregnant by Mars, her uncle gave orders that her offspring should be drowned in the River Tiber after their birth. They were laid in a chest that fortunately floated towards the riverbank where it grounded next to a fig tree. A she-wolf who had recently given birth found and suckled the twins.

A naively drawn panel of controversial authenticity from Aldborough (Yorkshire), now in the collection of Leeds Museums and Galleries, shows a teatless she-wolf towering over the two diminutive figures of Romulus and Remus. A stylised tree to the left represents the fig tree. The crude draftsmanship has led some to regard this mosaic as a Victorian copy, particularly since Ecroyd Smith did not include it in his publication of the Aldborough antiquities. There are, however, close parallels for this mosaic in pavements from other provinces that were unknown at the time when the Aldborough mosaic is said to have been discovered in 1842. It seems improbable that a forger would have sought deliberately to create a mosaic as poorly drawn as this. The Aldborough panel is likely to be essentially Roman, albeit with some modern restoration both to the panel itself and of most of its borders. Its very crudeness lends it a special charm in the eyes of many of its admirers. It recalls the naivety with which the Rudston Venus has been drawn, and suggests that mosaicists operating in Yorkshire were of widely different standards.

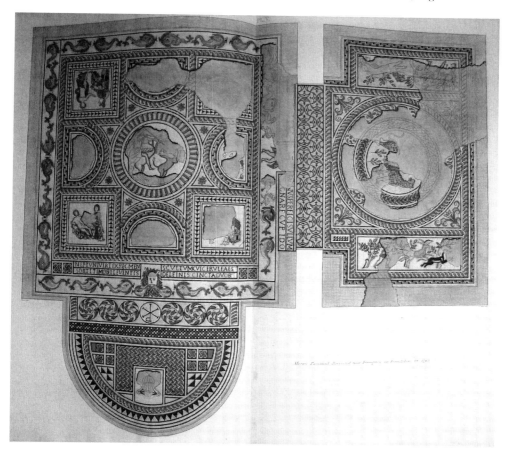

18 Mosaic in room B, Frampton (Samuel Lysons)

the apparently Christian elements of the Frampton and Hinton St Mary mosaics tend to reflect the personal standpoint of the commentator.

ALLUSIONS TO CLASSICAL CULTURE

Classical culture was epitomised by the Muses and by Orpheus who was, according to some of the most popular myths, the offspring of Apollo and one of the Muses.

The Muses

A mosaic with Muses was found at Aldborough (Yorkshire) in 1846 in a large apsidal room within a Roman town house. The figures were each contained in a series of individual compartments running across the chord of the apse (*19*).

Only half of this mosaic was excavated as the remaining half lay on the other side of a modern garden boundary and was in different ownership. Its condition has deteriorated since discovery, and the only piece visible today is the Muse who was originally placed at the end of the row on the right. The fragment has been lifted, conserved on several occasions, and is on display in the site museum. It is just possible to make out the Muse's left arm holding the remains of a scroll and her feet peeping out from under her striped robe.

The figures were identified by an inscription in blue glass tesserae below the surviving Muse's left elbow, which reads (in Greek letters) HELEKON and thus sets the scene on a slightly misspelt Mount Helicon, the home of the Muses. The surviving Muse was long thought to represent Clio, who, as Muse of History, held a scroll. In recent years, however, English Heritage has acquired a glass slide taken in the late nineteenth or early twentieth century when the mosaic was more complete than it is now. It shows that this Muse was also accompanied by a theatrical mask which no longer survives. This suggests that instead of Clio she was perhaps Thalia, the Muse of Comedy, or Melpomene, the Muse of Tragedy. Both Muses' attributes traditionally included a mask. As the latter was

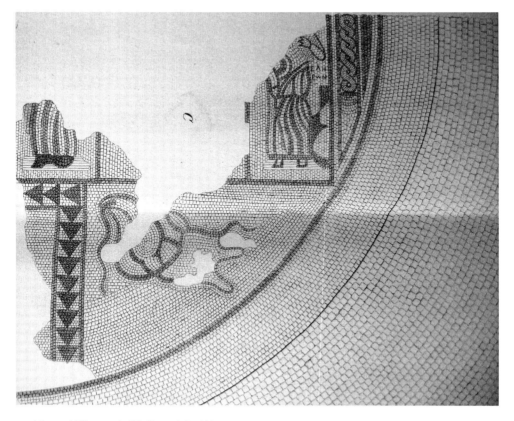

19 Muses, Aldborough (H. Ecroyd Smith)

usually shown wearing boots, as another now lost Aldborough Muse may have done, the surviving Muse is likely to be the former. This is reinforced by the suggestion that lettering on the scroll, revealed by the slide, is the name of the Muse Thalia.

Illustrations made at the time of discovery recorded a series of curved lines below the row of Muses. For many years unrecognised, these lines have now been identified as depicting a water nymph reclining with her head to the left and legs to the right. This was an appropriate image to accompany the Muses as, according to Hesiod, they danced around and washed in a spring (*Theogony*, 1–8). The nymph was no doubt mirrored by a similar figure on the other side of the mosaic.

An unusual mosaic from a villa at Brantingham (Yorkshire) might also represent Muses with water nymphs. Fragments of it are now in the Hull and East Riding Museum. It originally showed busts of eight female figures arranged in two rows of four in an arcaded setting, with a larger, ninth, bust in the centre of the mosaic (*20*). The water nymphs recline in semicircular compartments and rest their elbows on overturned urns (*21*).

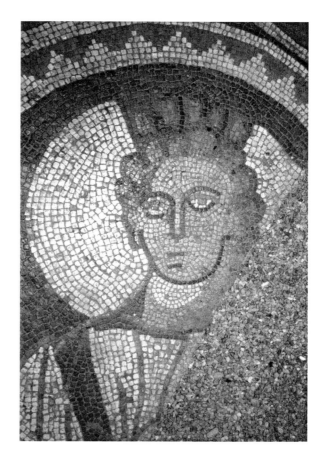

20 Tyche or Muse (?), Brantingham.
Courtesy Hull and East Riding Museum

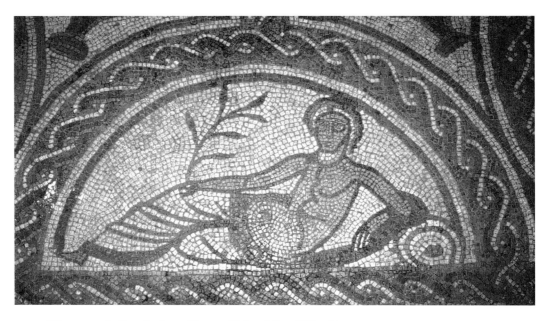

21 Water nymph, Brantingham. *Courtesy Hull and East Riding Museum*

Based on the number of busts, some scholars contend that they are the Muses. They lack attributes that would put their identity beyond doubt, and the headdress worn by the nimbed central figure resembles a mural crown. This has led others to identify her as a Tyche, a city goddess. On the other hand, the apparent mural crown could be a misinterpretation of the feathers often wore by Muses in their hair. The outline created by feathers in the headdresses of Muses in mosaics from other provinces often looks like the crenellations of a mural crown. The hair of the busts in the arcades, however, is dressed in a conventional 'top-knot' and seems to match neither the mural crown of a Tyche nor the feathered headdress of a Muse. The correct interpretation of this mosaic remains unclear.

Orpheus

The popularity of Orpheus as a subject for mosaics is easy to appreciate. His lyre evoked the delights of music and was highly appropriate in rooms used for dining and entertainment. Such was his skill as a musician that wild beasts were drawn to and soothed by his music. This provided the opportunity for depicting an attractive and sometimes exotic array of animals. Many of the Romano-British mosaics employed a circular scheme in which quadrupeds, and in some mosaics birds, processed around the central figure of Orpheus. This design seems to have been a provincial speciality. It was thought for some time to be unique to Roman Britain but a similar scheme has since been found in Spain.

Orpheus was typically shown fully clothed, wearing a Phrygian cap and playing a lyre or cithara. Among the animals, a canine was usually shown immediately next to him and seems to have been his special companion. Often described as a dog, it has been convincingly shown that this animal is more likely to represent a fox. It recalls the fox-skins worn by Thracians and signifies Orpheus' Thracian origins. It also alludes to his relationship with Bacchus, whose epithet *Bassareus* means 'fox fur'.

Instead of the typical Romano-British circular design, a panel in the entrance corridor at the Brading villa shows the animals clustered around Orpheus in a type of composition popular in the eastern part of the Roman empire (*22*). Orpheus is seated on a rock. A bird perches on his lyre next to which a fox squats attentively. To Orpheus' right are a peacock and a monkey with a misplaced ear resembling a cap.

An elegant example of the concentric circular design was found in 1824 in a Roman house built just outside the walls of *Corinium* (Cirencester, Gloucestershire)

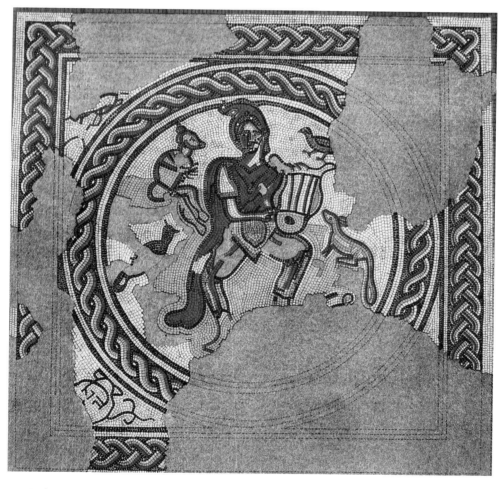

22 Orpheus mosaic, Brading (J. Price and F.G.H. Price)

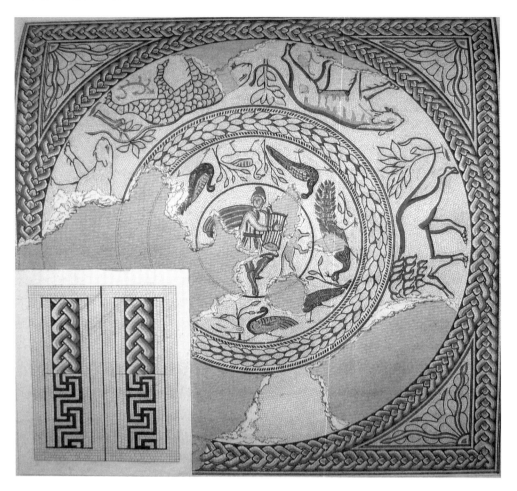

23 Orpheus mosaic, Barton Farm, Cirencester (J. Buckman and C.H. Newmarch)

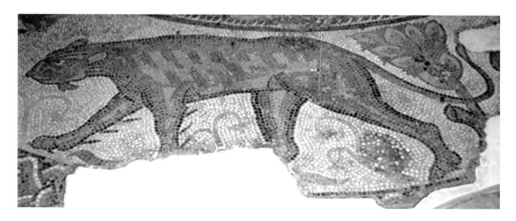

24 Feline from Orpheus mosaic, Barton Farm, Cirencester. *Courtesy Corinium Museum, Cirencester*

at Barton Farm. It is now in the Corinium Museum and is a particularly attractive rendering of the subject (*23*). Orpheus is shown playing his cithara in the central medallion. His cloak streams out behind his right shoulder and his cap is decorated with white crosses perhaps representing stars and emphasising his semi-divine nature. He is accompanied by his fox, which appears to be walking around the inner rim of the medallion.

Proceeding clockwise in the surrounding circle, and separated from one another by small trees or shrubs, are a series of birds. There is no unanimity among the scholars who have sought to identify the species. The most likely identifications, starting with the fragmentary bird near Orpheus' cloak and proceeding clockwise, are a guineafowl identified by the white crosses on its dark breast, a swan with its long neck, a peahen turning to look at the swan, a peacock, perhaps a pheasant with its forked tail, a crane with its fluffy tail feathers and perhaps a goose.

The outer circle, which is separated from the bird circle by a laurel wreath, contains a procession of strikingly drawn quadrupeds. Above left of Orpheus is a leopard whose spots have been transformed into a scale pattern. The leopard is followed by an animal of which only fragments survive, variously described as a tiger or bear; by comparison with similar mosaics, it is probably a tigress. In front of the leopard, a pale-coloured feline might have been intended as a lioness although no teats are shown (*24*). This animal follows a splendid lion, in front of which are the remains of a griffin (not shown in the engraving).

Another Orpheus mosaic was said to have been found beneath Dyer Street, Cirencester, in 1820 and is known only from a plate published many decades after discovery. In the plate, the way in which Orpheus has been drawn is not only unusual, but he is shown accompanied by a fish-tailed creature wielding an axe and spear or arrow. This creature has been interpreted as Abraxas or Scylla, neither of whom was a normal companion of Orpheus. The birds and quadrupeds in the surrounding circles are so similar to the Barton Farm creatures that some scholars consider the plate to be an inaccurate and misattributed rendering of that mosaic. Others contend, however, that the apparently unique iconography of the central panel is an argument for the authenticity of the Dyer Street mosaic despite the absence of contemporary accounts of it.

The craftsmen who made the Barton Farm mosaic are also thought to have worked on the Orpheus mosaic at the palatial villa at Woodchester (Gloucestershire), often referred to as the 'Great Pavement' (*25*). This mosaic is buried under a churchyard and was first recorded in the seventeenth century when grave digging revealed 'tesseraik work of painted beasts and flowers'. It was last uncovered in 1973. The centre of the mosaic was apparently decorated with 'fish and a Star about the Centre' and is thought to have featured a small pool. This would explain why Orpheus has been displaced from the centre of the mosaic and straddles the inner circle, flanked by a peacock and fox. The remainder of this circle is filled with a variety of birds.

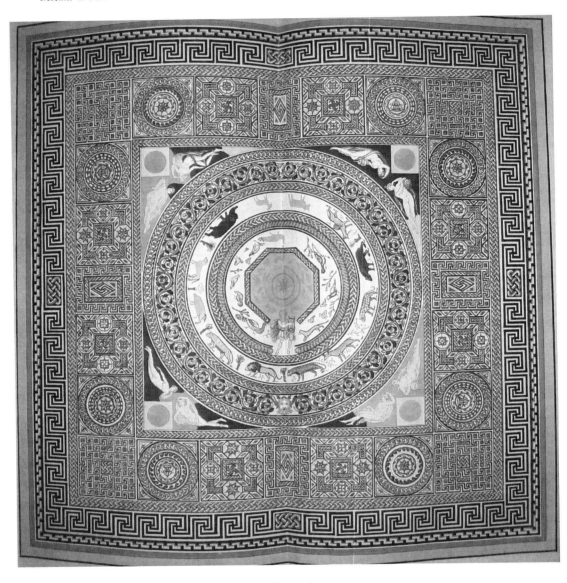

25 The 'Great Pavement', Woodchester (Samuel Lysons)

As on the Barton Farm mosaic, a laurel wreath border separates the bird circle from a band of slinking quadrupeds. Starting at top right and proceeding clockwise, the surviving animals are a griffin, a bear, a leopard, a stag, a tigress and a lion, with the remains of a lioness, a wild boar and probably a wild ass. Antiquarian drawings show that the circle also contained an elephant (*26*) and a feline, probably a tiger, that have since been lost. Pairs of water nymphs recline languidly in the spandrels where columns once rose up to support the inner part of the roof. Outside the columned area is an accomplished and highly ornate series of geometric panels.

They have an exact parallel in a mosaic at Trier but it is a moot point whether the Trier craftsman travelled to Woodchester or vice versa.

The Great Pavement is buried *in situ* but a replica painstakingly constructed by Robert Woodward and his brother John is occasionally put on display. Thoroughly researched and with the missing portions plausibly restored, the replica gives an excellent idea of just how impressive the original floor must have been. It is thought that the roof was heightened over the central part of the room to provide light by way of a clerestory. The room lay at a focal point at the centre of the inner range of the villa buildings, and the whole complex was of considerable size and grandeur.

A similar but less elaborate composition was found at the Withington villa (Gloucestershire) in 1811 (27). The central medallion is lost but Samuel Lysons'

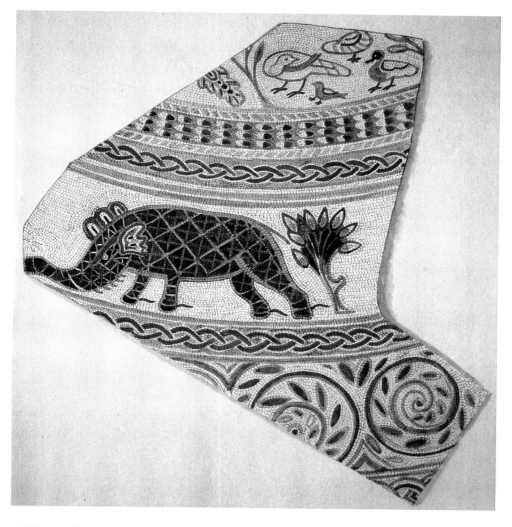

26 Elephant from the 'Great Pavement', Woodchester. *Courtesy Society of Antiquaries*

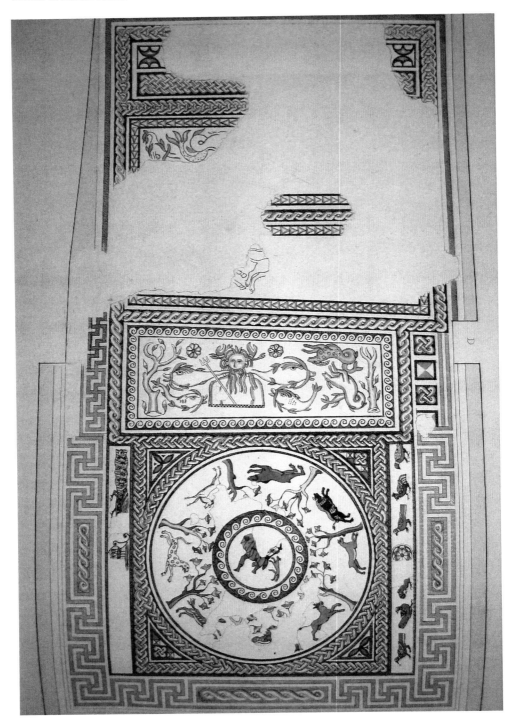

Above: 27 Orpheus mosaic, Withington (Samuel Lysons)

Opposite: 28 Orpheus mosaic, Newton St Loe. *Courtesy Bristol City Museum*

Orpheus panel was incomplete when found and the surviving fragment is in the Hull and East Riding Museum. It shows the head of a wild boar, a bear and an elephant. The birds are often described as peacocks but their short necks suggest that perhaps pheasants were intended. The black animal with a white patch in the inner register is a hunting dog and it is followed by a hind or hare.

The much-restored Orpheus mosaic at the Littlecote Park villa is another example of a radial design with quadrupeds circling around the central figure (*30* and *colour plate 2*). Orpheus, apparently standing but in reality seated as the lines on his drapery show, plays his cithara in the usual way and is accompanied by a fox. The mosaic is unusual, however, as the surrounding animals have human companions. They are thought to represent the seasons and are discussed in the next chapter. Some scholars consider that Orpheus is here conflated with Apollo and that the room was a cult chamber.

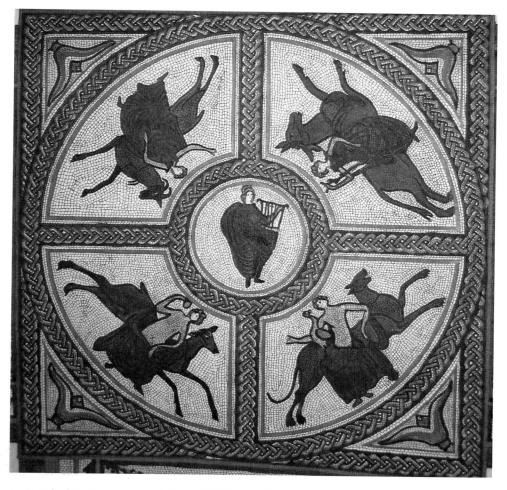

30 Detail of Orpheus mosaic, Littlecote (William Fowler). *Courtesy Society of Antiquaries*

Another unusual radial mosaic with Orpheus was discovered at Winterton (Lincolnshire) in the eighteenth century. It was re-excavated in 1958-9 when it was found that much, including the central compartment, had been lost. The surviving fragments are buried *in situ* and confirm the broad accuracy of antiquarian drawings (*colour plate 12*) although there are some discrepancies. The illustrations of Orpheus show him as naked and apparently sitting within a harp-like lyre. The excavated fragments include a wild boar recognisable from its ridge of bristles. Wings indicate a griffin. An animal with a long tongue, distinctively drooling spittle, is likely to be a hound. A striped animal with teats is accompanied by a spherical object and is a rare depiction in Roman Britain of a tigress with a mirror. The 'mirror trap' was used by hunters to distract the mother while her cubs were snatched. It is depicted, for instance, in the Great Hunt corridor mosaic at the palatial villa of Piazza Armerina in Sicily. A leopard is identifiable from its spots and the remaining fragment is of a stag.

Antiquarian records indicate that another panel adjoined the Orpheus mosaic. This was confirmed by the discovery of fragments of mosaic in the 1958-9 re-excavation, showing part of a medallion above the remains of a tree. Other fragments appear to show a hound pursuing a stag. The journal of George Stovin, a local antiquary, in the Lincolnshire Archives gives an eye-witness account of the initial excavation of the Winterton mosaics in 1747. The first discovery was of a bust of a lady with a stag below, presumably the fragments located in the re-excavation. Having enlisted help, Stovin returned a few days later and found the bust of a figure he described as a man holding a sceptre. He referred to this figure in his published account, on the basis of which it has since been suggested that the two busts might have been placed side by side and formed a series, perhaps of the seasons. The extra detail in his journal makes it clear, however, that the 'man' with the 'sceptre' was the figure subsequently identified as 'Ceres' and discussed in chapter 8. We are left with the mystery of the bust of the lady and whether she had any attributes or companions. The only known illustrations of the fragment with the stag omit her, but Stovin mentions further drawings by an artist who is otherwise unknown. To date, attempts to trace those drawings have not proved successful but the quest continues. It is a tantalising example of how knowledge of centuries-old excavations might yet be expanded.

A similar tale concerns the first Orpheus mosaic discovered in Britain, which was only identified some 300 years after it had been found at the Wellow villa (Somerset) and subsequently lost. John Aubrey included two short accounts of this pavement in his manuscript, *Monumenta Britannica*, giving the year of discovery as 1683. From an ink drawing Aubrey added to his papers with a note that the discovery date was about 1685, it looked as if the central compartment contained some rocks, a tree and two box shapes with two curvilinear objects. Regarded for centuries as virtually unidentifiable, it has since been convincingly demonstrated that the box shapes belong to Orpheus' cithara with its snake-like terminals. A pair of birds, probably peacocks, decorated a corner of the central square, and rectangular panels on either side showed felines in a leafy setting.

In addition to the known Orpheus mosaics described above, there are a number of incomplete mosaics where animals have been recorded. This naturally raises the possibility that they too could have featured Orpheus, but in most cases the evidence is too sparse to tell. They might have depicted hunting scenes instead. In the mosaic found at the Whatley villa (Somerset), however, an elephant and a griffin were among the animals in a square border (*31*). These animals often accompanied Orpheus and would be uncommon, although not unknown, in a hunting scene. This factor, coupled with the way in which the animals were displayed alternating with trees, makes it virtually certain that Orpheus was the subject of the lost central panel. Similarly, the design of a fragment from Pit Meads (Wiltshire), showing part of an animal processing around a circle, is thought to be indicative of another Orpheus mosaic.

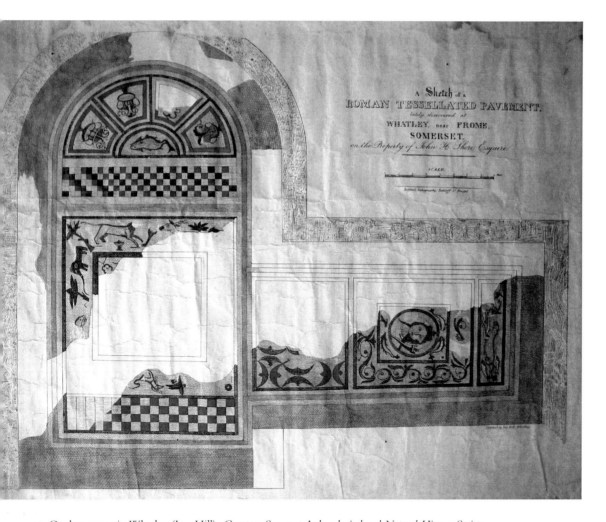

31 Orpheus mosaic, Whatley (Ino Hill). *Courtesy Somerset Archaeological and Natural History Society*

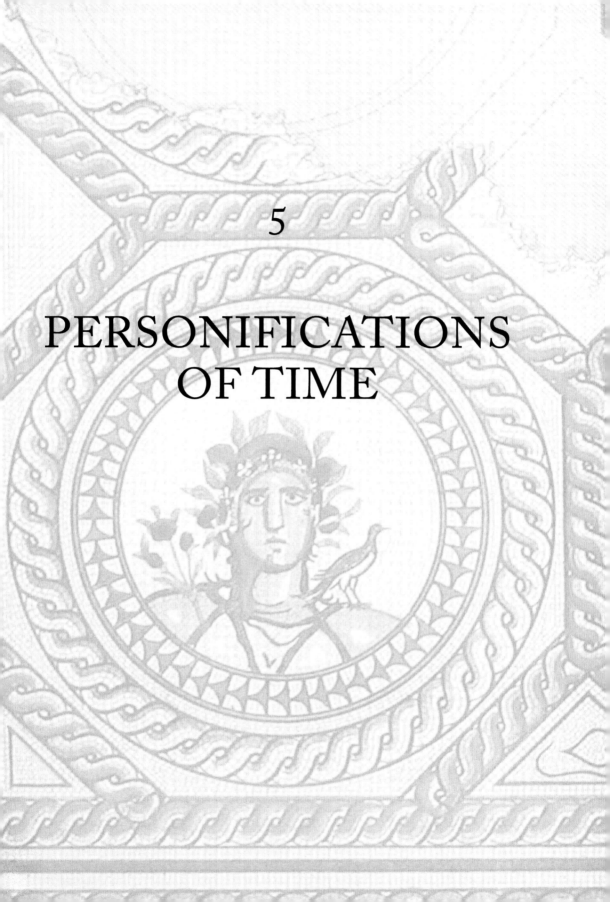

5

PERSONIFICATIONS
OF TIME

The divisions of the year – seasons, months and days – were a fertile source of imagery for Roman mosaics. In recent years, there has been increasing recognition of festival scenes celebrated at certain times of the year. The mosaics of Roman Britain have provided many examples of mosaics depicting the seasons, a disputed reference to months, one pavement showing the days of the week, and a fragmentary scene that might depict a festival.

DAYS OF THE WEEK

A fine collection of the deities representing the days of the week was shown in a mosaic at the Bramdean villa (Hampshire) (*colour plate 10*). Busts of the sun god, moon goddess and then-known planetary deities surrounded a central medallion decorated with the head of Medusa. Like the Hercules and Antaeus mosaic from the same site, it was found in 1823 and recorded by John Lickman but has since been lost.

The gods and goddesses were depicted in the order of the days they represented, as listed by the fourth-century writer Ausonius (VII, *The Eclogues*, viii, *On the Names of the Seven Days*). They started with Sol (Apollo) in the compartment above Medusa. He wore a crown replicating the sun's rays and had a whip for driving his horses across the sky. Proceeding clockwise, next came Luna (Diana), the moon goddess, who wore a headdress decorated with a crescent moon. It is likely that there was a torch across her shoulder in the area of the mosaic that did not survive. Mars was dressed as the god of war. He wore a helmet and had a spear. Mercury, in his role as messenger, wore a winged cap to speed him on his way and had a caduceus, his herald's staff. Jupiter was bareheaded. As he appeared to hold a trident, this bust was initially identified as Neptune, but the context shows that he must have been Jupiter with a poorly rendered thunderbolt. Venus wore a necklace and had a mirror.

Only a fragment survived of the seventh bust. This will have been Saturn, who represented the remaining planet known at the time and who appears on days of the week mosaics from other provinces. The identity of the missing eighth figure remains uncertain. A castration clamp found in the Thames in 1840 and now in the British Museum shows busts of the planetary deities with Ceres, representing agriculture. She would have been an appropriate choice. Other suggestions have included Bonus Eventus and Fortuna.

MONTHS

Fragmentary lines on the edge of the central part of the Orpheus mosaic at Winterton, not shown on Fowler's engraving (*colour plate 12*), have been tentatively regarded as the remains of inscriptions referring to the months of June and December. No inscriptions were noted when the mosaic was discovered in 1747 nor when it was re-excavated in 1958-9, and it is difficult to see why the months would be used as labels in an Orpheus mosaic. It seems likely that the putative 'inscriptions' should bear the much more prosaic interpretation of parts of Orpheus' anatomy: the shapes are consistent with the outlines of his head and knee, and the fragments were found in the areas of these parts of his body.

SEASONS

Unlike the single example of a mosaic showing the days of the week and the one doubtful example of months, the four seasons were abundantly represented in Romano-British mosaics. Their number made them an obvious and practical choice for the corners of a mosaic, but convenience was not the only reason they were chosen, as they were often linked thematically to other images on the same floor.

In earlier Graeco-Roman art, seasons were normally shown as full-length female figures, but by the time mosaics were being laid in Roman Britain they were commonly depicted as female busts. They could also be represented as masks, as at Colliton Park in Dorchester (Dorset), or as full-length figures in the special case of Littlecote Park. Cupid-seasons were also popular.

The only example of a male bust is recorded as being found in or around 1882 in the bath-suite of the Spoonley Wood villa (Gloucestershire). It cannot now be located, but a drawing shows a naïve figure accompanied by a rake. This was the only bust found in the Spoonley Wood mosaic, and the placement of the tesserae shown in the drawing looks more like Victorian restoration than Roman workmanship. No other Romano-British mosaics with seasons have been found in baths. The context suggests that the original mosaic perhaps showed Neptune with his trident, inaccurately restored as a season with a rake.

Seasons can be distinguished from one another by the attributes characterising the season in question: a swallow, leaves or flowers with Spring; corn or flowers with Summer; grapes with Autumn; and a dead animal or bare branch with

Winter. Other attributes found in Romano-British mosaics related to agricultural implements used for seasonal activities: for instance, a sickle in summer and a pruning-knife and rake or hoe (an apparent regional speciality) in autumn. Mosaics from other provinces show seasonal activities being undertaken, but no such scenes of activity are known from Roman-British examples.

Clothing was sometimes used to indicate the temperature at different times of the year. This is most noticeable with Winter who often wore a hooded cloak, but generally there is little difference between the amounts of clothing worn by the other three seasons. As Ovid has demonstrated, age could operate as an apt analogy for the progression of the year (*Metamorphoses* XV, 199-213). In the case of mosaics showing the seasons as female busts or figures, the cycle starts with Spring as a young girl and ends with Winter as an old woman. Seasons were usually, but not invariably, shown in sequence and read in a clockwise direction.

The two sets of seasons at the Bignor villa are illuminating because they belong to different phases of the villa and demonstrate radically different styles and standards of execution in the same building (*32* and *33*). Like most of the Bignor pavements, the Seasons mosaic from the bipartite room at the northern end of the west wing dates to the fourth century. Only Winter survives, a gaunt hooded figure with a bare branch over her left shoulder. The delightful dolphin next to a bunch of grapes and an inscription TER (the E and R being ligatured) (*1*), belong to the southern part of this mosaic, much of which had already been lost by the time of discovery in 1811. Inscriptions are rarely found in mosaics. This one is usually thought to represent the abbreviated signature of the designer or craftsman responsible for the mosaic and is the most likely explanation. A number of other possibilities have been considered, including an abbreviation for 'Terpsichore', one of the Muses. In this case, the Muses themselves might once have graced the lost central octagon and its eight surrounding hexagons, but nothing survives and this can be nothing more than speculation.

Nearby, but at a lower level, the seasons in the mainly black and white mosaic at the bottom of the corridor steps are crude and stylised. This mosaic, thought to date to the third century, is similar in concept to its much more accomplished later counterpart: it too has a dolphin and both mosaics had birds that have since been lost. The dolphin together with a fish can be seen near the hooded bust of Winter (top right in figure *33*). The remaining seasons are so schematic that it is impossible to tell them apart.

Traces of similar sketchily drawn seasons were found in the spandrels of the Orpheus mosaic at the Brading villa but no longer survive (*22*). Although some doubt has been expressed, the identity of the busts as seasons seems secure. Winter had a bare branch and a hood with two protruding shapes probably representing pine cones, an appropriate attribute for this season and shown with Winter, for instance, on a mosaic from Vienne in France. The second bust had flowers or foliage in the headdress and was probably Spring.

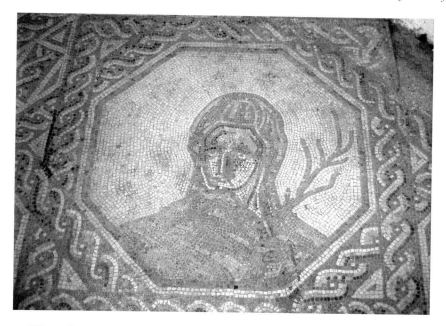

32 Winter, Seasons mosaic, Bignor. *Courtesy Bignor Roman Villa*

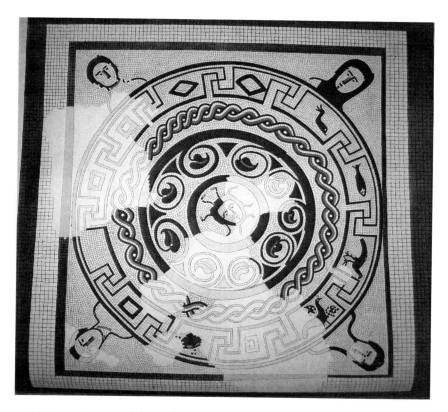

33 Medusa and seasons, Bignor (Samuel Lysons)

A second set of seasons at Brading are more detailed and colourful (*16*). They decorate the corner compartments of the mosaic in the western part of the eponymous Seasons mosaic (the upper part of figure *16*). Hooded Winter is easily recognisable. A dead bird is suspended from the bare branch lying across her left shoulder. Proceeding clockwise, next comes Spring with a headdress of protruding leaves, and then Summer with two ears of corn sticking out of the top of her headdress and four red poppies at the sides. The panel above Summer contains a peacock, a piece of fruit and a pedestalled bowl. Autumn does not survive but a vine leaf, bunches of grapes and a fragmentary peacock can just be discerned in the panel above.

The late second- or early third-century Seasons mosaic from a town house below Dyer Street in Cirencester (Gloucestershire), now in the Corinium Museum, contains three particularly detailed busts, Winter having been lost (*34*). Spring, to the left of Silenus on his ass, has a swallow perched on her left shoulder and a flowering stem lying across her right shoulder. She wears a headdress of flowers and leaves. The seasons progress anticlockwise on this mosaic and Summer is to the right of Silenus. Her leafy headdress is decorated with flowers and ears of corn (*colour plate 13*). The attributes lying across her shoulders are a sickle and two ears of corn. Autumn wears a leopard-skin tunic recalling the feline companion of the wine-god, Bacchus. Grapes and leaves adorn her headdress and there is a pruning-knife over her right shoulder. The attribute over her left shoulder is damaged and its identity is uncertain. In colour and shape, it resembles the leaves in the headdress to which it is apparently connected, making it likely that here were more vine leaves, perhaps with a bunch of grapes.

At the Lullingstone villa, seasons surround the cushion-shaped panel with Bellerophon slaying the Chimaera (*colour plate 3*). Winter with her hooded cloak is seen at top left and Spring with a swallow perched on her shoulder at top right. The next medallion did not survive but apparently showed Autumn. She must have been out of sequence as Summer is visible at bottom left with stalks and ears of corn in her hair.

In the Bacchus mosaic from the Thruxton villa, now in the British Museum, the busts of the seasons are flanked by leaf sprays resembling wings. The overall effect is as if the seasons are growing out of clumps of foliage (*colour plate 14*). Hooded Winter is visible at top left. Spring and Summer are virtually indistinguishable on the right as both have floral headdresses. Autumn did not survive.

Victorian restoration has subtly changed the appearance of the Seasons mosaic from Toft Green, York, now in the Yorkshire Museum. The seasons surround the central compartment, which evidently once held a depiction of Medusa as traces of snakes from her hair are still visible. Winter has a leafless branch and is unusually shown bare headed and naked save for a cloak over her right shoulder. The swallow on the right shoulder of the next season, proceeding clockwise, identifies her as Spring. The identity of the remaining seasons proved a puzzle for many years. The next season in sequence has a bunch of grapes apparently

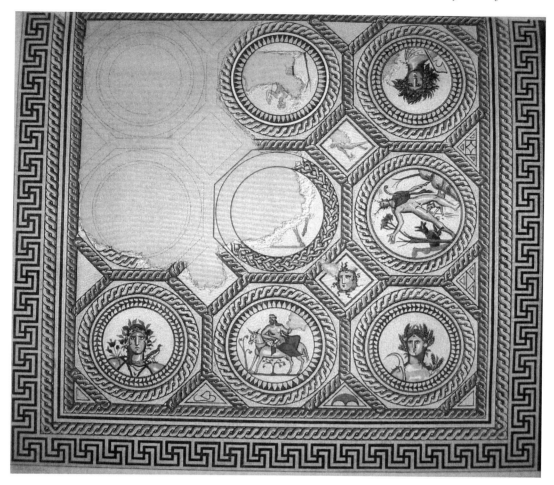

34 Seasons mosaic, Dyer Street, Cirencester (J. Buckman and C.H. Newmarch)

indicating Autumn even though Summer would be expected here. Interestingly, an account published soon after the mosaic was discovered in 1853 described fruit and flowers and identified this bust as Summer. The mosaic was the subject of restoration in the nineteenth century. It has been convincingly argued that the grapes are modern, and that this bust was intended to be Summer. It has also been shown that the rake with the remaining season is an attribute of Autumn and a Romano-British peculiarity.

A rake or drag-hoe is also shown with the season at the bottom left of the Victorious charioteer mosaic from the villa at Rudston (Yorkshire), now in the Hull and East Riding Museum (*35*) and fits her identity as Autumn. Missing Winter was at top left. A small surviving area of brown tesserae could be part of her hood. Spring is at top right with a swallow perched on her right shoulder. Summer is at bottom right with prominent flowers in her corn-coloured hair.

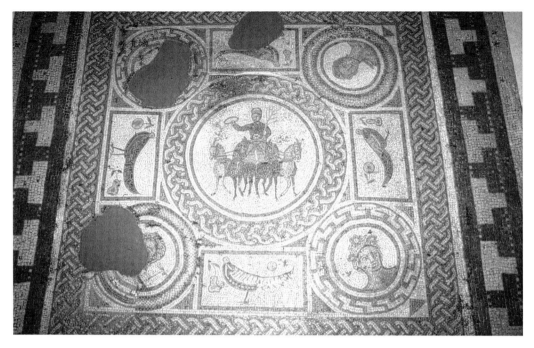

35 Victorious charioteer and seasons, Rudston. *Courtesy Hull and East Riding Museum*

A fragmentary Seasons mosaic was found in 1949 in an extra-mural town house at Malton (Yorkshire), and is buried *in situ*. Only Winter survived. She is heavily muffled in a hooded cloak and has a bare branch over her right shoulder. A stag and hound are shown in other panels.

A mosaic from Micklegate Bar, York, found in 1814 and since lost, is known from an engraving by William Fowler. The shapes in the four compartments around the central pair of deer were interpreted for many years as joints of venison. There are parallels for joints of meat being shown in xenia mosaics in other provinces but nothing remotely similar is known from Roman Britain. They are now thought to be the shoulders, heads and headdresses of busts, most probably seasons. They were no doubt disintegrating when seen by Fowler, who was accordingly unable to appreciate what he was drawing.

A fragmentary female bust found in 1901 in House XXVII.1 at Silchester (Hampshire) has recently been rediscovered in store at Reading Museum and put on display. Although no other figures survived from this mosaic, her corner position, floral headdress and a flower (?) over her left shoulder make it probable that she is a season, either Spring or Summer.

Busts of uncertain identification in other mosaics might also have depicted seasons. For instance, a bust in the corner of the rectangular part of the Muses mosaic at Aldborough had a jagged outline to her 'hair', perhaps indicating the folds of Winter's hood. Two of a presumed original four busts in the spandrels of the Orpheus panel from Horkstow are flanked by rosettes that might be a stylised indication of the flowers often shown with Spring and Summer (*29*).

Masks were used instead of busts for the two seasons that survived at the Colliton Park town house, Dorchester (Dorset) (*36*). They occupied small panels in the centre of the western and northern sides of the room. Winter, with her hood shown in jagged folds, has since been lost. The other season is *in situ*, partly restored. She is usually described as Summer with flowers in her hair and with ringlets. It has been suggested, however, that the 'flowers' are bunches of grapes and that this is Autumn, giving a consecutive sequence. A coloured tracing and painting made at the time of discovery support this interpretation. It shows four green 'petals' with a white and yellow centrepiece. The 'flowers' and 'ringlets' resemble vine leaves and ribbons, Bacchic attributes appropriate to Autumn, and the centrepiece might depict a prominent grape: its colour is matched by the grapes in the headdress worn by Autumn on the Seasons mosaic from Dyer Street at Cirencester discussed above.

The seasons at the Chedworth villa occupy triangular compartments in the corners of the triclinium mosaic discussed in chapter 2 (*7*). They are represented as Cupids. The famous figure of Winter is warmly dressed in a tunic, over-tunic, leggings and hooded cloak, the *Birrus Britannicus* mentioned Diocletian's Price Edict. He holds a bare branch in his left hand and a dead hare by its back legs in his right hand. Proceeding clockwise, Spring has a wisp of drapery around his waist. A swallow is perched on his right hand, while in his left arm he holds a basket whose stylised contents were perhaps intended to represent flowers. Summer is entirely nude. He holds a garland of flowers and a basket whose contents are larger than Spring's and might have been intended to represent ears of corn. Autumn is damaged and the attribute held in his right hand is lost. Like Spring, he wears a band of drapery around his waist and carries a basket.

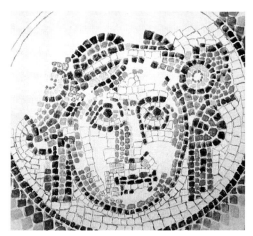 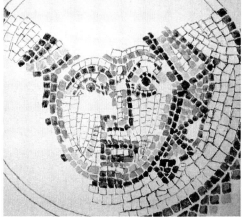

36 Masks of seasons, Colliton Park, Dorchester. *Courtesy Dorset County Museum*

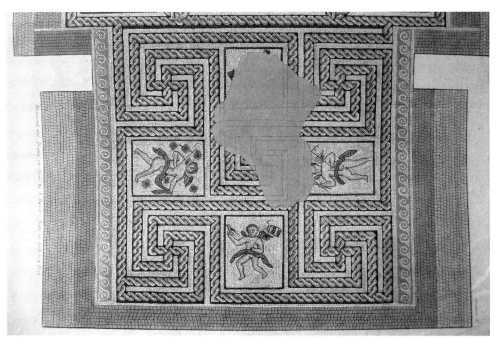

37 Seasons from 'Grand Mosaic', Pitney (Samuel Hasell). *Courtesy Society of Antiquaries*

Seasons were also depicted as Cupids in the lost Grand Mosaic at the Pitney villa (*37*). Spring had a swallow perched on his fingers and carried a pail, perhaps of milk, hanging from a pedum. Summer was surrounded by flowers and carried a pedum or sickle. The next season was lost save for traces of feet and drapery. He should have been Autumn if the figures were shown sequentially, but the season opposite Summer had a rake. He has therefore been interpreted as Autumn bearing vines or twigs, rather than Winter holding bare branches. Only the feet survived of the fourth season, along with a wedge-shaped feature at waist height. Most published illustrations of this mosaic reproduce one of the copies of the lithograph made of it (*colour plate 7*). On some but not all copies of the lithograph, the feet and wedge-shaped feature are coloured blue, implying a cold season. The most reliable illustration is the original watercolour by the excavator, Samuel Hasell, in the Somerset Studies Library in Taunton. This has been marked on the back (not in Hasell's handwriting) 'Mr Hassell's [sic] best Drawing of the Pitney Pavement'. It shows a black foot at the end of a fragmentary white leg, indicating that this Season was booted unlike his companions and was therefore Winter. The wedge shape was white, edged in black and fawn, and took the place of the other seasons' red drapery. The shape and location of this fragment is not particularly appropriate for part of a cloak and it might instead represent an implement held by Winter, perhaps an axe or a sarculum, a wedge-shaped hoe found as an attribute of Winter in the mosaics of North Africa.

The mosaic from House VII at Caerwent (Gwent), now in Newport Museum, depicts Cupids and seasons separately (*38*). When discovered in 1901, three of the seasons survived. The restored figure of Winter broadly resembles her appearance as recorded in tracings and lithographs made at the time of discovery. She is hooded and appears to be in the act of muffling herself further as the patch of white tesserae on her chest has been interpreted as her hand clutching the drapery. The tesserae from the two other seasons have been amalgamated to

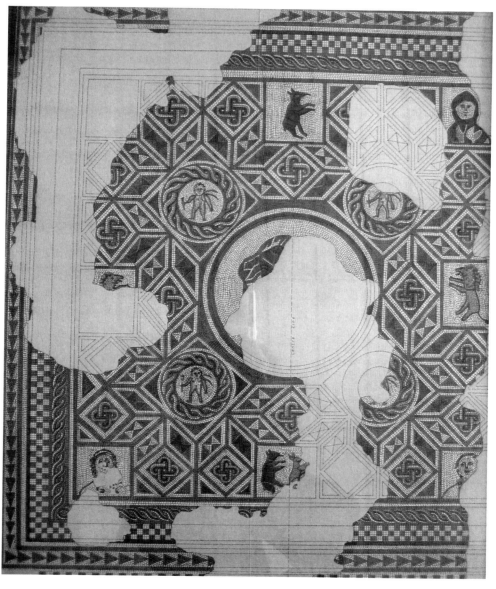

38 Seasons mosaic, Caerwent (S.J. Loxton). *Courtesy Newport City Council Museum & Heritage Service*

create the bust seen today. They were similar to one another and are thought to have represented Spring and Summer as they wore garlands in their hair. Four winged, torch-bearing Cupids were placed around the central compartment, of which only indeterminate fragments survive. The layout of the Caerwent mosaic is one of the clearest indications of a triclinium found in Roman Britain. Dining couches could have been accommodated on the U-shaped panels around the edge of the geometric pavement in the inner part of the room, while the Seasons mosaic decorated the outer part of the room.

SEASONAL ALLUSIONS

The busts in the western part of the Seasons mosaic at the Brading villa have been described above. They were immediately recognised as seasons when the mosaic was excavated in 1880. They might not, however, be the only seasonal element in this pavement. In the eastern part of the mosaic (the lower part of figure *16*) are four couples (*9* and *16*). Two of the panels have been discussed in chapter 2: Apollo and Daphne, and Attis with a water nymph. The remaining two are Ceres giving an ear of corn to Triptolemus who holds a plough, and Lycurgus attacking Ambrosia as she is transformed into a vine. The scene with Ceres and Triptolemus alludes to ploughing and sowing, activities that took place in the spring in the northern climates. As the sun god, Apollo's gift was strongest in summer and a major festival was held to him in that season. Lycurgus was a traditional enemy of Bacchus, who was linked to autumn, the season when the grape harvest took place. The vine itself, into which Ambrosia is being metamorphosed, is shown in the fronds surrounding the figures. The myth of Attis refers to the withdrawal of fertility in winter.

It therefore appears that the Brading mosaic has scenes alluding to the four seasons as well as busts of the seasons themselves. This double iconography can be explained by examining the pavement as a whole (*16*). Occupying a crucial position between the two parts of the mosaic is the figure of an astronomer (*39*). He is seated in a chair and points to a globe of the heavens. The globe is divided by lines into four sections, which recall the division of celestial time into the four periods marked by the summer and winter solstices and the spring and autumn equinoxes. Behind him is a sundial on top of a column. The vessel-like object on the right is probably a different sort of sundial. Only 15 Greek and Roman instruments of this nature, called horizontal planar sundials, are known to survive and in each case the gnomon is missing, so it is difficult to find an exact parallel for the Brading object. Comparisons can, however, be drawn with later sundials whose bowl-like base and angled gnomon are strikingly similar to the Brading example. The astronomer is critical to the interpretation of the Brading mosaic, for he occupies a significant position at the transition from one set of figured scenes to the other. He is indicating, quite literally, the character of what follows, namely time and the stars.

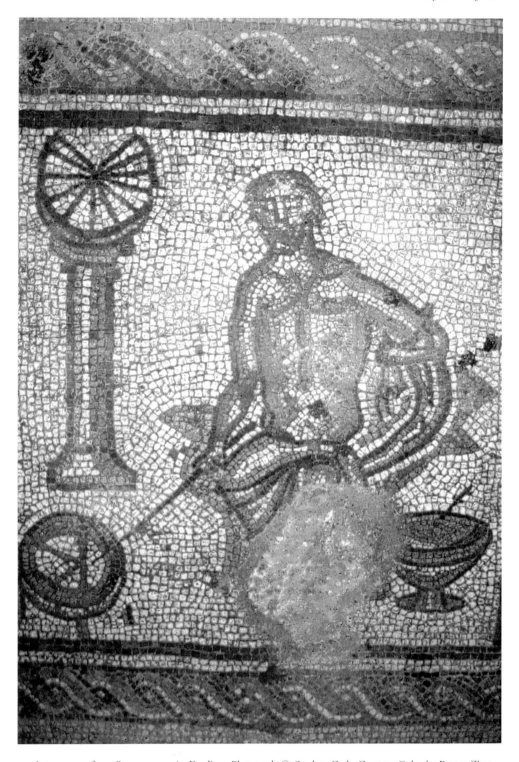

39 Astronomer from Seasons mosaic, Brading. *Photograph:* © *Stephen Cosh. Courtesy Oglander Roman Trust*

Because of the astronomer's preoccupation with time and the heavens, it is probable that the seasonal busts represent not just seasons but Tropai. They are indistinguishable iconographically from normal seasons, but their specific role is to personify the seasons as they turn around the sun. The word 'trope' means 'turning', and they refer to the solstices and equinoxes. They are clearly found in mosaics in the eastern part of the empire where they are identified by inscriptions. In the west, inscriptions are rare and we are reliant on the context to grasp the full meaning.

The identification of the busts as Tropai explains why there are two sorts of season in one mosaic. It is reinforced by the nature of the myths portrayed in the western part of the Brading pavement (the upper part of figure *16*). They have been discussed in chapter 3: Perseus and Andromeda, Cadmus, and probably Hercules. Their significance is that they all have allusions to the circumpolar, non-seasonal constellations; in other words, the constellations visible for all or most of the year. The story of Perseus and Andromeda spreads over six constellations, giving this myth extensive coverage in the night sky. One of the most easily recognisable constellations is the W-shape of Cassiopeia, Andromeda's mother, whose imprudent boasting instigated the chain of events. The prominent constellation of Draco, the serpent coiling around the north pole, is evoked by the well-known myth of Cadmus and the serpent. Another constellation was named Hercules.

The Brading mosaic thus arguably alludes to the seasons on earth in the eastern part, and then transfers to the heavens via the connecting figure of the astronomer. He points out what is happening on the next part of the pavement, where the turning points of the year (solstices and equinoxes) are shown revolving around allusions to the circumpolar constellations.

Another Romano-British mosaic containing references to seasonal myths is the Orpheus pavement at Littlecote Park. It was found in 1727 and subsequently feared lost. Excitingly and unexpectedly rediscovered in 1977, it was re-excavated the following year and completely restored based on eighteenth-century records (*30* and *colour plate 2*). A female figure accompanies an animal in each of the four segments surrounding the central medallion. The posture of these figures is disputed. Some see them as dancing or standing in front of the animals, while others note the apparent laps and conclude that they must be riding the beasts even though their bodies are low in relation to the beasts' backs. The position of their feet suggests that they are turning on the spot as the beasts proceed in a circle behind them.

The female figures are interpreted as goddesses evoking the different seasons of the year: Venus at bottom left with a mirror, representing rebirth and spring; Leda at bottom right with a swan, representing youth and summer; Ceres with a staff entwined with leaves, representing maturity and autumn; and Proserpina gesturing towards her mother Ceres with her arm, representing death and winter.

SEASONAL ANIMALS

Some animals have seasonal connotations. For instance, the leopard's connection with Bacchus alludes to autumn, the season of the grape harvest, while the boar is associated with winter, as that is the season in which boar-hunting takes place. It is not always clear, however, whether a Romano-British viewer would have attributed seasonal significance to any given set of animals. Much depends on the context and, even where the context is clearly seasonal, there seems to have been no consistency between the animals linked with each season. It has been suggested that the important factor was for the season to ride or drive an animal: the identity of the animal itself was not necessarily vital.

The significance of the Littlecote animals – deer, leopard, bull and goat – has been linked to the animals into which Bacchus (Zagreus-Dionysus) transformed himself when he fled from the Titans. However, they do not match the transformations set out in the account of this myth given by the fifth-century writer Nonnos (lion, horse, serpent, tiger and bull as well as various human forms) (*Dionysiaca* VI, 174-205). On the other hand, a general examination of the types of animal appearing in seasonal iconography shows that the Littlecote beasts could have been selected to create a seasonal sequence: the goat is sometimes but not exclusively found with Spring; the bull, although usually found with Spring, can be associated with Summer as on the Tourdan situla in the British Museum; the leopard is associated with Autumn; and the deer with Winter. If this was the intention of the designer of the Littlecote mosaic, the animals appear in a clockwise sequence, whereas the deities are shown proceeding anticlockwise. It is hard to tell whether this is deliberate or whether it is merely coincidental, but it makes it more likely that the figures are not meant to be seen as riding the beasts since there appear to be two separate processions taking place.

Similarly, the animals in the Seasons mosaic from House VII at Caerwent do not have a direct link with the season closest to them (*38*). At the time of discovery all four animal panels survived in whole or in part. Various identifications have been proposed but they appear to have been a boar on the left (identifiable from the ridge of hair along the back), a hound at the top (its identity confirmed by the loop of its leash, a detail omitted from the lithograph) and an easily recognised lion on the right. One animal in the pair at the bottom has the long ears of a hare. The context suggests that its companion is probably a hound although it looks somewhat like a bear. The boar is usually associated with winter, the hound with spring, the lion with summer, and the hare-hunt with autumn. The Caerwent animals have been depicted in the correct seasonal order and form a seasonal cycle distinct from the female busts.

A fragment of mosaic showing a lion in a shell niche walking towards a basket was found in the coincidentally named Lion Walk in Colchester (Essex) in 1975. Its whereabouts are currently unknown. Excavated in difficult circumstances from a roadside verge, the lion fragment was only part of a much larger mosaic.

It has been plausibly suggested that the lion represented Summer, in which case the remainder of the mosaic would have contained images of other seasonal animals.

The human and divine figures in the Venus mosaic from Rudston (Yorkshire) will be discussed in future chapters but here it is appropriate to consider the four animals, the very number raising the possibility that they were intended to evoke the seasons: the bull for Spring, the lion for Summer, the leopard for Autumn and the stag for Winter (*73*). If the Rudston animals are seasonal, they are not shown in sequence as the positions of Winter and Autumn are reversed. Although the seasonal theory is an attractive one, the presence of the animals at Rudston is already explained by their context in amphitheatre scenes, making a seasonal connection unnecessary and far from certain: it is questionable whether an animal representing a season would be shown injured or slain as is the case with the Rudston lion.

FESTIVALS

The depiction of a festival that took place at a certain time of the year was another way of referring to a month or season. No certain examples of such scenes are known from Romano-British mosaics, but a festival scene is a possible interpretation of another fragmentary mosaic found at Lion Walk, Colchester, in 1972, and now in Colchester Castle Museum (*colour plate 15*). As the mosaic had been discoloured in antiquity by burning, its details are not easy to make out. The design is thought to have comprised eight panels, probably all with figured scenes, alternating with eight narrower panels of acanthus, arranged in a circle.

Radial schemes were popular for mosaics whose subject related to the passing of time as they evoked the turning cycle of the year. The largest fragment showed traces of two female figures walking in profile one behind the other, holding out their arms as if carrying an object in their lost hands. The meaning of a damaged inscription above these figures, and another fragmentary inscription from a panel on the opposite site of the mosaic, is unclear. One suggestion is that the eight panels could have been accompanied by another four panels in a circle nearer the centre of the mosaic, with all twelve depicting the months of the year. As the two female figures seem to be in a procession, they are perhaps participants in a religious festival. An alternative interpretation, based on close examination of the fragmentary inscriptions, is that the mosaic depicted scenes from a play.

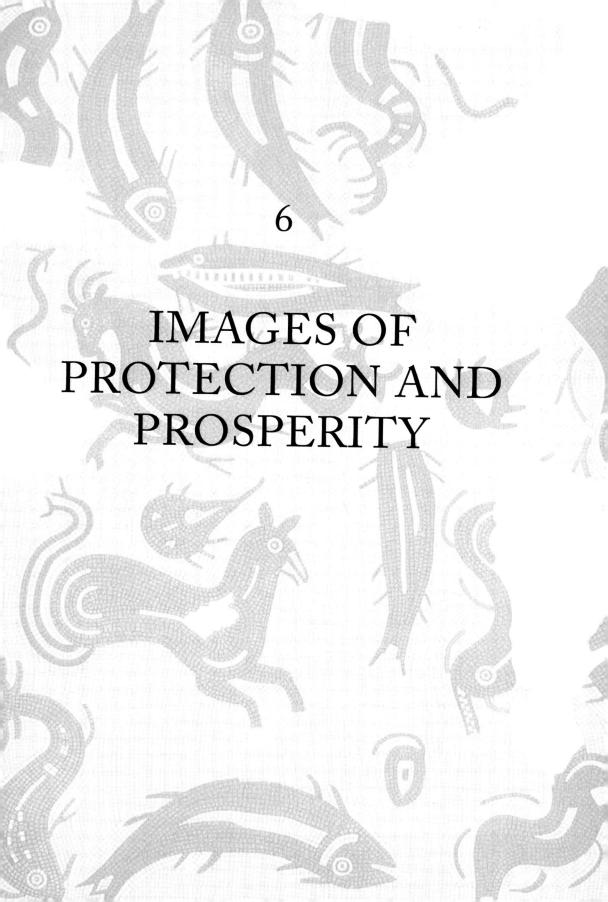

6

IMAGES OF PROTECTION AND PROSPERITY

As the previous chapter has shown, personifications of or allusions to time were plentiful. Closely allied to the reassuringly repetitive subject of the seasons were themes concerned with averting bad luck, promoting good fortune, or evoking the natural phenomena on which prosperity so often depended.

MEDUSA

Medusa, one of the three Gorgons, was once renowned for her beauty, especially her lovely hair. Her fortunes changed when she was seduced by Neptune in a temple dedicated to Minerva. The shocked goddess decided to punish Medusa for the impiety by changing her hair into writhing snakes. Eventually, with help from Mercury and Minerva, Perseus slew Medusa by cutting off her head. He presented it to Minerva who wore it thereafter on her breastplate.

The belief that sight of Medusa's head would paralyse an enemy made it a powerful protective amulet, and it was used widely in mosaics as well as other media. Medusa was often represented with wings as well as snakes in her hair, and this is the case with some, but not all, of the depictions of her in Romano-British mosaics.

The potent image of Medusa was the sole figure in a number of mosaics. She appears as a beautiful and benign mask in the baths at the Bignor villa (Sussex) with snakes issuing attractively from her hair (40). In the apsidal mosaic from the villa at Dalton Parlours (Yorkshire), now in the Yorkshire Museum, a ribbon in the shape of the letter 'M' dangles beneath her chin. It is unclear whether this was intended to refer to the initial letter of her name or is purely coincidental. This mosaic has been much restored. Medusa's eyes in particular look modern, and the constituent parts of the mosaic have been rearranged on several occasions since it was lifted and taken to the museum in 1854. At the palace of Fishbourne (Sussex), a second-century mosaic with Medusa was laid over an earlier pavement (41). Half of Medusa's face is visible, including her left eyebrow. Lines in the hair suggest a wing. A mosaic discovered at Whitley Grange (Shropshire) in 1996 provides another example of Medusa in the centre of an otherwise geometric mosaic.

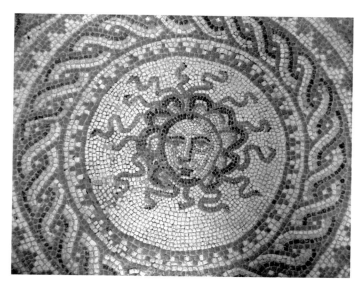

40 Medusa, Bignor.
Courtesy Bignor Roman Villa

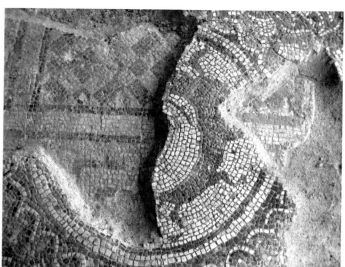

41 Medusa, Fishbourne.
*Courtesy Sussex
Archaeological Society*

Medusa was also a popular choice of image for the centre of mosaics showing other figures. She appears with the seasons in the third-century mosaic at the Bignor villa (*33*), and fragments of the snakes from her hair can still be seen in the central panel of the Seasons mosaic from Toft Green, York. She is surrounded by mythological scenes and winds in the eastern part of the Seasons mosaic at the Brading villa (Isle of Wight) (*9* and *16*), and might have featured in the centre of the western part as well (respectively, the lower and upper parts of figure *16*). The same mosaic contains a scene showing Perseus holding Medusa's head aloft as he and Andromeda look at its reflection in a pool. The deities of the days of the week were placed around Medusa in a mosaic from the Bramdean villa (Hampshire) (*colour plate 10*), and she was also shown with theatrical masks in a mosaic at the Halstock villa (Dorset). Neither of these mosaics survives.

Two second- or third-century mosaics from Cirencester (Gloucestershire) are unusual because they feature heads of Medusa not as a central image but in minor positions. She appears next to Summer in the Seasons mosaic from Dyer Street, the surviving wing drawn in black and white with an upper edge of yellow (*34*). In the Hunting dogs mosaic she is shown near one of the Neptune masks (*42*). The wings and snakes are especially detailed, with the tails of two snakes neatly knotted beneath her chin, making this one of the finest of the Romano-British Medusas.

It is probable that a small, fragmentary mask from room K at the Keynsham villa (Somerset), known from a tracing and an oblique photograph, represented Medusa. A small fragment recently discovered at Dinnington (Somerset) could be part of a Medusa head as the black lines protruding from the face might represent stylised snakes. An alternative interpretation is that they depict the upswept hair of a wind.

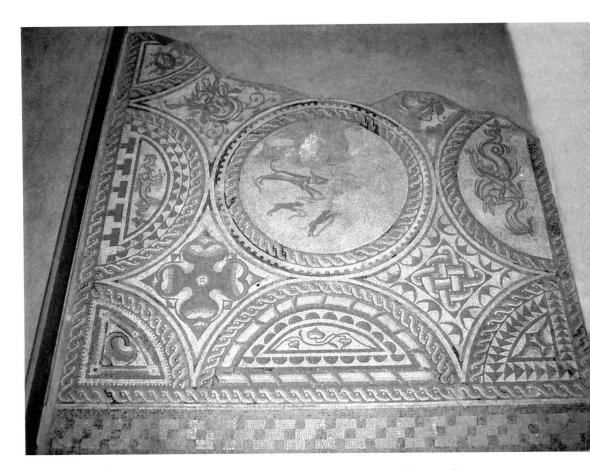

42 Hunting dogs mosaic, Dyer Street, Cirencester. *Courtesy Corinium Museum, Cirencester*

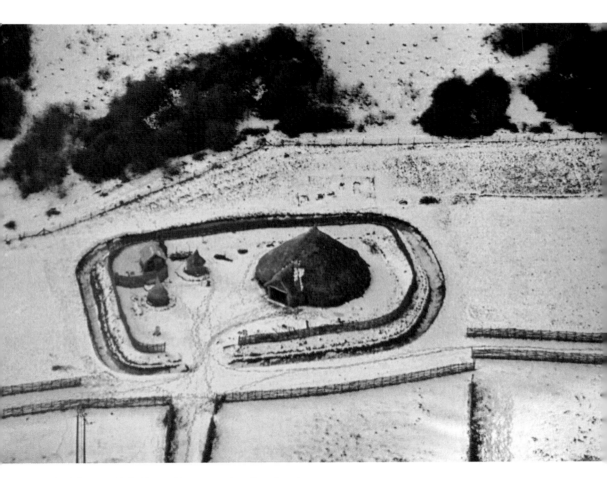

1 Aerial view: Little Butser Demonstration Area in winter

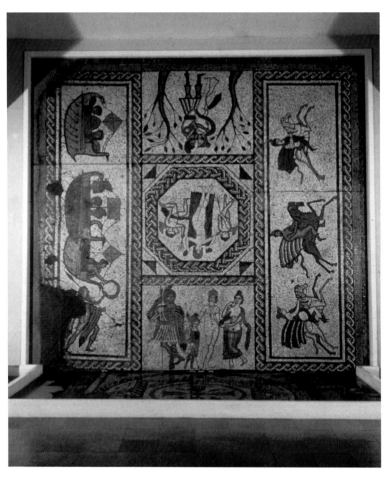

Left: 2 Mosaic depicting the story of Dido and Aeneas from the Low Ham villa possibly commissioned by someone with an appreciation of classical learning. Taunton Museum

Below: 3 Hadrian's Wall from Steel Rigg. The Wall follows the highest part of the crests

Opposite above: 4 An imaginative reconstruction of Hadrian's Wall at Walltown Crags, Northumberland. *Illustration by Alan Sorrell*

Opposite below: 5 Letocetum (Wall, Staffordshire) was an important mansio for couriers travelling along Watling Street that developed into a small town. The bathhouse is in the background, the guesthouse in the foreground. *Illustration by Ivan Lapper*

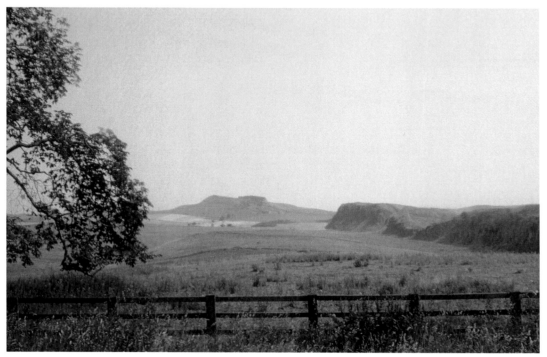

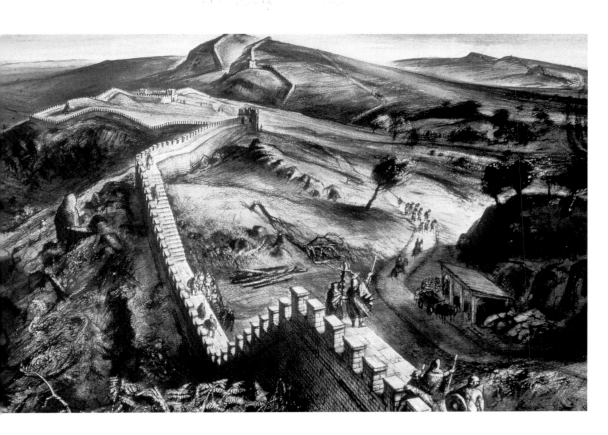

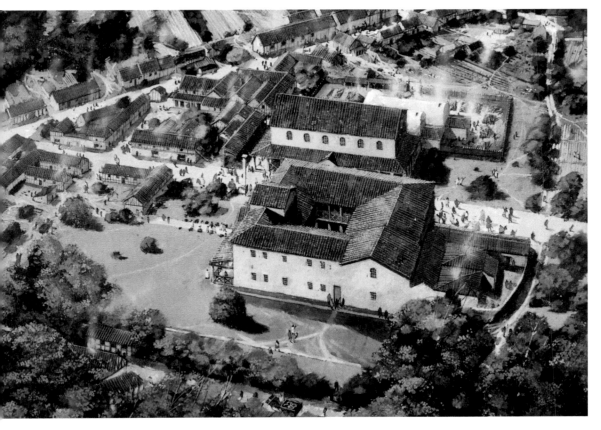

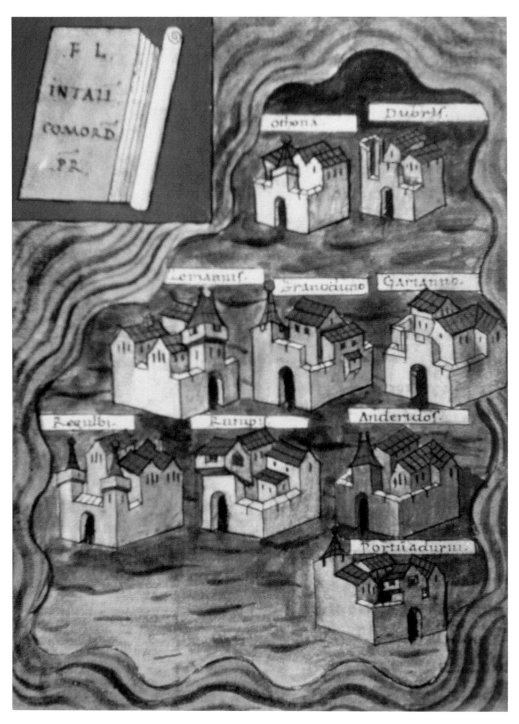

6 Illustration showing the Saxon Shore forts from a manuscript (MS Canon Misc 378, fol. 153r) in the The Bodleian Library, University of Oxford

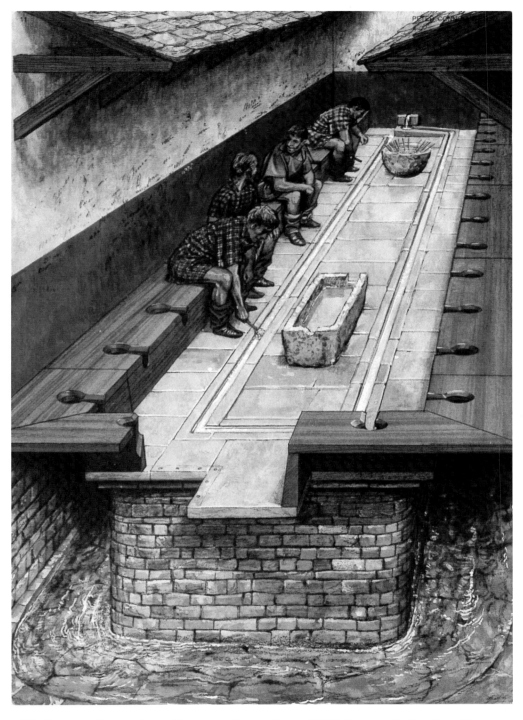

7 The Roman military latrine at Housesteads fort on Hadrian's Wall. *Illustration by Peter Connolly*

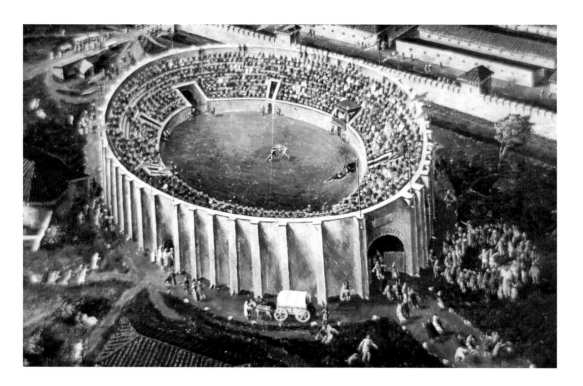

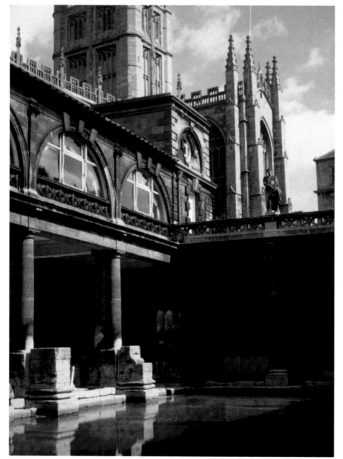

Above: 8 An imaginative reconstruction of the amphitheatre at Caerleon fort. *Illustration by Alan Sorrell*

Left: 9 View of the Great Bath at Bath

Opposite above: 10 View of the 'Old Work', Wroxeter, which was once part of the original south wall of the basilica. In front of it are the hypocausts under the warm room and the hot room

Opposite below: 11 Reconstructed round house, Little Butser Demonstration Area

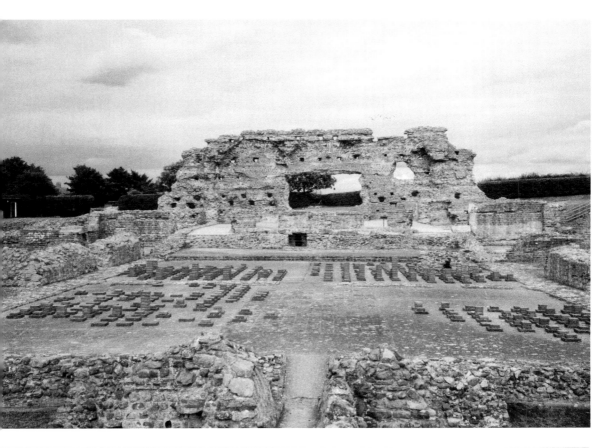

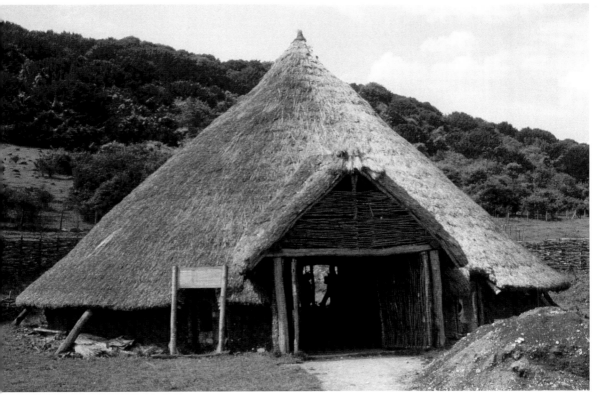

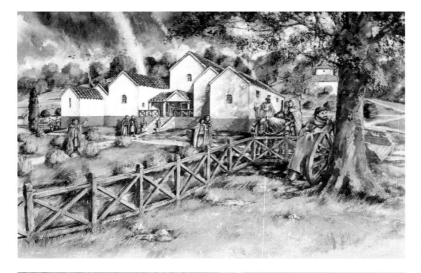

12 Imaginative view of the Lullingstone villa as it might have appeared about AD 380. *Illustration by Peter Dunn*

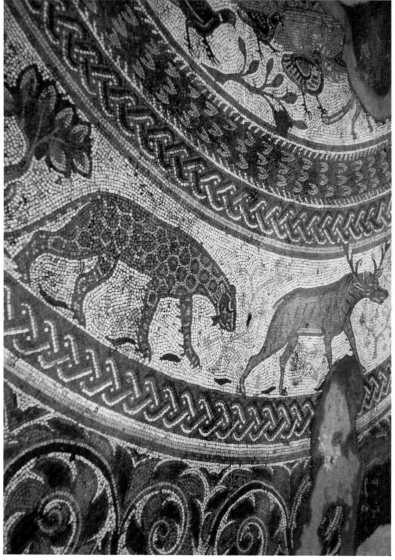

13 Detail of the Woodchester mosaic, Gloucestershire, showing a deer and a panther. The photograph was taken when the mosaic was uncovered for public viewing in 1974

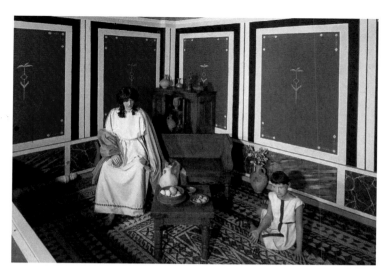

Right: 14 Reconstruction of a reception room based on finds made at the Castle Hill villa site, Ipswich. The floor mosaic is restored from the original and the wall plaster is typical of the period, third century AD. Ipswich Museums and Galleries

Below: 15 Imaginative drawing of a butcher's shop. *Illustration by Judith Dobie*

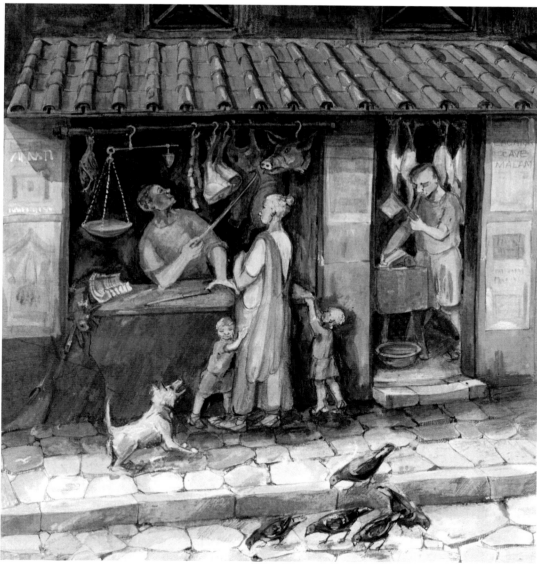

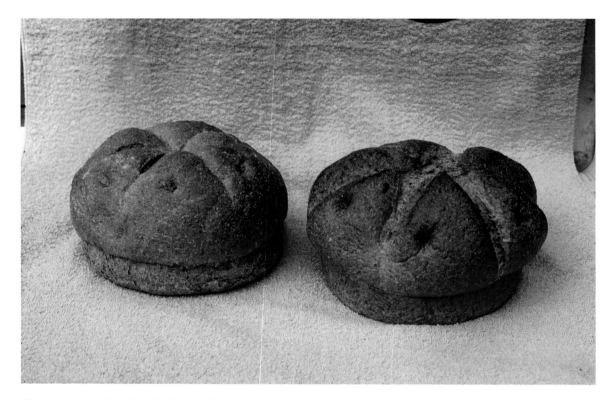

Above: 16 Loaves baked in the form of Roman ones

Opposite above: 17 A Roman kitchen reconstructed for educational purposes at the Fishbourne villa, West Sussex

Opposite below: 18 Attractive Samian ware from the Newstead fort. National Museums of Scotland, Edinburgh

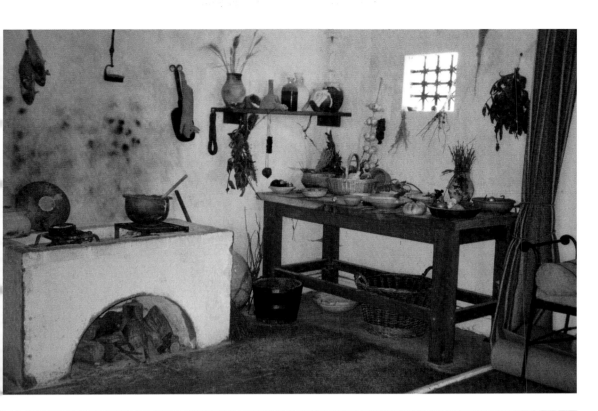

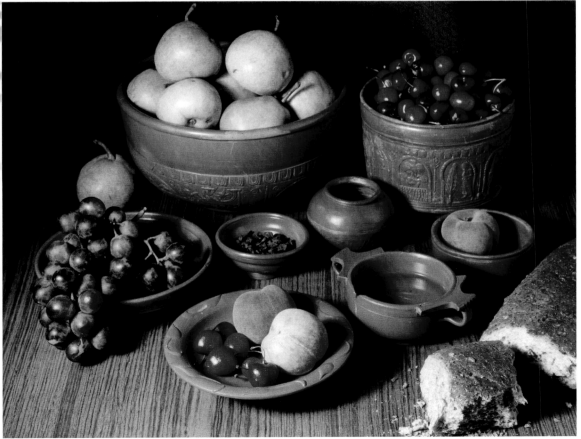

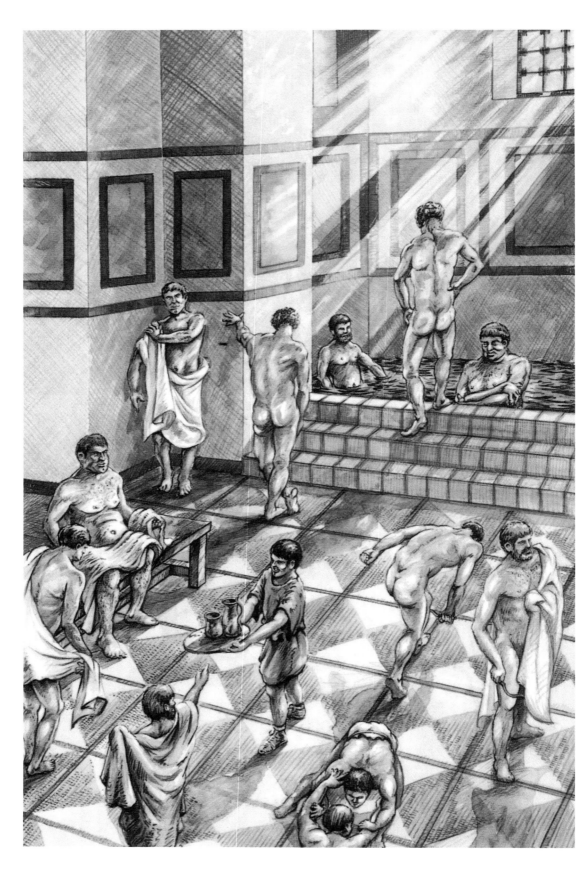

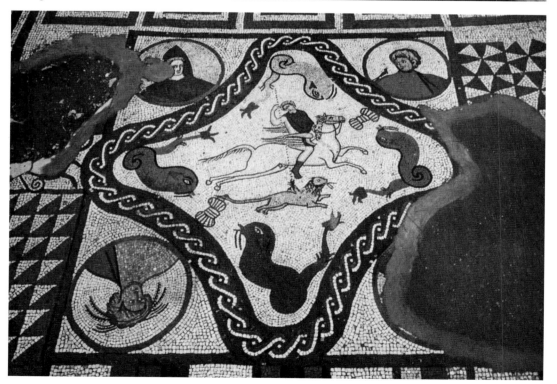

Opposite: 19 A lively scene in a bathhouse at Verulamium. *Illustration by Peter Dunn*

Right: 20 Model of a mosaic worker. Corinium Museum, Cirencester

Below: 21 Mosaic of Bellerophon slaying the Chimaera, fourth century AD. Lullingstone villa

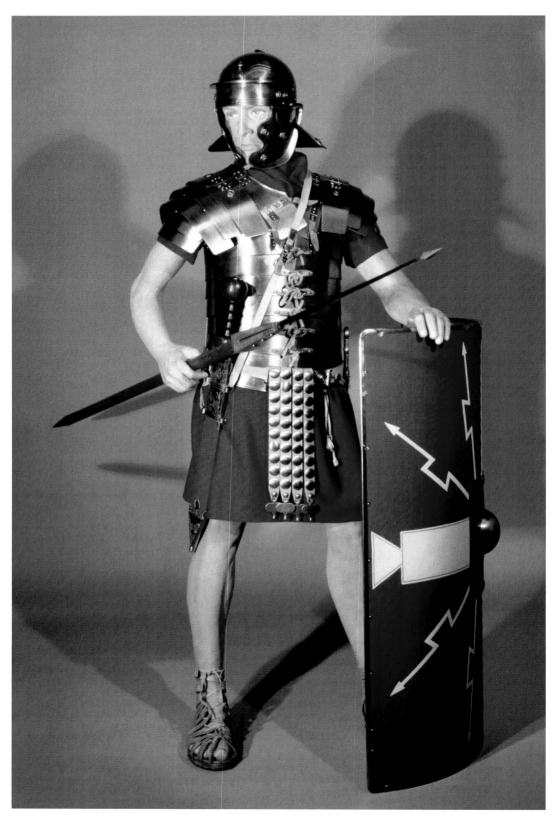

22 Model of a Roman legionary. Grosvenor Museum, Chester

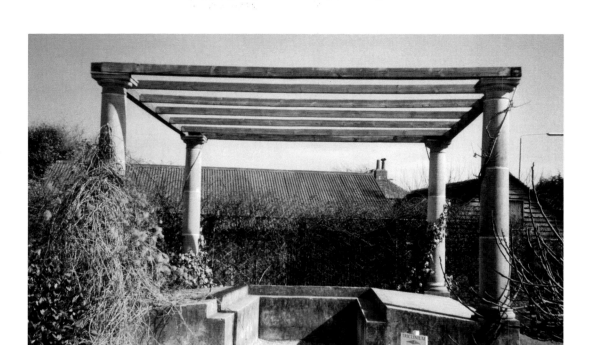

23 Sometimes dining took place in outdoor triclinia. One has been reconstructed at the Fishbourne villa. The diners would recline on cushions, three diners to each side. A table would be put in the middle on which food would be placed

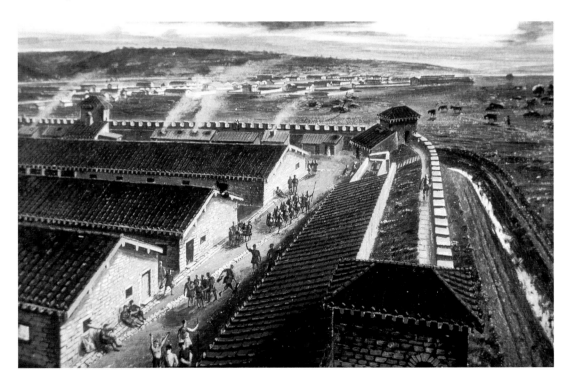

24 Reconstruction of the western angle of the Caerleon fort. The smoke indicates the position of the bake houses or ovens. The *via sagularis* runs between the walls and the barrack blocks. The defences include a rampart backing a wall and a ditch. *Illustration by Alan Sorrell*

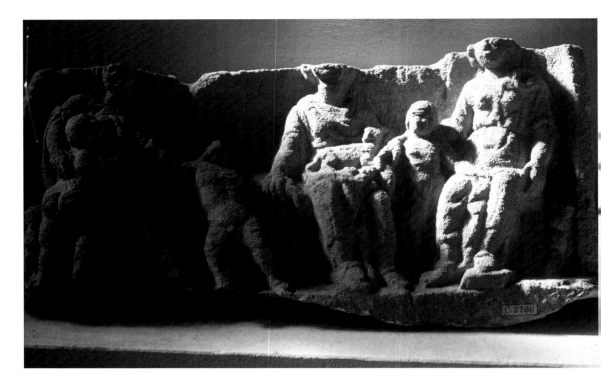

25 Relief of Mother Goddesses in the Corinium Museum, Cirencester. This is an unusual depiction. The relaxed group of Mothers indulging their children contrasts with the more usual stern hierarchical poses

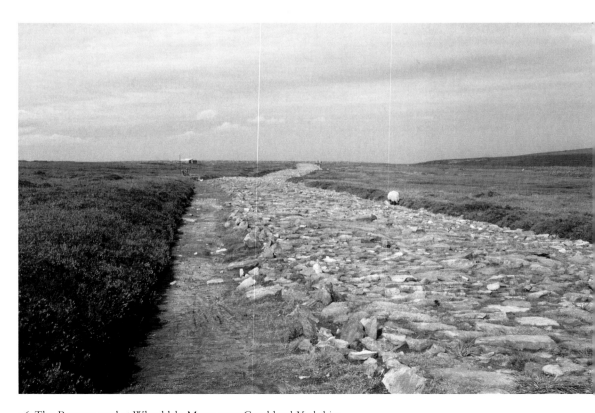

26 The Roman road at Wheeldale Moor, near Goathland, Yorkshire

GOOD LUCK SYMBOLS

As well as employing images to offer protection from bad luck, mosaics used figures to promote good luck, prosperity and fruitfulness. Bonus Eventus, Fortuna and Tyche were all deities who had good luck and material prosperity at the heart of their concerns, while aspects of many of the traditional Olympian gods and goddesses related to fertility, especially of crops. They are discussed in the next chapters.

From ancient times, dolphins have been recognised as helpful to man. They famously rescued the musician Arion after he had been thrown into the sea by robbers, and one is said to have carried a boy to school on his back. When the Tyrrhenian pirates tried to take advantage of Bacchus, not knowing who their divine passenger was, they were driven mad with fear and were transformed into dolphins, in which repentant guise they became friendly to men.

Dolphins are one of the most popular images in Romano-British mosaics. Nearly 200 are known or inferred from over 50 mosaics. In some cases, they appear with Neptune. In others, they are included among a variety of marine creatures as an appropriate decoration for a room in the baths, as in the second- or third-century mosaic at Great Witcombe (Gloucestershire) (*43*) and in the fragment with the delightfully tetchy dolphin from Dewlish (Dorset), now in the Dorset County Museum (*colour plate 16*). In the only figured mosaic to have survived from Bath (Somerset), now appropriately housed in the Roman Baths Museum, Bath, a dolphin swims with a sea horse and a sea panther (*44*). In most instances, however, they seem to have functioned as good luck symbols.

At Fishbourne, dolphins are shown on three probably first- to third-century AD pavements in addition to the famous dolphin ridden by a Cupid (*45*). The first to greet modern visitors is the colourful mosaic of two scallop shells in room N5a (*46*). The black and white area between the two shells has a series of lozenges (perhaps a stylised net) above which are the tails of two dolphins. The significance of the straight and curved lines between the dolphins' tails is uncertain, but these shapes might represent floats. The imaginative suggestion that the whole mosaic shows a knobbly-kneed peacock with an outstretched tail can be discounted, not least because the radial flutes realistically replicate scallops and bear no resemble to the 'eyes' of a peacock's tail.

More scallop shells appear in the corners of the mosaic in room N8, which also has lozenges in the panels at either end. Here each pair of dolphins is shown flanking a cantharus, another good luck symbol. Finally, in room N20 the visitor sees a fragmentary polychrome mosaic whose centre, now lost, is surrounded by alternating flowers and leaves. The remains of the long neck of an amphora can be seen in one corner with a fish, while the adjacent corner has an elaborate long-necked vessel (an amphora or cantharus?) flanked by dolphins (*47*). Fishbourne's location close to the sea no doubt prompted the interest in marine creatures and in the vessels in which commodities were imported, though scallop shells

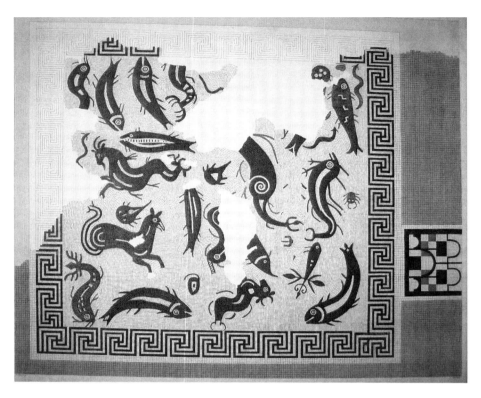

43 Marine mosaic, Great Witcombe (C.H. Stothard). *Courtesy Society of Antiquaries*

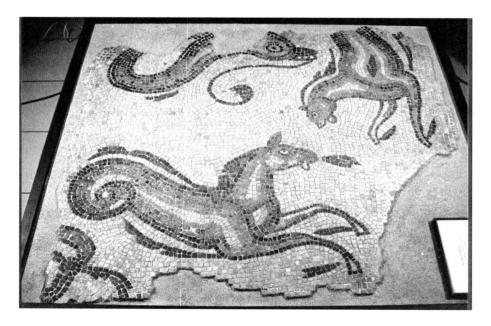

44 Marine mosaic, Bath. *Photograph: © Stephen Cosh. Courtesy Roman Baths Museum, Bath and North East Somerset Council*

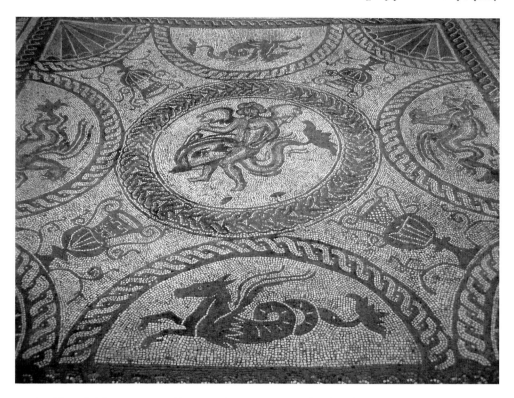

45 Cupid on dolphin mosaic, Fishbourne. *Courtesy Sussex Archaeological Society*

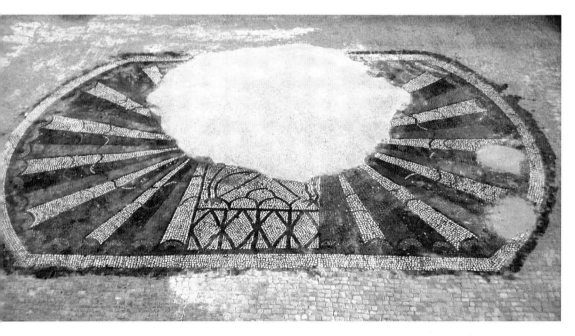

46 Dolphins and scallop shells, room N5a, Fishbourne. *Courtesy Sussex Archaeological Society*

and dolphins featured in inland mosaics as well. For instance, the same subjects are shown in a mosaic from Ilchester Mead (Somerset), now in the Museum of South Somerset, Yeovil.

The introduction of scallop shells into a mosaic is sometimes subtle. In the pavement from Sparsholt (Hampshire), now in Winchester City Museum, unusual scallops with the centre flute coming to a point are placed in diagonally opposite corners of the mosaic (*48*). This pavement contains another reference to water in the form of the wave pattern border around the central medallion.

The bodies of dolphins in some mosaics were depicted undulating in a sinuous shape as if to imitate the movement of the beast as it swam through the water. Others were shown in a rather more dramatic form, with tails twisted into a coil. There was generally no attempt to achieve a zoologically correct rendition although most dolphins, whether sinuous or coiled, conformed to a standard iconography with flukes, fins and a tail (tripartite, unlike the real creature) usually drawn in red.

A good example of a 'coiled' dolphin appears in part of a mosaic of uncertain date from Little Minster Street, Winchester (Hampshire), now in Winchester City Museum (*49*). The tail of a second marine creature to the right is perhaps another dolphin or some form of sea beast. This fragment formed part of a large

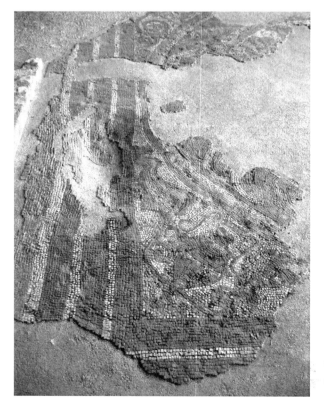

47 Dolphins and amphora, room N20, Fishbourne. *Courtesy Sussex Archaeological Society*

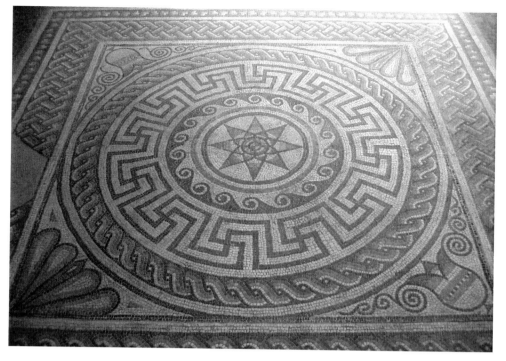

48 Scallop shells, Sparsholt. *Courtesy Winchester Museums Service*

design based on interlaced squares. The hint of a bust can be seen within the remains of the interlaced squares above right of the dolphin although we can only guess at his or her identity.

The concept of a pair of dolphins flanking a cantharus combined two exceptionally popular motifs. The drinking cup reinforced the good luck message and incorporated a reference to Bacchus and his gifts. The most recent such mosaic to have been discovered was found at Bradford on Avon (Wiltshire) in 2002 (*colour plate 1*). This spectacular find consists of an almost perfectly preserved pavement with two lively dolphins and a cantharus in the semi-hexagonal apse, with a large rosette in the centre of the main floor and unusual lotus urns consisting of three buds, one on top of the other, in the corners.

Not all the mosaics with a cantharus and dolphins survive, but two that can still be appreciated are of particular interest. The second-century mosaic from House XXVIII.3 at Verulamium (Hertfordshire), now in the Verulamium Museum, shows the dolphins leaping through the handles of a cantharus that functions as a fountain with jets of water spurting forth (*50*). The association between the dolphins and the cantharus handles is taken a step further in the mosaic from Downton (Wiltshire), now in the Salisbury and South Wiltshire Museum (*colour plate 17*), where the dolphins actually form the handles of a narrow-necked cantharus.

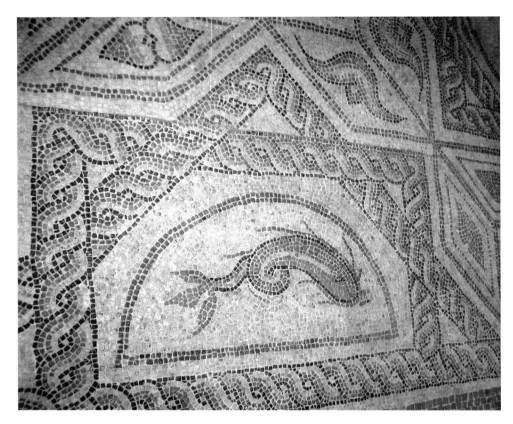

49 Mosaic from Little Minster Street, Winchester. *Courtesy Winchester Museums Service*

In some mosaics, the dolphins were shown separately from the cantharus. The pavement from Admiral's Walk in Cirencester (Gloucestershire), for instance, had a cantharus in the centre with other motifs in separate compartments around it. They include dolphins, a heart-shaped leaf and a possible crown, and these fragments are now in the Corinium Museum. The Brislington mosaic from Bristol, whose fragments are stored in Bristol City Museum, had a splendid cantharus in the central square panel which was bordered by wave pattern (*51*). The dolphins were only a small part of the design, with one in the centre of each side. They were less dominant than the elegant peltae and lotus buds that were such a feature of this mosaic.

The cantharus was not only associated with dolphins. Sea panthers as well as dolphins flank canthari in the Littlecote Park mosaic (Wiltshire) (*colour plate 2*). The presence of the felines underlines the Bacchic imagery in this pavement. In a large mosaic from Durngate Street, Dorchester (Dorset), now laid in the main gallery of the Dorset County Museum, crested snakes emerge from the mouths of two canthari occupying diagonally opposite spandrels. Snakes and Bacchus both symbolise rebirth so the combination here is particularly appropriate. There is, however, another explanation. Reptiles were traditionally associated with the month of September in calendar imagery, and it has been suggested that snakes served as an apotropaic symbol protecting the new wine.

The cantharus was also associated with birds. They are often featured separately in the same mosaic, as in the floor in the west wing baths at the Chedworth villa (Gloucestershire).

In other mosaics, the birds flank the cantharus, as in the threshold panel of the Hare mosaic from Beeches Road, Cirencester (*52*). The imagery in this panel originally faced the opposite direction from the hare, but the panel has been turned round for ease of viewing in the Corinium Museum. The short necks with ring-markings and the long pointed tails of the birds suggest that they are probably pheasants although they are often described as peacocks. They perch on leaf scrolls flowing from the bud-shaped cantharus and are accompanied by bunches of grapes. Like these game birds, the hare could represent the fruits of the chase but is seen here crouching to nibble a shrub. This peaceful depiction, coupled with the prominence given to the image, suggests that the hare was chosen for this mosaic primarily as a symbol of fertility. This role is stressed by Philostratus, who refers to its fecundity and comments that the hare was the offering that Aphrodite (Venus), herself a fertility goddess, found most pleasing (*Imagines* I, 6, 31–34).

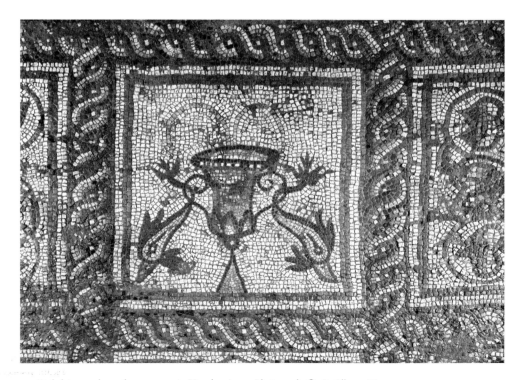

50 Dolphins and cantharus mosaic, Verulamium. *Photograph:* © *St Albans Museums*

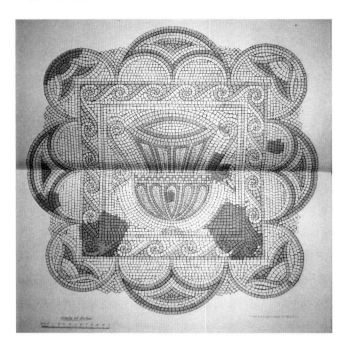

51 Cantharus from the
Brislington mosaic.
(W.R. Barker)

The Beeches Road hare is one of the most attractive and accomplished animals in a Romano-British mosaic. Clear glass tesserae have been employed to highlight the fur on the creature's back, while the surrounding geometric design is laid out to focus attention on this central image.

Birds perched on scrolls or pecking fruit are ubiquitous. Colourful examples appear in the centre of the foliate scroll in each side of the second-century Middleborough mosaic from Colchester (Essex), now in Colchester Castle Museum (*colour plate 8*). At the Bignor villa, birds perch on leafy swags either side of Venus as they peck fruit from leafy branches, while cornucopiae placed below them underline the message that these motifs evoke plenty (*58*). In the Seasons mosaic from the same site, busts of the seasons occupied one part of this bipartite room, while the scheme around the lost centre of the other part seems to have consisted of a dolphin in the centre of each side flanked by panels each with a bird perched on a cornucopia overflowing with fruit. At Keynsham, the kite-shaped panels between the mythological scenes in the mosaic from room W each have birds perched on branches and show a piece of fruit above each bird. Pheasants pecking fruit decorate panels in the Victorious charioteer mosaic from Rudston (Yorkshire) (*35*), while doves and fruit are featured in the corners of the Venus mosaic from the same site (*73*).

Peacocks were particularly auspicious as it was thought that their flesh was incorruptible and they were thus regarded as symbols of immortality. Magical significance was also attached to the 'eyes' in their tails, which were considered powerful symbols that could be harnessed in opposition to the Evil Eye.

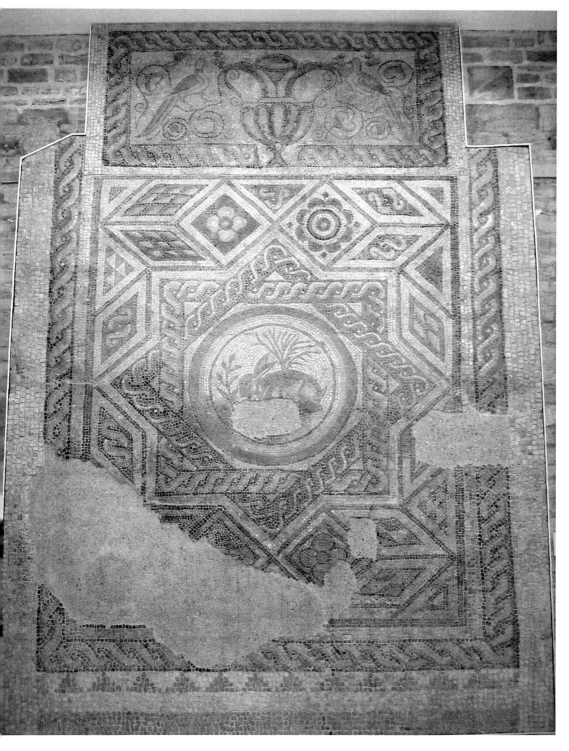

52 Hare mosaic, Beeches Road, Cirencester. *Courtesy Corinium Museum, Cirencester*

The only peacock shown with an outstretched tail in a Romano-British mosaic was found at Leicester. This second-century mosaic is now in the Jewry Wall Museum. When a long-tailed bird is shown in profile with its tail closed, it is difficult to tell whether it represents a peacock. Such a description is often employed, but unless the bird has the distinctive peacock's crest it might represent a pheasant instead. The birds above the busts in the corners of the western part of the Seasons mosaic (upper part in figure *16*) at Brading are clearly peacocks as the surviving examples are decorated with crests (*16*). The peacock above the lost bust of Autumn is accompanied by a bunch of grapes. It would seem that in this mosaic the pieces of fruit differed according to the season, but fruits are often difficult to distinguish from one another or even to identify as a particular type.

It is a moot point whether small motifs such as flowers, leaves and Solomon's knots were used as simple decoration or whether they held a special meaning for their Roman viewers. They occur with such frequency in figured and non-figured mosaics and are so suitable as filling motifs for small spaces that we need to exercise caution before ascribing particular significance to them.

The colourful panel lying between Europa and Bellerophon in the mosaic at Lullingstone (Kent) employs familiar decorative motifs in an unusual composition (*colour plate 3*). Among the heart-shaped leaves, petals, swastikas, chequers and crosses is a Solomon's knot and a two-handled undecorated drinking cup. It has been suggested that this panel was used as a game board, while others see a prophylactic element in the use of some of the motifs, especially given the appearance of the word 'INVIDA' in the adjoining inscription (discussed in chapter 2), a word usually connected with the Evil Eye.

The prominence of the Solomon's knot in the border immediately above Venus at Bignor (*58*) hints that it might have been inserted for reasons that were more than purely decorative. The visitor to museums and sites will, however, often spot this motif in a less focal position. More research is needed before we can properly assess its significance.

NATURAL FORCES

A good supply of water was important to service Roman houses and baths, while rain-bearing winds were important for making crops grow. Too little rain, too much, or rain falling at the wrong time could cause major problems. It is no surprise that the weather was a vital concern.

Winds not only brought rain but were linked with the seasons in literature as well as in art. As there were four main winds they, like the seasons, were a convenient decoration for the corners of a mosaic. They were usually represented with wings in their hair and had a conch shell as an attribute.

The naked busts of winds in the corners of the mosaic in room A at Frampton (Dorset) conformed to the standard iconography (*5* and *colour plate 6*). Wings sprouted from their upswept hair and a conch shell lay across their shoulders. In the Seasons mosaic at Brading, winds are shown blowing their conch shells (*9* and *16*). They have cloaks over their shoulders and wings in their hair.

The special case of Hinton St Mary (Dorset) has been noted above (*14*). Although the corner busts have upswept hair, they lack wings or shells and are enveloped by their cloaks. Some scholars have interpreted them in a Christian context. Recalling St Irenaeus, who compared the number of winds with the number of gospels being carried to the four corners of the earth, they suggest that standard figures of winds were altered to represent the evangelists.

Wings growing out of the hair of a wind resemble the winged cap worn by Mercury. The drawing of the lost mosaic from East Coker (Somerset) of Bacchus discovering Ariadne showed four Mercury figures in the corners, each with a cloak, a winged cap and a caduceus. It is usually thought that these were winds, misinterpreted by the eighteenth-century draftsman, as it is unlikely that an image of Mercury would have been relegated to a corner position and repeated four times.

In the Grand Mosaic at Pitney (Somerset), the corner busts lacked wings and two of them had long hair, suggesting that they were female (*6* and *colour plate 7*). One wore a small diadem and had a leaf, perhaps representing a fan instead of a conch shell. It is not clear why the attribute of one bust should have been different from the attributes of the others. Given that, as discussed above, two of the main panels seem to have been displaced, and that the seasons were also shown out of order, perhaps the explanation for the mismatched fourth wind lies not in the iconography but in a more mundane reason. The bust could have been prepared for another mosaic entirely, and employed here for convenience.

A mosaic found in room D at Frampton, now buried *in situ* or lost, depicted naked busts with upswept hair and conch shells but no wings (*53*). Most scholars describe them as winds, but the alternative identification as Tritons seems more probable given the marine theme of this pavement: the main subject was Neptune and the other panels were decorated with dolphins.

Unlike the examples discussed above, the head of a wind is shown in profile in the corner of a mosaic of uncertain date found in a town house at Silchester (Hampshire), and now in store in the Museum of Reading. The remains of a second head were visible at the time of discovery and it is probable that there would have been four originally, one in each corner. Although apparently unique in a Romano-British mosaic, depictions of winds in profile were the norm in other provinces.

Winds are mentioned in the inscription flanking the head of Neptune in the mosaic in room B at Frampton (*18*), and there is a reference to Aeolus, the ruler of the winds, in the Lullingstone couplet accompanying Europa and the bull (*colour plate 3*).

In another reference to natural phenomena, several mosaics incorporate small heads thought to represent spirits of nature. The design in the apse of a mosaic

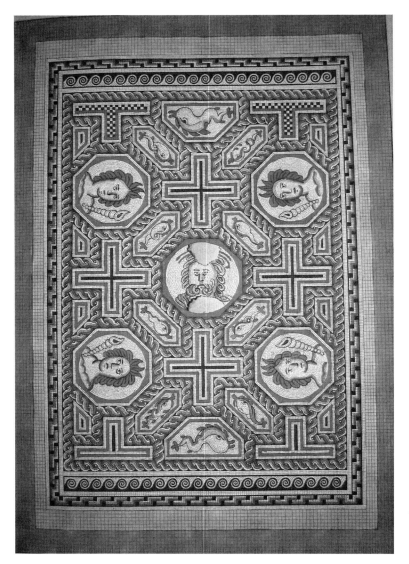

53 Neptune
mosaic, room D,
Frampton (Samuel
Lysons)

excavated in the 1970s at Dewlish (Dorset), and now reburied, is divided into
five segments, each with an exotic 'candelabrum' of foliage. A small human
head or mask peeps out from three of the candelabra. Similar heads or masks
appear flanked by tendrils in the circular border around Bacchus in the centre
of the Seasons mosaic from Thruxton (Hampshire) (*colour plate 14*) and above
the Achilles panel at Keynsham. Another, probably of second-century date, was
found and lost in 1969 during construction work in Gloucester. It formed the
termination of a volute in an acanthus scroll. A small Cupid-like figure emerging
from a clump of acanthus in the border of the Winds mosaic from Silchester,
mentioned above, seems to evoke a similar concept.

7

GODS

Deities have been discussed in the previous chapters where they feature in narrative scenes. In this and the following chapter, the portrayals of each deity in Romano-British mosaics will be brought together, including those representations where the deity is the sole image. In this way, their relative popularity can be assessed along with the styles of depiction and the ways in which the image of each deity was used.

APOLLO

As the sun god, Apollo was essential to the course of the day and of the year. Along with the deities of the other days of the week, he was included in the Bramdean mosaic (Hampshire) (*colour plate 10*). He and Daphne are probably the figures shown in the scene of pursuit in the Seasons mosaic at Brading (Isle of Wight) alluding to summer (*9* and *16*).

His cultural role as god of music was exemplified by the popular story of his musical contest with the satyr Marsyas. This scene is shown in a mosaic from Lenthay Green (Dorset), now at Sherborne Castle (*colour plate 19*). Marsyas had become skilled at playing the flutes and challenged Apollo to a competition. The god accepted on condition that whoever lost would submit himself to whatever punishment the winner chose. In the Lenthay mosaic, Apollo is calmly seated on the left, playing the lyre that rests on his knees. On the right, Marsyas dances as he plays the flutes. The unusual rectangular tesserae making up the figure of Apollo and the straight lines in which they are laid has led experts to conclude that this figure is of modern workmanship, restoring the original figure which perhaps disintegrated on lifting.

The outcome of the contest, not shown here but represented in other media and in mosaics from other provinces, was that Apollo was declared the winner. In some versions of the story, he achieved his victory because, unlike Marsyas, he was able to play his instrument upside down. He punished Marsyas by having him flayed alive. The myth is often regarded as an allegory for the contrast between savagery, exemplified by Marsyas, and civilisation, embodied in Apollo.

In another link with music, Apollo was the father of Orpheus according to some versions of the myth. Some scholars equate him with Orpheus in the

Littlecote Park mosaic (Wiltshire) (*30* and *colour plate 2*), an argument based largely on writings contained in the Orphic Fragments. The cithara player at Littlecote has even been identified by some as Apollo rather than Orpheus, but the presence of the fox indicates the latter. The radial decoration in the three apses at Littlecote is often likened to the sun's rays, and would thus provide a further connection with Apollo. Although Roman visitors to this room might well have been reminded of the sun, the hinges depicted along the straight sides of the apses show that the designs were based on scallop shells.

Given Apollo's association with laurel, the link between Apollo and Orpheus is also perhaps displayed in the laurel wreaths shown in some of the other Orpheus mosaics.

Apollo played a role in other myths depicted in Romano-British mosaics although he himself was not shown. He turned Cyparissus, depicted in the mosaic panel at Leicester (*colour plate 5*), into the cypress tree after Cyparissus had accidentally killed his pet stag and was so grief-stricken that he no longer wished to live. Apollo featured in the myth of the invention of the syrinx by Mercury, a scene discussed below and possibly portrayed in the Grand Mosaic at Pitney (Somerset) (*6* and *colour plate 7*). He was also instrumental in helping Ceres when she was searching for her lost daughter, Proserpina. It was Apollo as the all-seeing sun who was able to tell Ceres that Proserpina had been abducted by the god of the underworld. The Littlecote Park mosaic, with its figures of Ceres and Proserpina, thus has another link with Apollo.

BACCHUS

Primarily remembered today as the god of wine, Bacchus was an agricultural deity regarded as master of nature and of the seasons. He was usually portrayed naked save for a cloak and was accompanied by his attributes of a drinking cup and thyrsus. His hair was long and he wore a wreath decked with ivy or vine leaves and grapes. According to Ovid, his face resembled a young girl (*Metamorphoses* IV, 20), while one of Nonnos' characters likened him to a woman (*Dionysiaca* XVI, 171-173). Because of his effeminate appearance, he is often misidentified.

Bacchus' involvement with Ariadne was the most popular story from his life to receive artistic expression. The lost mosaic of East Coker (Somerset) showed him discovering her on the island of Naxos after she had been abandoned by Theseus, underlining his role as a saviour god. As a couple, Bacchus and Ariadne are shown regally seated in the focal position of the triclinium mosaic at Chedworth (Gloucestershire) (*7*).

In non-narrative contexts, Bacchus was usually the sole subject of a mosaic or was given prominence in the central panel with other figures disposed in compartments around him. He was often accompanied by his panther. As god of wine, he was a particularly appropriate choice for a dining room.

One of the most sybaritic images of Bacchus is found in a mosaic of uncertain date from Leadenhall Street, London, now in the British Museum. It shows him languidly reclining on a tigress. The beast paws the air as she turns her head to look up at her master (*colour plate 20*). The inclusion of the tigress alludes to the Indian triumph of Bacchus. He holds a one-handled drinking cup in his right hand and a thyrsus in his left hand. His toes peek out from his leopard-skin boots. Paintings made shortly after discovery of this mosaic in 1803 show that the medallion not only had the undulating ribbon border visible today, but also borders of wave pattern and an uncommon awning border. Two of the spandrels had large canthari or craters. This mosaic is notable for its variety of colours, including the use of blue and green glass tesserae in the cloak.

Although the medallion is complete, the mosaic appears to have been subjected to substantial restoration and polishing in Victorian times. The authenticity of the upper part is particularly suspect as Bacchus' head is disproportionately small in relation to his body and its top is missing. The leaves of his wreath are also truncated. By contrast, the illustrations made at the time of discovery show him as an attractive and accomplished figure.

A second Bacchus mosaic in the British Museum comes from Thruxton (Hampshire) (*colour plate 14*). This pavement has already been discussed in relation to the seasons in the spandrels. It was found in 1823 and, like the Leadenhall Street example above, illustrations made at the time of discovery show it in a more complete state than it is today. Bacchus appeared in the central medallion wearing a cloak, boots and a leafy headdress. He held a thyrsus and was seated on a leopard that turned its head to catch the drops of wine he poured from his cup. The beast was small and had a rather squashed appearance, perhaps because it had been compressed to fit the available space. Four large vine leaves, some with tendrils, formed a backdrop to the scene. Today all that survives of this central part of the mosaic are two vine leaves and part of Bacchus' knee and foot. The medallion is enclosed within a wheel-like border with the areas between the 'spokes' filled with bands of wave pattern and foliage, the latter incorporating small heads or masks.

An inscription runs across the top of the mosaic. It was matched by another line of text below, of which very little survived at the time of discovery. The upper line, giving the name of a person or persons, reads:

QVINTVS NATALIVS NATALINVS ET BODENI

Experts are divided as to whether this refers to 'Quintus Natalius Natalinus, also known as Bodenius' or whether it means 'Quintus Natalius Natalinus and the Bodeni'. There is also no consensus about the status of this person or persons: the mosaicists, the villa owner, or the owner and his clients or tenants?

A Bacchus mosaic found at Stonesfield (Oxfordshire) in 1711 and since lost was primarily an accomplished and attractive geometric pavement (*54*). The god was featured in the centre of the southern part, mounted somewhat precariously on his feline. As usual, he had his attributes of cantharus and thyrsus but despite this he was identified as Apollo by some early commentators. The location of Stonesfield within walking distance of Oxford meant that it attracted much attention from members of the university, and the debate about the mosaic generated considerable vitriol and controversy in the eighteenth century.

Another Bacchus mosaic that no longer survives was found on the site of the New Market Hall in Gloucester, its loss being all the more surprising as it was discovered as recently as 1966. The fragments showed parts of a leopard, Bacchus' arms, his cloak and a thyrsus.

Bacchus also featured prominently in two important mosaics at Frampton (Dorset). The pavement in the main part of room B has already been discussed in relation to its Chi-Rho monogram and some of the figured scenes. Other images will be considered below and in the next chapter. The mosaic in the antechamber showed Bacchus seated on a leopard (*18*). The animal turned its head towards its master, of whom all that remained at the time of discovery were traces of a cloak and thyrsus.

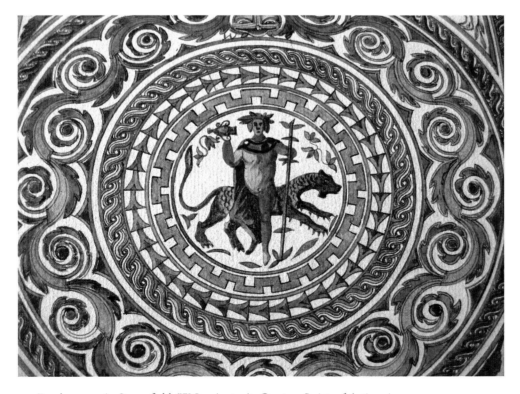

54 Bacchus mosaic, Stonesfield (W. Lewington). *Courtesy Society of Antiquaries*

The mosaic in room A at Frampton had the standing figure of Bacchus in the centre of the best preserved part (5 and *colour plate 6*). He held a bunch of grapes in his right hand, which was extended over his head as if in ecstasy, and a thyrsus in his left hand. Unusually, he was not accompanied by a feline.

The feline was also omitted from the Grand Mosaic at Pitney, where Bacchus appeared in the central octagon holding a cup and thyrsus (6 and *colour plate 7*). As he was shown in a seated posture, however, it has been suggested that his portrayal was based on the standard image but the animal was simply omitted through lack of space. The truncation of Bacchus' feet hints at practical problems with the layout, and further problems have been noted above in relation to one of the winds and the placement of some of the figured panels.

When Bacchus is portrayed as a full-length figure his identity is usually apparent, especially where he holds a cantharus or is accompanied by a panther. Establishing whether a bust represents the god is more difficult. Grapes and/or a thyrsus signify a Bacchic connection, but they could indicate a satyr, maenad or a personification of Autumn.

If the bust occupies the central position within a design, it seems probable that Bacchus was intended; a subsidiary location would suggest one of his attendants. This seems to be the case in the Bacchus mosaic at the Brading villa (55), where the central bust is usually interpreted as Bacchus and the surviving corner bust as a satyr. Each has a thyrsus. A bust with an apparent thyrsus in the centre of a lost mosaic from Fifehead Neville (Dorset) might also have represented Bacchus. The details shown in the paintings of this mosaic are unclear, but what has been described as a helmet on the head is perhaps more plausibly interpreted as poorly drawn leaves, hair or ribbons. Blue-green glass tesserae have been employed to indicate grapes in the headdress of a bust of Bacchus from the centre of an otherwise geometric mosaic from House XXVII.2 at Verulamium (Hertfordshire), now in store in the Verulamium Museum. Although small in relation to the overall mosaic, the lively sideways glance of the god animates this representation.

Somewhat more difficult to identify are two busts in the Yorkshire Museum, the first on display and the second in store. One found in Aldwark, York, is invariably described as female. The large 'bunches' of hair at the side of the face are consistent with a male hairstyle, and the end of a cloak on the bust's right shoulder is shown in the way used with male figures. The prominent location in the entrance corridor of the house makes it probable that an important figure was meant. Given Bacchus' effeminate appearance, he is the most likely candidate, especially as the overall shape of the hair recalls stylised bunches of grapes in a headdress. Rows of tesserae across the top of the head might have been intended as the bands of such a headdress, although the limited colour scheme employed in this mosaic makes it impossible to be certain. Similar comments apply to a bust from Oulston (Yorkshire), described as a 'wide eyed female' but also likely to be male. He has a cloak on his left shoulder and protrusions on either side of the face possibly representing ribbons and grape-clusters.

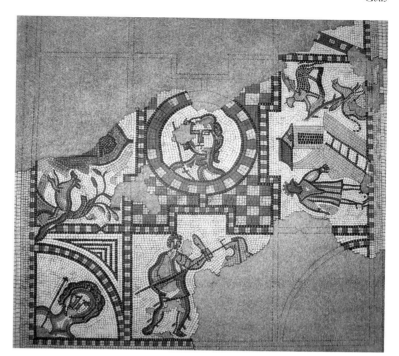

55 Bacchus mosaic, Brading (J. Price and F.G.H. Price)

Another confusion of gender has occurred with the Old Broad Street mosaic from London, sadly destroyed in the Crystal Palace fire of 1936 (*colour plate 21*). The figure in the central compartment was mounted on an animal and was regarded as female for many years. Europa with Jupiter in the guise of a bull, or a maenad reclining on the back of a panther, were among the most popular interpretations. A detailed painting of this mosaic shows, however, that the animal was spotted, indicating that it must have been a leopard and therefore that the mosaic had a Bacchic theme. Bacchus was often represented reclining on a leopard. Given the central position of the figure in the Old Broad Street mosaic, it is probable that Bacchus himself was depicted here rather than a maenad.

Other mosaics might also have shown Bacchus. A written account of the lost mosaic of Littleton (Somerset) describes 'a male figure, supposed to be a Bacchus'. The badly damaged figure in the centre of the Bonus Eventus mosaic in room 10 at Woodchester (Gloucestershire), with its satyrs, maenad, Cupids and inscription, had a tress of long hair or a ribbon on the shoulder, which would be consistent with a depiction of Bacchus (*56*). It has been suggested that Bacchus was depicted in the largely lost central medallion of the Seasons mosaic from House VII at Caerwent (Gwent) (*38*).

In all the examples above, Bacchus was the only or the major figure in the mosaic. In the second- or third-century Seasons mosaic found at Dyer Street in Cirencester (Gloucestershire), however, he merely featured in one of the side panels, now lost, where he was shown with his leopard, thyrsus and headdress of

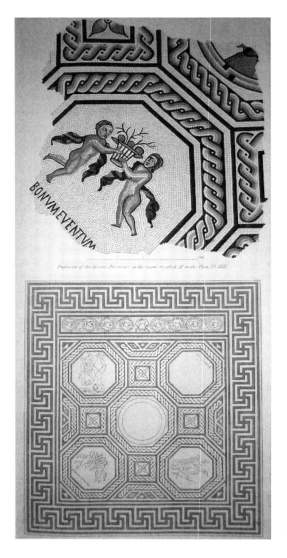

56 Bonus Eventus mosaic, Woodchester (Samuel Lysons)

vine leaves (*34*). Perhaps at this earlier date he had not acquired the prominence and potency he was later to enjoy.

Finally, the thyrsolonchus at Caerleon (Gwent), now displayed in the Caerleon Roman Fortress Baths, is so unusual that it merits a mention. The bulbous shape in the spandrel of this fragmentary mosaic terminates in a point and is crossed by diagonal bands of coloured tesserae. It is thought to represent the tip of a spear disguised in a Bacchic thyrsus, bound with ribbons that stream out on either side. Ovid describes such a spear being brandished by Bacchus when he encountered the Tyrrhenian pirates (*Metamorphoses* III, 667). Although there is nothing in the surviving fragments of the Caerleon mosaic to tie it to a specific myth, it seems clear that the imagery was Bacchic.

Bacchus' followers

The Seasons mosaic from Dyer Street, Cirencester, not only showed Bacchus but also his rotund companion, Silenus, who slumps drunkenly on the back of a donkey (*34*). This is the only certain portrayal of Silenus known from a Romano-British mosaic and it is notable that he is accorded the same prominence as Bacchus himself. The absence of Silenus from the later mosaics suggests that the hedonistic aspect of the Bacchic cult had waned in influence and that the deity was regarded in a more serious light. A small female figure in a square panel adjacent to Actaeon in this mosaic appears to be another Bacchic follower: a maenad holding a bunch of grapes and vine leaves.

A tale related by Nonnos, although otherwise obscure, concerns the Bacchante Ambrosia and is depicted in the Seasons mosaic at Brading (*9* and *16*) (*Dionysiaca* XXI, 1-154). Ambrosia is being attacked by Lycurgus, an enemy of Bacchus, who brandishes a double-headed axe. In the myth, Ambrosia cried out for help and the Earth responded to her plea by turning her into a vine that throttled Lycurgus. Vine leaves can be seen sprouting in the background of the Brading panel. Lycurgus was only saved from death by the intervention of Juno.

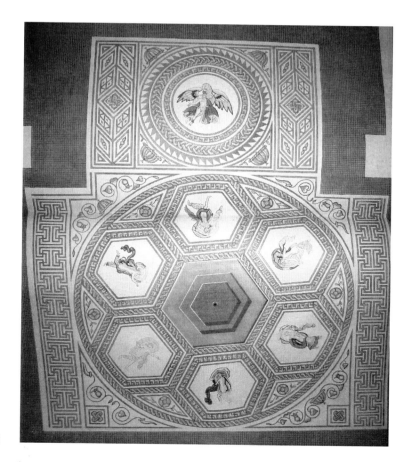

57 Ganymede mosaic, Bignor (Samuel Lysons)

Satyrs and maenads, the male and female members of the Bacchic thiasos, were a pleasing and popular decoration. They are depicted in the Seasons mosaic in the triclinium at Chedworth (*7* and *8*), the Bonus Eventus mosaic at Woodchester (*56*) and a small panel in a corridor mosaic from the same palatial dwelling. Satyrs surround Mars in a mosaic found at Fullerton (Hampshire), now in private hands, and maenads dance around the pool adjacent to the Ganymede panel at Bignor (*57*). As discussed above, the figures in the medallions in central part of the Horkstow pavement (Lincolnshire) (*12* and *colour plate 11*) are regarded by many as Bacchic. It is unfortunate that the centre of this mosaic did not survive as it may well have informed us about the character of the whole panel.

BONUS EVENTUS

Bonus Eventus was a god of rural prosperity who came to enjoy a more general meaning of good fortune and a lucky outcome.

An inscription 'BONVM EVENTVM' in the buried mosaic in room 10 at Woodchester (*56*) has been interpreted as an exhortation to worship this god. Another inscription in the mosaic has been restored as 'BENE COLITE', translated as 'enjoy yourselves'. It suggests that the message of the mosaic was simply to convey a wish for good fortune and happiness. The fragmentary central bust might have represented Bonus Eventus himself. Alternatively, given the Bacchic character of the other figures in this mosaic – the three surviving corner octagons are decorated with dancing satyrs, a maenad, and Cupids bearing a basket of fruit and foliage – it would have been appropriate to show Bacchus here.

CUPID

Originally the god of love and son of Venus, Cupid came to be represented in the plural in the form of children, often with wings but frequently without.

There are many depictions of Cupids in Romano-British mosaics, some shown in a playful or light-hearted vein. In the lost mosaic from room B at Frampton, however, the fragmentary figure of Cupid seems to have been imbued with a serious and profound meaning (*18*). He was flanked by water birds and by lines from an inscription. The lettering was wholly missing on one side and slightly incomplete on the other, where it read:

[NEC MVN] NVS PERFICIS VLLVM
[SI DI] GNARE CVPIDO

This has been translated as '… and you do not perform any service, if you deem it fit, Cupid.' The mosaic appears to show the two realms of Neptune (whose appearance in the mosaic was also accompanied by an inscription) and Cupid, whose name is derived from the Latin word for desire.

Cupid appears as an instrumental character in some of the stories discussed in previous chapters. A single winged Cupid aims an arrow in the Cyparissus mosaic from All Saints Church in Leicester (*colour plate 5*). Similarly, a pair of winged Cupids accompany Europa and the bull in the mosaic at the Lullingstone villa (Kent) (*colour plate 3*), and flank Venus in the central panel of the Low Ham mosaic (Somerset) (*13*). Eros, Cupid's Greek antecedent, appears wrestling his brother Anteros in the mosaic from Middleborough, Colchester (Essex), where they represent requited, reciprocal love (*colour plate 8*).

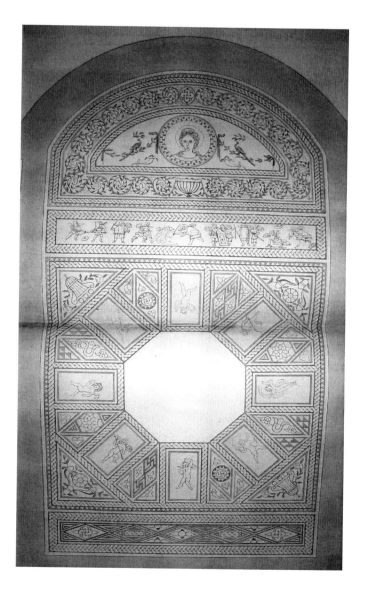

58 Venus mosaic, Bignor (Samuel Lysons)

Cupids were often used in Roman art in a pastiche of human activities. The most famous examples are perhaps the wall-paintings in the House of the Vettii at Pompeii. A similar spirit pervades the panel with the Cupid-gladiators in the Venus mosaic at Bignor (*58* and *colour plate 22*). Cupids were also used to represent the seasons. They appear in this guise in the triclinium mosaic at Chedworth (*7*) and in the lost Grand Mosaic at Pitney (*37* and *colour plate 7*). The Bignor and Pitney Cupids have wings, but curiously at Chedworth only Summer is so endowed.

Cupids also featured in mosaics where the seasons were shown as female busts. A small wingless Cupid, now lost, occupied an oval panel in the southern part of the fourth-century Seasons mosaic at Bignor, while the Caerwent Seasons mosaic originally had four winged Cupids placed around its central medallion (*38*).

A pair of wingless Cupids hold a basket of fruit and foliage in the 'Bonus Eventus' mosaic at Woodchester (*56*). The winged Cupids dancing around the

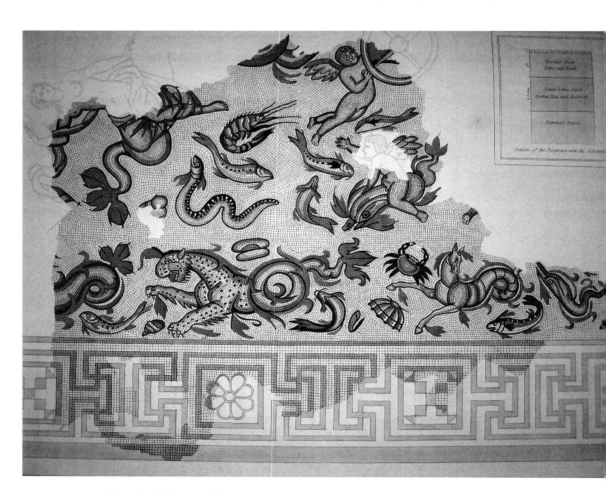

59 Triumph of Neptune, Cirencester (Samuel Lysons)

lost centre in the rectangular part of the Bignor Venus mosaic hold Bacchic objects (*58*), while more winged Cupids dance around a basket of fruit (?) in the only fragment to survive from the inner circle of the central panel from Horkstow (*12* and *colour plate 11*).

As well as their association with the seasons and fruits of the earth, Cupids featured in marine contexts. The winged Cupid holding a trident and riding a bridled dolphin is one of the best known images at the Fishbourne palace (Sussex) (*45*). The marine imagery is here reinforced by the scallop shells in the corner panels and by the sea beasts in the semicircular compartments. The latter are particularly unusual as the sea horses are primarily black and white, while the sea panthers are polychrome.

The fragmentary mosaic thought to have shown the triumph of Neptune from Dyer Street, Cirencester, now virtually lost, included two winged Cupids, one riding a dolphin and the other holding the wheel of Neptune's chariot (*59*). The marine mosaic from Dewlish (Dorset), part of which is on display in the Dorset County Museum (*colour plate 16*), originally included a winged Cupid. Swimming Cupids, some winged and some wingless, accompany the marine thiasos in the outer circle of the central panel from Horkstow (*12* and *colour plate 11*).

GIANTS

Children of the Earth, Giants were divine beings whose legs took the form of snakes. With their raised arms, they held up the circle in the central panel of the Horkstow mosaic (*12* and *colour plate 11*). It has been suggested that similar figures supported the central roundel of a mosaic with hunting scenes from Dewlish. If the excavated fragment is interpreted in this way, the Giant's girdle did not hang straight down as would be expected but swung to one side. Others have suggested that the fragment shows a bird or griffin.

JUPITER

Jupiter was shown representing one of the days of the week in the Bramdean mosaic (*colour plate 10*). Despite his role as the greatest god and father of many of the other deities, the other depictions of him in Romano-British mosaics show him participating in amorous adventures: with Europa at Keynsham (*4*) and Lullingstone (*colour plate 3*), with Ganymede at Bignor (*57* and *colour plate 4*), and perhaps with Danaë at Frampton (*5* and *colour plate 6*).

MARS

The role of Mars as the father of Romulus and Remus often overshadows the equally important role he played as a god of nature, protecting crops and herds. This seems to have been more significant than his original role as god of war.

The agricultural aspect of Mars is probably recalled in the Fullerton mosaic (Hampshire), now in private hands, in which satyrs cavort not around Bacchus, as we might expect, but around a figure wearing a cloak and helmet and holding a shield and spear. Although some scholars have suggested that the central figure is Virtus, the personification of military virtue, the context suggests that this figure is Mars.

Mars also represented one of the days of the week at Bramdean (*colour plate 10*), and perhaps appeared in mosaics at Calne (Wiltshire) and Caerwent (Gwent) as accounts of mosaics at those sites refer respectively to 'a Roman soldier … armed with a spear' and 'a man in armour'.

A mosaic, now lost, was found in a temple dedicated to the god Mars Nodens at Lydney Park (Gloucestershire). Its inscription indicated that here Mars had been conflated with Nodens, a local deity.

MERCURY

Mercury was the messenger of Jupiter and was renowned for his inventiveness and cunning. His attributes included the caduceus, a winged hat or sandals, and a purse.

Mercury was shown with his caduceus and wearing a winged cap as one of the days of the week in the Bramdean mosaic (*colour plate 10*). A bust of Mercury also appears flanked by vines in a narrow panel bordering the Venus mosaic from Rudston (Yorkshire) (*60*). The caduceus by his right shoulder is well drawn but his cap has a leaf emerging from either side. The leaves are often regarded as misunderstood wings, but the wings already seem to be present in the two dark lines sprouting tuft-like from the top of the head, resembling those on Mercury's cap at Bramdean. Instead of a poorly understood depiction of Mercury, perhaps the Rudston bust was closer to the traditional representation but with the addition of vine leaves to complement the grape-laden vines on either side.

In the Grand Mosaic at Pitney, the naked male figure holding a small crook in his right hand with a purse or bag hanging over his left wrist has been interpreted as Mercury. Some scholars explain his appearance in the mosaic as one of the lesser known consorts of Venus (*6* and *colour plate 7*). Although the purse was an appropriate attribute for Mercury, the crook shown in the Pitney pavement was distinctive and unlike a caduceus. As I have explained above, I believe the key to interpreting this mosaic lies in establishing the original scheme. If the seated shepherd had been paired with regal-looking female with the voluminous red cloak, Mercury would have faced the female who held a syrinx in her left hand. This couple are numbered 4 and 7 on Hasell's watercolour.

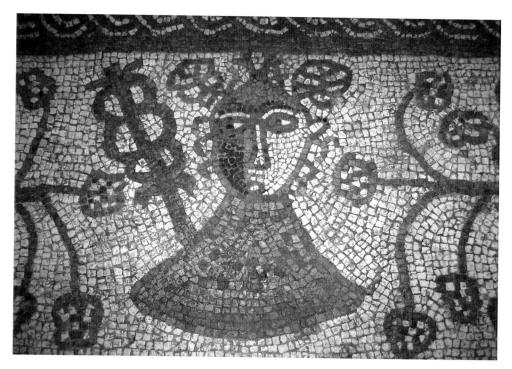

60 Mercury, Venus mosaic, Rudston. *Courtesy Hull and East Riding Museum*

The *Homeric Hymn to Hermes* — Hermes being Mercury's Greek antecedent — relates the amusing incident of how, while a child, Hermes stole some cattle belonging to Apollo and cunningly drove them backwards to confound Apollo's attempts to trace them. An old man told Apollo that he had seen an infant who had a staff driving some cattle, and the reference to the infant alerted Apollo to the identity of the thief. Hermes soothed Apollo by playing on the lyre which he had just invented. Apollo was so impressed by the instrument that he gave Hermes the cattle in exchange for it. Hermes then invented the syrinx to play while pasturing his newly-acquired beasts.

In later legend, the syrinx became associated with Pan and was personified in the form of a nymph of that name. In the *Metamorphoses*, Ovid puts the tale of Pan and Syrinx into the mouth of Mercury (I, 689-712), maintaining the link between the god and this musical instrument. It seems likely that the panels in the Pitney mosaic showed Mercury holding his cattle-driving staff, paired with Syrinx who held the instrument that gave her her name.

Mercury played a role in the famous episode of the judgement of Paris. On Jupiter's instructions, he conducted the three goddesses to Paris who was to act as judge. He is shown as part of the scene in an accomplished mosaic from Antioch, now in The Louvre in Paris, although he is not depicted in any of the Romano-British mosaics featuring Paris.

NEPTUNE

Neptune, the god of the sea, used his trident not only to stir up the waves but also to make water flow forth from springs. This, and his ability to send storms or favourable winds, made him important as a fertility god. Among his accomplishments, he was renowned for creating and taming the horse. He was often shown holding the trident and with crab's or lobster's claws or legs sprouting from his head.

The trident identified Neptune and distinguished him from Oceanus, although it was not essential that he should be accompanied by this attribute. The Frampton inscription, discussed below, named Neptune even though no trident was in evidence. One school of thought suggests that a bust or mask of an aquatic deity in a Romano-British mosaic, even without a trident, was almost certainly intended to represent Neptune rather than Oceanus.

Like the exploits of his brother Jupiter, Neptune's love life was recorded in mosaic, as in the Grand Mosaic at Pitney discussed above (*6* and *colour plate 7*), but his image was also popular in its own right. His connection with water unsurprisingly made him a suitable choice for baths, although he also graced the floors of a number of Romano-British reception rooms.

A panel on the left of the mosaic in room A at Frampton showed a man wielding a trident as if about to slay the small creature scrabbling at his knees (*5* and *colour plate 6*). Originally identified as Neptune because of the trident, the figure was subsequently reinterpreted as Perseus. The pose, with left hand resting on hip, was typical of that adopted by Perseus in the act of slaying the sea monster during his rescue of Andromeda. The left hand usually held the bag containing the head of Medusa, but the mosaic was damaged at this point and it is impossible to tell whether the hand held an object or simply rested on the hip. A figure in a similar pose depicts Perseus in a mosaic at Conímbriga in Portugal, in which the sea monster resembles the Frampton beast.

A factor influencing the identification of Perseus in the Frampton mosaic was the youthful, beardless appearance of the male figure. This is more in keeping with the way a young hero would be depicted rather than a god. Evidence has, however, been assembled for youthful portrayals of Neptune, and the fact that the Frampton figure wielded a trident rather than the short sword used by Perseus makes it probable that he was Neptune. The curiously puny, and apparently winged, sea creature might be a misrendered version of Pegasus, his son.

The Triumph of Neptune was a popular and striking subject for mosaics in other provinces, especially in Italy and North Africa, in which the god was shown being drawn through the sea in his chariot. The fragmentary scene found in a second- or third-century mosaic beneath Dyer Street, Cirencester, in 1783 and recorded by Samuel Lysons was probably of this type (*59*). A lively scatter of marine creatures, one ridden by a Nereid and another by a Cupid, swam around a lost centrepiece of which only a winged Cupid holding or pushing a wheel survived. The context

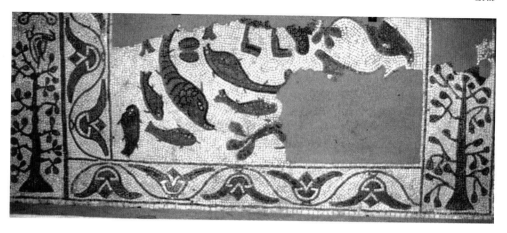

61 Neptune mosaic, Rudston. *Courtesy Hull and East Riding Museum*

suggests that this belonged to Neptune's chariot. This mosaic must once have been a sumptuous floor comparable to any found in the Mediterranean. Although virtually lost, small portions have been rediscovered in the cellars of existing buildings in recent years, and confirm the accuracy of Lysons' record.

A surviving, albeit fragmentary, mosaic showing the head or bust of Neptune surrounded by fishes and dolphins was found in the bath suite of the Rudston villa (Yorkshire) and is now in the Hull and East Riding Museum (*61*). The surviving side of Neptune's head is displayed horizontally; a fork of his curly beard curves outwards on the viewer's right. The two L-shapes to the left are stylised crab's legs emerging from his hair, similar to those in the Hemsworth bust described below. This mosaic has been described as creating the illusion of a pool or an imaginary aquarium surrounded by a border of lotus flowers whose bases give them the appearance of urns. A tree with a bird (short-tailed on the left and long-tailed on the right) is shown on each side of the scene. The curved feature above the bird on the left is thought to be the handle of a cantharus.

Another bust of Neptune, clearly identified as such from a small trident behind his head, was found in a Roman bath at Ashcroft Villas, Cirencester, in 1905 and recorded in an oblique black and white photograph. Dolphins, fishes and sea beasts accompanied him. Small fragments rediscovered in the store at the Corinium Museum in 1994 show that this mosaic employed glass tesserae to enhance the watery effect.

A panel from the Orpheus mosaic from Withington (Gloucestershire), now in the British Museum, has a similar representation of Neptune, but here the trident is more prominent and two of the dolphins swim out of the god's beard (*27*). Prominent crab's claws and pincers emerge from his hair. He is flanked by two flower-like motifs variously described as sea anemones, rosettes or jellyfish. The scene is completed by a pair of trees or, more probably, aquatic plants, and has a border of wave pattern, an appropriate choice for a marine subject.

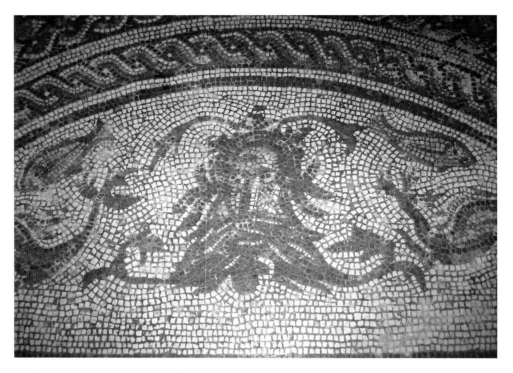

62 Neptune mosaic, Fordington High Street, Dorchester. *Courtesy Dorset County Museum*

The apse of the second- or third-century mosaic from Fordington High Street, Dorchester (Dorset), now in Dorset County Museum, has a simplified layout with a single dolphin and fish on either side of the head of Neptune (*62*). He wears a red band around his forehead. The shapes sprouting from the band and from his beard are probably strands of seaweed rather than the legs or claws of a crustacean as some descriptions suggest.

Dorset County Museum is also the home of a majestic bust of Neptune found in the bath suite of the Hemsworth villa (Dorset) in 1908 (*63*). The jagged shapes around his head originally led to suggestions that this was Jupiter with bolts of lightning or Apollo with the sun's rays. In recent years, some scholars have identified these shapes as reeds, suggesting a river god, but they are probably crab's legs. The face of Neptune can be regarded as superimposed on the body of a crab whose folded claws can be seen in the two orange shapes on the top of the head. The unusual chevron border around the medallion recalls the zigzag panels often used to indicate pools of water as, for instance, in the mosaic at Littlecote Park (*colour plate 2*).

Another bust sometimes described as a river god is the figure recorded by Samuel Lysons in the centre of the mosaic in room D at Frampton (*53*). The red lines protruding from the top of the head look less naturalistic than the crab's claws in the figures of Neptune discussed above, but the context with dolphins shows that he was probably intended here.

The well-known second-century mosaic from House IV.8 at Verulamium (Hertfordshire), now in the Verulamium Museum, shows an impressive bust of Neptune with a pair of crab's claws on his head (*64*). In the past, the prominence of the claws has caused some scholars to regard them as antlers and to propose a Celtic horned god, perhaps Cernunnos. Such a non-classical figure would have been unique and surprising in a Roman mosaic, and the bust is now generally accepted as Neptune. The conical shapes emerging from the canthari or craters in the borders above and below the bust are sometimes described as ladles. It is more likely that they represent jets of water playing in fountains shaped as drinking vessels, complementing the watery theme of this mosaic.

Neptune was also associated with a drinking vessel in the mosaic in room B at Frampton, where the bust of the god was the focus of the border facing the apse (*18*). He was aligned with a prominent cantharus or crater and with the Chi-Rho monogram discussed in chapter 4. An inscription either side of

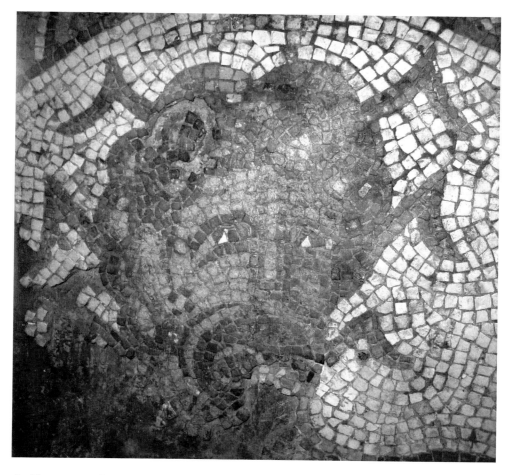

63 Neptune mosaic, Hemsworth. *Courtesy Dorset County Museum*

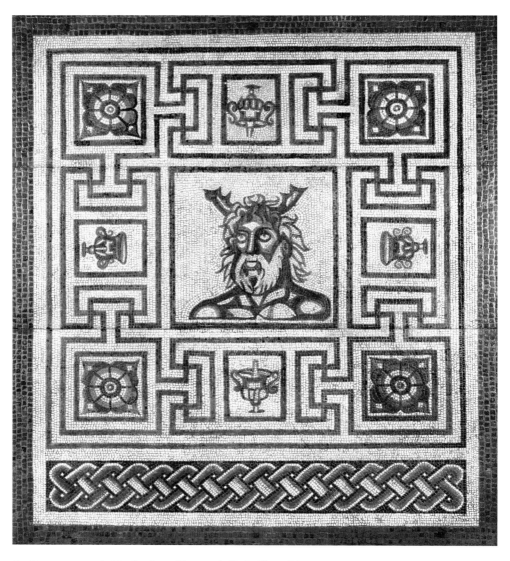

64 Neptune mosaic, Verulamium. *Photograph: © St Albans Museums*

the bust was echoed by the inscription flanking Cupid, who was positioned in the centre of the opening to the anteroom. The inscription accompanying Neptune read:

NEPTVNI VERTEX REG[I]MEN

SORTITI MOBILE VENTIS

SCVL[P]TVM CVI C[A]ERVLEA ES[T]

DELFINIS CINCTA DVOB[VS]

This has been translated as 'The head of Neptune allotted the domain stirred by the winds, whose dark-blue figure is flanked by two dolphins'. In addition to the dolphins swimming out of his beard, it is estimated that a further 24 dolphins decorated the border. Despite the sophistication of the inscriptions in this mosaic, the bust of Neptune seems poorly proportioned: according to Lysons' drawing, the crab's claws in his hair were of unequal length, and the hair was shown in greater profusion on one side of the face than the other.

A Neptune mask, again with crab's claws in the hair, appears in alignment with Orpheus in the outer circular border of the Great Pavement at Woodchester (*25*). It would have faced visitors as they entered the room through what is thought to have been the main doorway. Although the mask is associated with an acanthus scroll and not with aquatic imagery, the mosaic has clear references to water: it was reported that at the time of discovery in 1693 the lost centrepiece included a fish, and the spandrels of the mosaic are decorated with four pairs of reclining water nymphs.

A similar mask, also in an acanthus scroll, was positioned above Bacchus in the lost mosaic of Stonesfield (Oxfordshire) (*colour plate 23*). This pavement is known from a plethora of antiquarian drawings and from an embroidery. Although the details vary between the different records, the Neptune mask appears to have had crab's claws on top of the head, a strand of seaweed on either side of the face, and a flowing blue and white beard recalling streams of water.

In all the examples above, the image of Neptune was an important part of the mosaic. In the second- or third-century Hunting dogs mosaic from Dyer Street, Cirencester, however, two Neptune masks are used as incidental decoration (*42*). Despite the relatively unimportant position of the deity in the design here, the masks have been drawn in great detail. A coloured band around the head has crab's claws at its base and incorporates strands of seaweed, while the beard terminates in further strands notable for the realism with which they are depicted.

Neptune's attendants

In the same way that Bacchus was often accompanied by satyrs and maenads, Neptune was frequently shown with his male and female entourage of Nereids and Tritons. The latter had human upper bodies terminating in fish- or dolphin-tails; sometimes they had equine-like front legs and a single tail. They were often depicted blowing into shells as horns.

The easternmost panel of the Seasons mosaic (the lowest panel in figure *16*) at Brading shows two types of Triton (*16*). The Triton in the centre has a human head, arms and torso, with coiled legs terminating in dolphin-tails. He holds an oar in his right hand and a bowl of shellfish (?) in his left hand. He is flanked by a pair of Nereids who recline languidly on the tails of Tritons who each have equine forelegs ending in flippers and a long tail terminating in a single fin. The

Triton on the left holds a pedum, while the tapering rod held by the Triton on the right is probably intended to represent a conch shell. The Nereid on the left holds a leaf-fan.

The Nereids and Tritons swimming around the outer circle of the central panel of the Horkstow mosaic (*12* and *colour plate 11*) are difficult to disentangle from one another: some Nereids seem to be superimposed over, rather than mounted upon, their accompanying Triton. One of the Nereids recalls depictions of Venus in a shell. The figures seem to have been drawn by a mosaicist who was uncertain of what he was trying to depict.

A curious Triton accompanies Venus in the central panel of the Rudston mosaic (*73*). His role here primarily alludes to the birth of the goddess from the sea. The object he holds has been variously described as a 'back-scratcher', a torch or a conch shell. Although a shell is a common attribute, the Triton is not placing it to his lips but is holding it up as if it is a torch. The red lines at the upper end seem to indicate a torch's flames, and it has been suggested that this Triton should be seen as a type of marine Cupid attending Venus. Busts of four Tritons with conch shells accompanied Neptune in the mosaic in room D at Frampton (*53*).

SATURN

Saturn, the father of Jupiter, appeared representing one of the days of the week in the Bramdean pavement (*colour plate 10*), but is otherwise unknown in Romano-British mosaics.

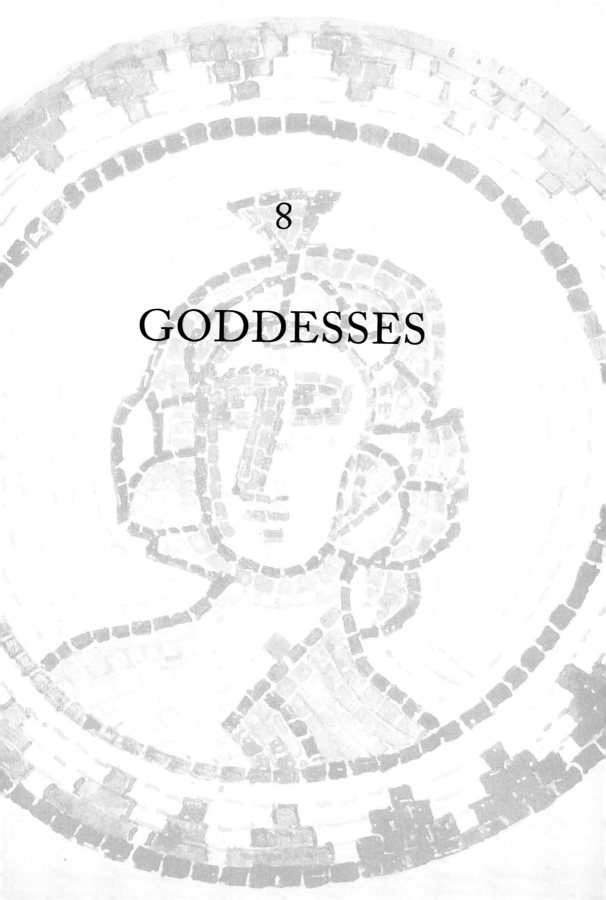

8

GODDESSES

Only Venus rivals some of the most popular male deities in terms of the number of mosaics in which she is depicted. She is also usually easy and unambiguous to recognise. This is not the case with many of the other goddesses, some of whom were concerned with similar themes to one another and whose precise identity is accordingly unclear.

CERES

Ceres was the goddess of agriculture who bestowed the gift of corn on mankind and taught Triptolemus how to use the plough.

We have seen in chapter 5 that the Seasons mosaic at the Brading villa (Isle of Wight) has a depiction of Ceres standing on the left of the panel, handing an ear of corn to Triptolemus who stands on the right holding a plough (*9* and *16*). This scene appears to represent an allusion to Spring when seed was sown. Ceres has also been identified in another seasonal role, this time Autumn, accompanied by the bull in the Orpheus mosaic at Littlecote Park (Wiltshire) (*30* and *colour plate 2*), where she is paired with Winter, represented by her daughter Proserpina.

A bust usually referred to as 'Ceres' enjoys the unusual distinction of gracing a mosaic in the foyer of Scunthorpe's Civic Centre (*65*). When this pavement was discovered at Winterton (Lincolnshire) in 1747, an attribute over her right shoulder was initially thought to represent a sceptre and the bust was regarded as that of a man, perhaps an emperor. Later, the 'sceptre' was reinterpreted as ears of corn, and on this basis the bust was described as Ceres.

The accuracy of this identification and of the antiquarian engravings of the mosaic has subsequently been called into question. During re-excavations in 1958-9, it was found that part of the head and attribute still survived. Several blue and purple tesserae in the latter recalled the colour of grapes, and Bacchus was therefore proposed as the possible subject. However, the 'grapes' were clearly not part of a headdress nor were the tesserae arranged to form the shape of a bunch. Instead, they looked more like the top of a peacock feather, for which the colours of the tesserae would also be appropriate. As the peacock feather is an attribute often found with Venus, she might have been the subject of this

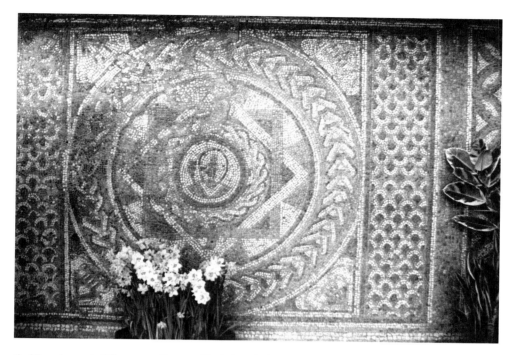

65 'Ceres' mosaic, Winterton. *Courtesy North Lincolnshire Council*

mosaic. Ironically, following lifting and inaccurate restoration of this mosaic, the bust is now far from being the embodiment of female beauty and has taken on a cartoon-like appearance.

DIANA

Diana was identified with the moon goddess, Luna, and appeared in this guise along with the other deities of the days of the week at Bramdean (Hampshire) (*colour plate 10*).

A well-known myth concerning Diana was the story of how she transformed Actaeon into a stag. While out hunting with his hounds one day, Actaeon accidentally chanced upon a pool in which the naked goddess was bathing with her attendants. Outraged at being seen undressed by a man, Diana threw a handful of water at Actaeon and turned him into a stag, whereupon he was pursued and torn apart by his own hounds.

One of the panels in the second- or third-century Seasons mosaic from a town house beneath Dyer Street in Cirencester (Gloucestershire), now in the Corinium Museum, shows Actaeon in the course of the transformation. Antlers sprout from his head as two collared dogs savagely bite his right leg (*34* and *colour plate 24*). Tesserae made of red glass were used to highlight his dripping blood.

The leafy tree on the left contrasts with the leafless tree on the right, underlining Actaeon's transition from life to death.

Representations of Actaeon's metamorphosis into a stag are commonly paired with a scene of the bathing Diana. It is therefore likely that she was the subject of the panel on the opposite side of the mosaic that did not survive. This supposition is strengthened by the fact that the other two side panels, showing Bacchus and Silenus, formed a thematic pair.

It has been suggested that Actaeon was the quarry in the second- or third-century Hunting dogs mosaic from the same house, again in the Corinium Museum (*42*). This is feasible, especially as the shape of a standing human would fit the available space better than an animal. As no trace of the figure survived, it is impossible to tell what the complete scene originally showed, especially as the mosaic has been repaired in antiquity.

Diana is the possible subject of two other mosaics, one buried *in situ* and the other privately owned. In the mosaic at Bratton Seymour (Somerset), the bust of a clothed figure apparently wears a helmet. An object by her left shoulder has been identified as Diana's bow, with the 'helmet' interpreted as a type of headdress known as a high stephane. This way of representing the goddess is closely paralleled in a mosaic depicting Diana from the Bruckneudorf villa near Carnuntum in modern Austria, and suggests that she is the deity represented in the Bratton Seymour pavement.

The female depicted in a mosaic found at Thenford (Northamptonshire) is unusual in that the upper body of her figure is shown as well as her head and shoulders. Lines on her body and arms could represent a dress or might delineate a necklace and armlets worn by an otherwise naked female. Strands of long hair cascade onto her shoulders. A red feature on the top of her head has been described as a cap, but it is more likely to be a semicircular diadem and to be indicative of a goddess. A leafy twig rests against her left shoulder, behind which is a red band with blue stripes. This band has been regarded as a cloak, but it is remarkably sparse for such a garment. The stripes run horizontally, whereas the folds of a cloak would be vertical. It is perhaps a quiver, as such objects are depicted striped in this way in mosaics from other provinces. The 'twig' could represent a bow or arrow. Alternatively, it has been suggested that this figure is Venus with a sprig of leaves to indicate her role as goddess of gardens.

FORTUNA/TYCHE

Fortuna, the goddess of good luck, was one of the most popular deities. She shared her attribute of the cornucopia with the Greek Tyche, a deified personi-fication of Chance who gave special protection to cities. For this reason, Tyche was shown wearing a mural crown. Abundantia and Providentia personify similar concepts, and it is not always easy to tell which figure was intended. Good fortune, whichever the deity chosen to personify the concept, was a constant concern, particularly as it was often elusive and unpredictable.

The central bust in the Brantingham mosaic (Yorkshire) has been discussed in chapter 4 (*20*). Is she a Tyche or a Muse? Much depends on the interpretation of the headdress but, whatever her identity, it should take into account the eight subsidiary busts who have no headdresses or attributes to provide a clue. The fact that the busts number nine in total makes it attractive to regard them as Muses, but perhaps there is another explanation to which we have yet to find the key.

In a mosaic from Winterton, found by chance in 1797 and now in Scunthorpe Museum, Fortuna is shown in the traditional way with a cornucopia over her shoulder. The position of the cornucopia is, however, unusual. It was normally placed over the left shoulder, whereas here it lies over her right shoulder. It contains three oval objects perhaps intended to represent fruit. The mosaic has been substantially restored and, like the 'Ceres' mosaic from the same site, looks far cruder today than was originally the case.

Another bust with a cornucopia, this time in the conventional position over her left shoulder, comes from Bailgate in Lincoln and is now in the City and County Museum, Lincoln. Here the identification as Fortuna is complicated by her headdress. It appears to contain ears of corn, suggesting Summer. The cornucopia is an attribute occasionally found with seasons as well as with Fortuna. However, as there is no surrounding border of guilloche, it is thought that this panel cannot have come from a corner of the mosaic. It is therefore unlikely to have formed part of a series of four seasons.

A bust from Itchen Abbas (Hampshire), known to have been the sole image in the mosaic and no longer thought to survive, is an example of a similar figure. It showed a woman whose headdress was decorated with flowers and leaves, possibly indicating Spring or Summer. As there were no other seasons in this mosaic, however, the figure was probably intended to evoke growth and prosperity in general rather than a specific season.

Another bust, found at Whittlebury (Northamptonshire) in the nineteenth century, showed a winged female with a fragmentary attribute that appeared to be the tip of a floral or foliate spray or a cornucopia. She was originally thought to depict Victory but it is more likely that she personified good fortune or growth. The mosaic was lifted after discovery and reportedly presented to Queen Victoria. Attempts to trace it have not been successful.

At right angles to the presumed Orpheus mosaic at Whatley (Somerset) discussed in chapter 4 was a panel with the bust of a long-haired female wearing a mural crown (*31*). The lithograph of this mosaic shows a cornucopia over her left shoulder but a sketch based on another drawing has ears of corn instead. A variety of identifications have been put forward but the presence of the mural crown indicates a Tyche. She evidently had connections with water as dolphins and fishes decorated the spandrels and there was an adjoining panel of marine creatures.

A fragmentary bust found in a mosaic possibly dating to the third century in House XIV.2 at Silchester (Hampshire) is known from a painting made at the time of discovery in 1895. She appears to have been a Tyche. Two crenellations of a mural crown are visible, and there was room for a cornucopia to have been shown in the missing area around her left shoulder. An adjoining panel showing a basket of fruit was lifted and is now in Reading Museum. As the putative Tyche has not been traced, it is probable that she has perished.

JUNO

Juno, the queen of heaven and wife of Jupiter, is not depicted in any known Romano-British mosaics although her name is mentioned in the inscription above the scene of Europa and the bull at Lullingstone (*colour plate 3*). She also played a role in some of the myths shown in other mosaics. For instance, she was one of the contenders in the famous beauty contest. She is shown with her competitors in mosaics of this scene from other provinces, but in the Romano-British pavements only Venus, the winner, is portrayed with Paris. Juno also played a crucial role in releasing Lycurgus from Ambrosia's grip when the latter was turned into a vine and entwined herself around her attacker, as shown in the Brading Seasons mosaic (*9* and *16*).

MINERVA

Among her many talents, Minerva was credited with inventing the flutes. She found the sound pleasing, but she caught sight of her reflection in a pool as she played the instrument and was displeased by the way her puffed up cheeks distorted her face. She threw the flutes away in disgust. They were found by Marsyas who became a skilled player and challenged Apollo to a musical contest. This is pictured in the Lenthay Green mosaic discussed in the previous chapter (*colour plate 19*).

Along with the scenes of Europa and the bull and Achilles on Scyros, the hexagonal mosaic from room W at Keynsham (Somerset), currently in store, included a panel showing two standing figures leaning over what looks like, and was originally interpreted as, a disembodied, helmeted head (*66*). This scene has since been recognised as Minerva looking at her reflection as she blows into the flutes. The figure on the right is a water nymph whose hand, pouring water from an urn, can be seen at the upper edge of the surviving part of the mosaic. Mosaics from other provinces often include Marsyas in the background, peeping at Minerva as she tries out her musical skills, and it is entirely possible that he was shown in the lost upper portion of the Keynsham panel.

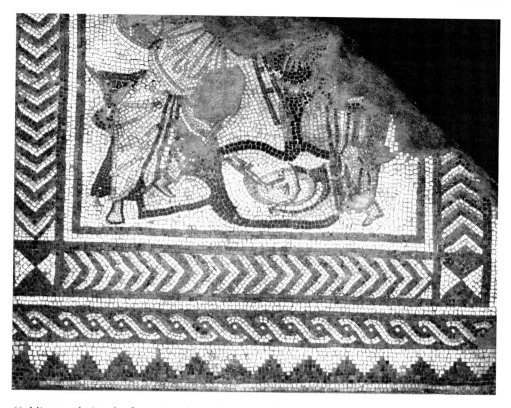

66 Minerva playing the flutes, Keynsham. *Photograph: © Charles Browne*

Given that Minerva wore the head of Medusa on her aegis once Perseus had slain the Gorgon, the Roman viewer of the many Medusa mosaics discussed in chapter 6 would no doubt have recalled this association.

PROSERPINA

Proserpina was snatched by the god of the underworld and taken to live in the nether regions. Ceres was disconsolate at the loss of her daughter and the earth became sterile. Jupiter decreed that Proserpina should be returned, but only on condition that she had not eaten anything. As it happens, she had eaten a pomegranate seed and by doing so had shown that she had not entirely rejected the underworld. In a compromise, she was allowed to spend part of the year above ground, returning to spend the other part in the underworld. The myth of Ceres and Proserpina is an allegory for the way in which shoots sprout from the earth and then, after a period of growth, die down again.

Proserpina is considered to represent Winter in the Littlecote Park mosaic, where she is shown with a goat (*30* and *colour plate 2*).

TELLUS

The earth goddess Tellus played a similar role to Ceres. In a number of mosaics from other provinces where her identity is established by an inscription, she is shown with a corn measure on her head.

The role of Tellus in the myth of her son Antaeus' wrestling match with Hercules in one of the lost mosaics from Bramdean has been related in chapter 3 *(colour plate 9)*.

The concern for the fruitfulness of the earth that Tellus shared with Ceres makes it possible that some figures described as Ceres might have been regarded as Tellus by their Roman viewers.

A small panel in an acanthus scroll below the Newton St Loe Orpheus mosaic (Somerset) (*67*) divided the outer part of the room with its Orpheus pavement from the inner part with a geometric mosaic. A female bust in the centre of this panel had an object shaped like an inverted triangle poised on her head. Often interpreted in the past as a diadem, this object more closely resembles the stylised shape of a corn measure and, if so, would identify the bust as Tellus. This panel cannot now be traced.

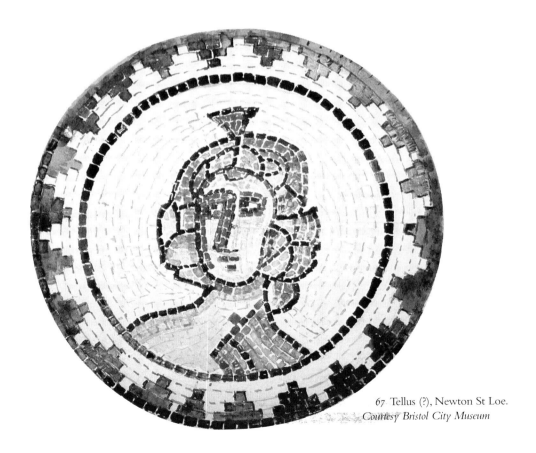

67 Tellus (?), Newton St Loe.
Courtesy Bristol City Museum

VENUS

Of all the female deities depicted in Romano-British mosaics, Venus was by far the most popular. Famous for her beauty and her role as goddess of love, she was also goddess of spring, of gardens, and of fertility. Depictions of Venus often allude to her birth from the sea. Her victory in the beauty contest judged by Paris had far-reaching repercussions, and her status as mother of Aeneas made her the mythical ancestress of the Roman race.

Venus appeared in a number of mosaics with narrative scenes. She was probably intended to be paired with Paris in the Grand Mosaic at Pitney (Somerset) (*6* and *colour plate 7*). She addressed Paris in one of the panels of the mosaic from room B at Frampton (Dorset), and mourned Adonis in another (*10*). She is central, both literally and metaphorically, to the story of Dido and Aeneas depicted in the Low Ham mosaic (Somerset) (*13*), and appears in the guise of a dove with Eros and Anteros in the mosaic from Middleborough, Colchester (Essex) (*colour plate 8*). She represented one of the days of the week at Bramdean (*colour plate 10*), and stands for Spring in the Littlecote Park mosaic, where she is accompanied by a deer (*30* and *colour plate 2*).

One of the most accomplished Romano-British mosaics, and one that ranks among the finest mosaics from anywhere in the Roman empire, is the beautiful bust in the apsidal room at Bignor (Sussex), excavated in 1813 and famous ever since (*58* and *colour plate 18*). Although other identifications have occasionally been proposed, she is usually and plausibly regarded as Venus. Her hair is arranged in curls and crowned by a semicircular diadem and a tiara of small crosses. Tresses of hair cascade onto her shoulders. Some scholars have suggested that she wears a diaphanous dress, but she appears to be naked save for a pendant around her neck. Her head is shown against a pale blue nimbus on which the darker blue at the top indicates an area of repair carried out in 1929.

The bust is seen as if reflected in a mirror hanging from the leafy swags on either side. Birds perch on the swags and peck at fruit, while below each of them is a cornucopia. The birds are often described as pheasants or peacocks. The long necks and sleek, glossy blue of the feathers are more evocative of a peacock than any other bird, although it is possible that they were intended simply as generic game birds and that we need not struggle to identify a particular species. The flourishing acanthus scroll around the apse has tendrils terminating in leaves, lotus flowers and fruit. The imagery is redolent of fruitfulness, an appropriate accompaniment for a goddess of fertility. The mirror, the peacock (if the birds are peacocks) and the lotus all have associations with Venus, giving a coherent theme to the imagery in the apse.

It has been suggested that the Bignor bust is a portrait of the lady of house in the guise of Venus. A few mosaics from other provinces include a series of faces that are so different from one another that they might well have been portraits. Generally speaking, however, portraits do not seem to have been executed in mosaic. There is no reason to suppose that the serene figure at Bignor represented a living person, nor is it likely that the mistress of the villa would have been so presumptuous as to elevate herself to the status of a goddess.

Small Cupids dressed as gladiators enact realistic scenes of combat at Bignor in the delightfully detailed panel, discussed in the next chapter, in front of the apse. More Cupids, this time naked and wielding Bacchic attributes, cavort around the lost centrepiece in the remainder of the room.

Venus seems to have been the subject of the small square panels surrounding Bellerophon and the Chimaera in the mosaic in room B at Frampton (*10*). Two have been discussed above – Venus and Paris, and Venus and Adonis – and one did not survive. The remaining panel, at the lower right, was damaged. It showed a child standing in front of a woman who wore long robes, held a staff, and was seated on a chair or throne. All that was left of the child were its naked feet and lower legs.

Long thought to be another representation of Venus, this panel was reinterpreted as one of the children of Jason and Medea bearing poisoned gifts to Creusa, Jason's new bride. In other such scenes, however, there is more than one child, the children face the viewer to show what they are holding, and Creusa does not hold a staff. It is more likely that the scene showed Venus punishing Cupid. All the surviving elements are consistent with this interpretation, and it is particularly notable that the seated female was leaning forward as Venus does in similar scenes of chastisement.

Venus also appeared in the mosaic in room A at Frampton, where the southern part of the pavement contained a damaged medallion of a female bust wearing a diadem (*68* and *colour plate 6*). A large leaf was placed alongside her and the medallion had an inner border of wave pattern. For many years this part of the Frampton mosaic, unlike the northern part with its five male figures and four winds, received little attention. The bust has since been identified as Venus and the surrounding imagery refers to her marine origins: the wave pattern border alludes to the sea, the leaf is a lotus-leaf fan recalling the breezes that wafted her ashore in a scallop shell, and there is an allusion to the shell itself in the form of the decoration of her diadem as it replicates the 'eyes' on the edge of the shell. The marine theme is reinforced by the sea beasts processing around her.

Another bust of Venus decorates the central medallion of a mosaic from Kingscote (Gloucestershire), now in the Corinium Museum (*69*). She wears a diadem and has long hair cascading onto her shoulders. A mirror lies across her left shoulder and refers to the toilet of Venus, a common composition in which the goddess is shown beautifying herself. The medallion has an outer border of wave pattern and an inner border of ivy or lotus leaves, as if Venus is depicted in a pool. Further marine imagery alluding to her birth from the sea is contained in the threshold panel depicting a sea beast with an elongated, twisted neck and two dolphins.

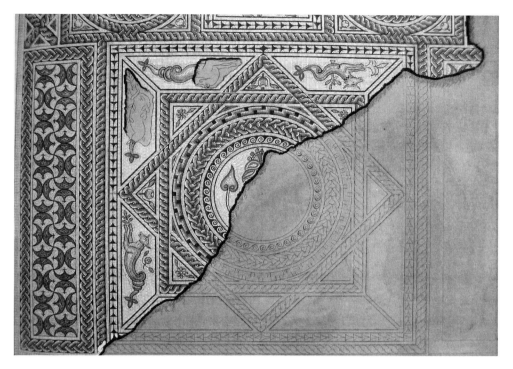

68 Venus from room A mosaic, Frampton (Samuel Lysons)

Venus' marine associations are also evoked, this time in the form of a Triton, in the Rudston mosaic (Yorkshire), now in the Hull and East Riding Museum (*73*). The goddess delicately holds in her right fingers the golden apple, her prize in the beauty contest judged by Paris. A mirror, again alluding to the toilet of Venus, is shown below her left hand. Although she is sometimes described as dropping the mirror, perhaps in alarm at encountering the Triton, it is likely that the attribute has simply been placed in this location to balance the composition. As at Bignor, birds are shown in the Rudston mosaic pecking fruit. Again, they might be generic but the fan-tails suggest that doves, birds sacred to Venus, were probably intended here. The Rudston Venus is wholly classical in concept although, like the wolf and twins from Aldborough (Yorkshire) whose standard of depiction was discussed in chapter 4, the draftsmanship suggests that the proprietor had difficulty finding a craftsman whose skills matched the sophistication of the iconography.

A more accomplished representation of the goddess is shown in the horseshoe-shaped panel from the Hemsworth mosaic (Dorset), now in the British Museum. Venus stands in front of a large scallop shell. She is flanked by a pair of prominent leaves similar to the Frampton example and again alluding to the winds blowing her ashore (*70*). A border of wave pattern and an outer border of dolphins, fishes and crustacea complete the marine theme.

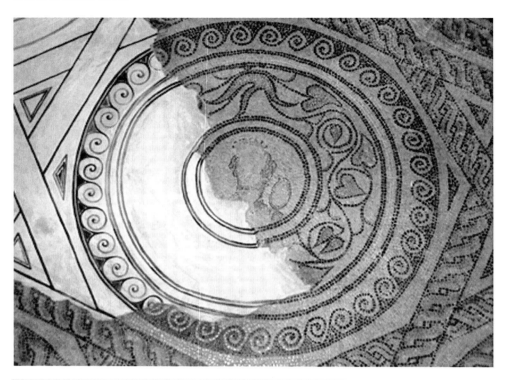

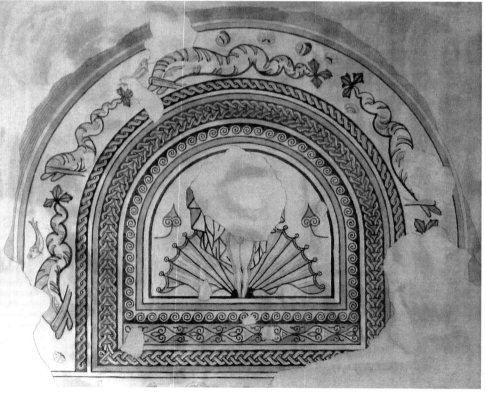

As discussed above, it is likely that Venus, and not Ceres, is the subject of the 'Ceres' mosaic from Winterton (65), and she might be the figure shown in the Thenford mosaic.

Large shells such as those in the mosaics from Bucklersbury in London, now in the Museum of London, and House II.1 at Verulamium (Hertfordshire) (71), now in the Verulamium Museum, were a suitable shape to decorate an apse. This factor alone might have prompted the choice of motif, but the well-established association between Venus and the scallop shell would not have been lost on the contemporary viewer. A prominent shell would call to mind the birth of the goddess, bringing a note of grace and beauty into the room.

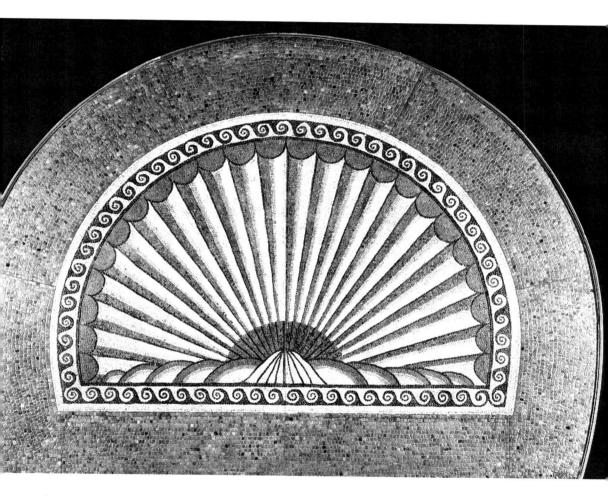

Above: 71 Shell mosaic, Verulamium. *Photograph:* © *St Albans Museums*

Opposite above: 69 Venus mosaic, Kingscote. *Courtesy Corinium Museum, Cirencester*

Opposite below: 70 Venus mosaic, Hemsworth (G. Brumell). *Courtesy Dorset County Museum*

9

THE ARENA AND
THE HUNT

An interest in the activities of the arena is primarily demonstrated by the depictions of scenes from the circus and amphitheatre in mosaics from the villas of Bignor and Brading in the south and Horkstow and Rudston in the north. As these mosaics are all well known, it is easy to overlook the fact that they are relatively few in number.

Hunting scenes were more widespread. It is, however, unclear whether such scenes were intended simply as a reflection of the types of entertainment enjoyed by the villa proprietors, or whether they had an allegorical significance.

THE ARENA

Only traces of one circus have been found from Roman Britain, suggesting that chariot racing was not an important sport in the province. Perhaps, therefore, other considerations prompted the choice of a chariot race for the first panel seen by visitors entering the large mosaic-floored room at Horkstow (Lincolnshire) (*72* and *colour plate 11*). In many other pavements throughout the empire, the chariot race is the only scene in the mosaic, but at Horkstow it was accompanied by two other panels discussed above: one with medallions set within a marine thiasos, and one with Orpheus and animals. The charioteers, the members of the thiasos and the animals all revolve around the centre of their respective panels, suggesting that perhaps the three panels were intended to be read together as parts of a wider, allegorical message.

The circus setting shown in the Horkstow mosaic is pared down to its barest essentials, namely the central spina decorated with two metae at each end. Unlike circus depictions in mosaics elsewhere in the empire, the spina is not adorned with pavilions and statues. The only indication of the shape of the arena lies in the two dark triangles at the top left and top right of the panel. They help the eye to envisage an oval.

The race is shown in full flight. In the bottom row, the charioteer on the left is urging his horses on with his whip, while the middle charioteer is giving his horses their head; one appears to stumble. The reins held by the charioteer on the right are taut and he leans back, reining in his steeds to make the turn around

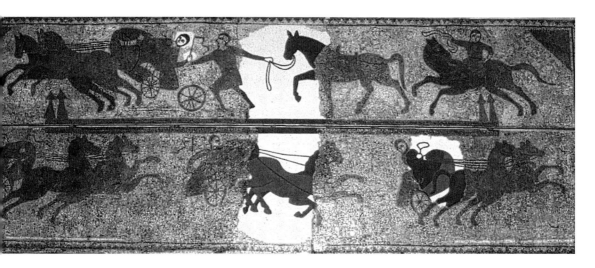

72 Chariot race, Horkstow. *Courtesy Hull and East Riding Museum*

the metae. It is sometimes suggested that he is pulling his horses to a stop having won the race, but there is nothing to suggest victory here. The fact that he is glancing over his shoulder at his competitors indicates that he is still interested in their progress and that the race is continuing.

The scene in the top row is full of incident. The charioteer on the left has lost a wheel from his biga and is about to take a tumble in the conventional scene known as the naufragium or 'shipwreck'. A man rushes forward on foot, leading a horse by the reins. Behind him, a horserider waves a lasso or a white piece of cloth. Some interpret this as the mappa, the cloth dropped by the presiding official to signal the start of the race, but this seems unlikely. The horserider appears to be a participant rather than in charge of the race, and the proceedings are already underway. Riders are shown in some other mosaics wearing scarves around their necks. Perhaps the Horkstow rider has taken off his scarf and this is what he is holding, although its purpose remains obscure.

Despite its simple appearance, the Horkstow chariot race manages to embody many of the details commonly found in racing scenes and also to display a number of unusual features. For instance, the charioteers appear to sit or kneel in their bigae whereas a standing posture was normal. Although there are four charioteers, they apparently do not represent the traditional four factions as there has been no attempt to display the factional colours: the kit worn by the charioteers simply alternates between red and yellow, a colour scheme perhaps determined by the availability of materials for the tesserae. It has been noted that the metae consist of only two cones at each end, rather than the usual three, and the dismounted rider is not found in any other circus mosaics. These discrepancies could indicate a regional peculiarity or might perhaps suggest that the mosaicist was not familiar with the model he was being asked to follow.

Frontal depictions of victorious charioteers were popular throughout the empire. The charioteer in a mosaic from Rudston (Yorkshire), also in Hull and East Riding Museum, is an accomplished example (*35*). He stands facing the viewer in a quadriga, holding the victor's palm in his left hand and a simple wreath representing the winner's crown in his right hand. The colour of his tunic shows that he belongs to the red faction. His clothing is shown in detail, including the bindings to protect his ribs and the 'crash helmet' he wears on his head. The mosaicist has also included the plumes on the heads of the horses and the coloured ribbons binding their manes. The Rudston charioteer is surrounded by busts of the seasons which alternate with panels showing long-tailed birds with fruit. The birds are usually described as peacocks or pheasants, the short necks perhaps indicating the latter.

Reports of charioteer mosaics from Abbotts Ann (Hampshire) and Colerne (Wiltshire), the latter apparently bearing an inscription giving the charioteer's name, show that circus mosaics were not confined to the northern part of the province.

Gladiatorial contests were another popular form of entertainment. Like chariot races, they are sparsely represented among the known Romano-British pavements, but the panel in the Venus mosaic at Bignor (Sussex) is notable for its wealth of realistic detail (*58* and *colour plate 22*). It shows a series of scenes involving Cupid-gladiators and their trainers. These were probably not intended to form a continuous narrative as details of the attire and shields vary from gladiator to gladiator, but they are accurately portrayed and document many of the stages found in a traditional combat. On the left, a secutor, wearing a helmet and carrying a shield and short sword, fights with a retiarius who is armed with a trident and dagger. An iron shackling ring is shown between them. They are supervised by a trainer who wears a white robe and wields a stick. In the next scene, a trainer rushes to aid a retiarius who has been defeated by a secutor. Then comes a secutor standing beside his shield and arming himself with the assistance of another gladiator. To the right, a trainer leads a retiarius forward; unlike the retiarius in the first scene, this one is still holding his net as well as his trident and dagger. In the final scene, a retiarius lies on the ground, blood gushing from the wound in his thigh, while his opponent, a secutor, charges towards him still holding his bloodied sword. The ground is strewn with the retiarius' trident and the secutor's helmet. Another iron shackling ring is shown above the scene.

The Cupid-gladiators of Bignor are executed in tesserae less than 0.5cm square and represent some of the finest workmanship in Roman Britain. The contrast with the standard of execution of the Venus mosaic from Rudston, another example of a mosaic with amphitheatre scenes, is stark, yet the Rudston pavement is one of the most iconographically sophisticated in the country (*73*). We have seen above that it contains allusions to the marine Venus, Venus at her toilet, and Venus as the winner of the beauty contest judged by Paris. It is not entirely clear why the goddess of love should be represented at the centre of a

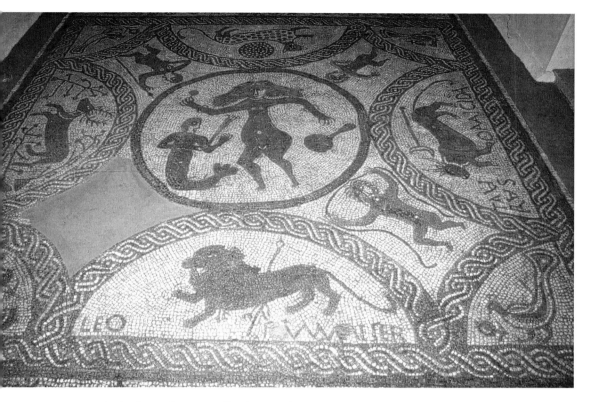

73 Venus mosaic, Rudston. *Courtesy Hull and East Riding Museum*

gory scene of beast-fighting. The suggestion has been made, drawing a parallel with a Tunisian mosaic depicting Venus among amphitheatre images, that she was a patroness of the amphitheatre. It is now thought, however, that the Tunisian mosaic commemorated games held at the festival of Venus, and perhaps a similar consideration lay behind the conception of the Rudston mosaic.

The amphitheatre combats shown in the Rudston pavement are *venationes*. These are not fights between gladiators, but between men and beasts. In the semicircles around Venus, clockwise from the top, are a leopard with a coloured disc above its back, a bull shown with a crescent on a stick, a lion (whose head is not original but is the result of modern restoration) pierced by a spear, and a stag running through a stylised wood. The curious human figures, three of whom survive, are the *bestiarii*. It has been observed that these are not the slick, professional beast-fighters seen on mosaics from other provinces, but appear to be as uncivilised and as wild as the animals they hunt. One (between the bull and lion) holds what looks like a length of rope but is probably intended to represent a net that he is in the process of throwing. Another (between the stag and leopard) has a spear and, judging from the prominence given to the nipples, is female.

Two of the animals are accompanied by inscriptions. The words 'TAVRVS OMICIDA' with the bull have been translated as either 'the man-killing bull' or 'the bull called man-killer'. The inscription with the lion does not survive in its entirety and has exercised the minds of a number of scholars. 'LEO FRAMMEFER' or 'LEO FLAMMEFER', or slight variations of these, are the most commonly suggested readings. A recent alternative of 'LEO FAMMEFER' has been put forward. The first phrase has been translated as 'the spear-bearing lion' or 'the lion called spear-bearer', while the second would read 'the fiery lion', and the recent suggestion would stand for a misspelling of 'fame-bearer' or 'hunger-bearer'. It has been cogently argued that the correct readings mean respectively 'man-killer' and 'fiery', and represent the names by which the beasts were presumably presented to the audiences in the amphitheatre. This seems far more likely than a stark description. It is unlikely that the patron would have wished to immortalise the fact that a lion had been speared, but lions were commonly regarded as 'fiery' (Aelian, *On Animals*, XII, 7) and such a name would have been regarded as an apt one.

The crescent on the stick shown above the bull's back is a unique appearance in a Romano-British mosaic of a symbol commonly seen in amphitheatre mosaics in North Africa. It was used as the emblem of the Telegenii, a team of animal fighters. More fundamentally, it represents an ox-goad which the Telegenii adopted as their emblem. It is more likely that a simple goad was intended at Rudston rather than a direct link with a North African troupe. The nature of the chequered disc shown above the leopard's back is uncertain, but it was perhaps another device used for exciting otherwise sluggish animals.

The appearance of Mercury in the narrow rectangular panel at the top of the mosaic (*60*), discussed in chapter 7, recalls the amphitheatre attendants who dressed in the guise of this deity to remove the dead from the arena: one of Mercury's functions was to conduct souls to the underworld. The panel at the bottom of the mosaic appears to have been similar but is now vestigial.

Both types of combat, gladiatorial as well as venationes, are depicted in a mosaic at Brading (Isle of Wight) (*55*). In the panel below the central figure of Bacchus, a retiarius holding a dagger and trident attacks a secutor of whom only the helmeted head survives. Nothing is known of the opposite panel but it is likely that it would have complemented the gladiatorial scene.

Interpretation of the remaining side panels has proved controversial. One shows a pedimented building flanked by a cock-headed figure and a pair of griffins. The other shows a canine running in front of a tree towards a centrally placed domed building. The cock-headed figure was, for many years, identified as Abraxas although it lacks his characteristic snake-legs. Subsequent interpretations have suggested that this figure is guarding a ladder leading up to a house beset by griffins, or is part of a Nilotic scene. An alternative view draws comparisons between the Brading figure and fabulous creatures known from literature and from mosaics elsewhere to suggest that it is a misreading of a kynokephalos, a dog-headed creature, and that this mythical animal is shown in a hunting scene.

I have argued elsewhere that, as the pedimented building matches temples set within arenas in mosaics from other provinces, even down to the barely discernible wreath on the pediment itself, the scene appears to be a venatio in the arena rather than a hunt in the wild. The cock-headed figure is likely to be a punning reference to a venator named Gallus, as this popular name means 'cock' in Latin. The rows of red and yellow tesserae parallel to the griffins' wings represent millet stalks. They were used, in the same way as the Rudston crescent on stick, by an amphitheatre faction and are found in North African mosaics of venationes. Millet was regarded as the most prolific kind of corn (Pliny, *Natural History* XVIII, X, 55) and was therefore an appropriate choice for an emblem.

The domed building shown in the panel on the opposite side of the mosaic has been regarded as a native hut or bulbous hill of a type often found in hunt mosaics. There are, however, parallels for this form of construction appearing in scenes set in the arena. Pavilions of this shape decorate the spina of a circus in a number of mosaics from other provinces. It seems likely, therefore, that this panel also depicted a hunt in the arena with a fox-like dog whose quarry was originally depicted in the lost half of the panel. The wooded setting suggests that it was probably a deer. Even where there is no imagery specifically relating to the amphitheatre itself, the inclusion of non-native beasts in the hunting scenes shown in some mosaics suggests that the scenes should be regarded as taking place in the arena.

The well-known second-century mosaic from House XXI.2 at Verulamium (Hertfordshire), now in the Verulamium Museum, shows a lion with the gory head of a stag in its jaws (*74*). A panel from Withington (Gloucestershire), since lost, apparently showed a figure on horseback hunting a lion or lioness (*27*). A fragment from Dewlish (Dorset) in private hands contains a realistic depiction of a leopard or cheetah pouncing on the back of a gazelle. Another panel has traces of a human hunter with a spear. Each of the panels flanking Bacchus in the mosaic from room B at Frampton (Dorset) included a human hunter, confronting a leopard in one case and pursuing a stag in the other (*18*). The black and white creature bounding in front of the stag was probably a hunting dog similar to those shown in the Horkstow and Malton mosaics, although it is unusual that it is not positioned as if in pursuit of the stag.

THE HUNT

While hunts in the arena refer to a spectator sport, other hunt mosaics could remind the contemporary viewer of hunts in which he had participated in the wild. They might also have had a symbolic significance.

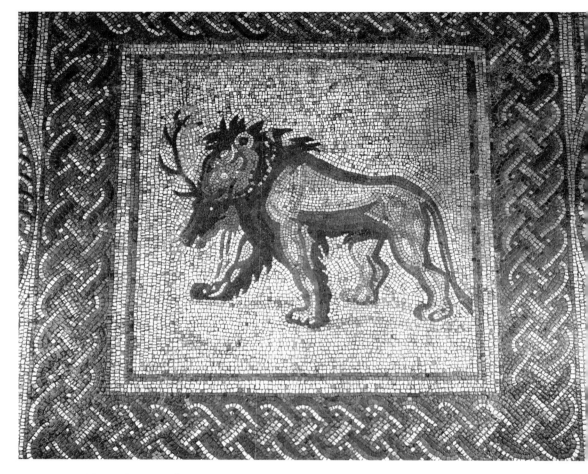

74 Lion and stag, Verulamium. *Photograph: © St Albans Museums*

Hounds hunting deer seem to have been particularly popular among the craftsmen of mosaics attributed to the Durnovarian school. Five such hunting panels appear in the Hinton St Mary mosaic (Dorset) (*14*), and the mosaic from room A at Frampton had at least one hunting panel (*colour plate 6*). In the lost mosaic of East Coker (Somerset) a hound hunted a stag while another pursued a hare. A fragment from Cherhill (Wiltshire), now in Devizes Museum, shows a hunting dog evidently from a similar type of scene. In each case, a tree or trees serves to indicate that the hunt is taking place in a wood.

The mosaics discussed above all show the chase, but a scene in which the quarry has been cornered appears in the centre of the second- or third-century Hunting dogs mosaic from Cirencester (Gloucestershire) (*42*). The possibility that the quarry here might have been Actaeon turned into a stag by the goddess Diana, as in the Seasons mosaic from the same town, has been mentioned. Whether a mythological scene or not, it evocatively captures the baying hounds.

A fragment from a second mosaic found at East Coker in or around 1820, now in the Somerset County Museum, Taunton, depicts the return from the hunt (75). Two men are shown almost life-size, wearing typical fourth-century tunics decorated with orbiculi. They carry a deer slung from a pole. A dog sits expectantly beneath the dead animal. The poor appearance of this mosaic is explained by the fact that it disintegrated on lifting and was subsequently reconstituted. A painting made before lifting shows, however, that the modern appearance is not far removed from the original.

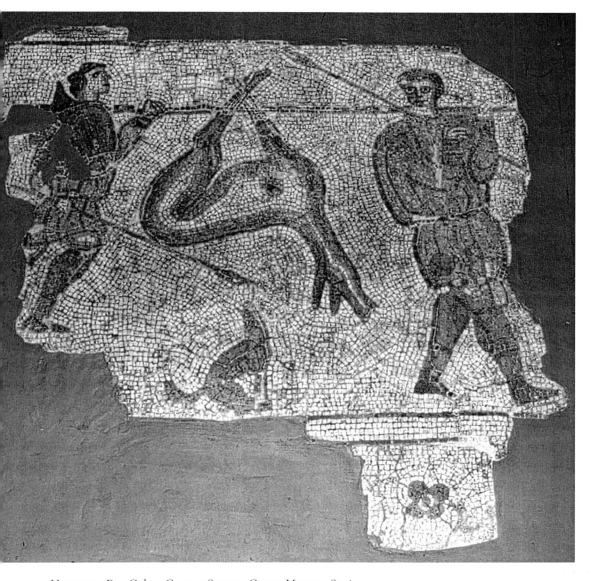

75 Huntsmen, East Coker. *Courtesy Somerset County Museums Service*

10

THE MESSAGES IN
THE MOSAICS

From a swift appraisal of the mosaics discussed in this book, we could conclude that mythology was one of the most fertile sources of inspiration. Daily concerns such as the turning of the seasons and the wish to encourage good luck or to avert bad fortune were particularly popular choices. As a number of mosaics depict Orpheus whereas few are known of the Muses, perhaps esoteric aspects of the Orphic cult attracted patrons, or perhaps they simply liked animals. Gods were chosen more often, and depicted in a greater variety of situations, than goddesses. There was less enthusiasm for scenes from the arena and the hunt than in many other provinces.

Well-known love stories and the adventures of heroes seem to have been appreciated even more in Roman Britain than in many provinces nearer to the centre of the empire. Could this be because patrons living on the fringes of the civilised world felt it was important to display their knowledge of classical culture to reinforce their sense of belonging? Another area where mythological subjects were depicted in greater than average numbers is the eastern Mediterranean, especially Antioch, which mirrored Britain in its geographical place on the edge of the empire.

Although many of the mosaics are of indifferent quality, Britain has one of the richest and most varied collections of figured mosaics from the Roman world. Stories were depicted in mosaics throughout the Roman empire, but the British examples are notable in three respects.

First, over a third of the figured mosaics show mythological characters, either alone or in narrative scenes, to which can be added the many mosaics depicting the seasons. This is a high proportion. The visitor to museums in other countries might be bowled over by the sheer number of mosaics on display – the Bardo in Tunis is an outstanding example of a museum with a breathtaking quantity – but will be hard pressed to find more than a handful of mythological scenes. What was it that caused so many Romano-British patrons to decorate their homes in this way?

Secondly, a number of the mosaics included not just one character or scene but several: the Seasons mosaic at Brading (*16*), the Seasons mosaic from Dyer Street in Cirencester (*34*), the mosaics from rooms A and B at Frampton (*colour plate 6* and *18*), the complex Horkstow mosaic (*colour plate 11*), the panels from the hexagonal mosaic in room W at Keynsham (*4*, *11* and *66*), the colourful expanses of the Lullingstone floor (*colour plate 3*), and the Grand Mosaic of Pitney (*colour plate 7*) are just some examples of mosaics fascinating enough when considered individually, but constituting an exceptional collection for one relatively small province. Can we conclude that there was a particularly high level of classical education on the part of the patrons, and perhaps even an element of competition between them?

Thirdly, some of the scenes are ones that were rarely depicted in mosaics elsewhere. Ceres giving corn to Triptolemus in the Seasons mosaic at Brading (*9* and *16*) is a case in point. Does this suggest that the patrons were especially involved in the creation of the schemes, rather than choosing from designs in mosaicists' pattern books?

Whatever the answers to these questions, it seems clear that the mosaic resources of Roman Britain have great potential for further study. In particular, where more than one figure or scene is shown in a given pavement, it provides us with scope for assessing whether the images were intended to convey an overall message or, alternatively, whether they should be regarded simply as a collection of isolated pictures displaying the owner's cultural standing along with his artistic enthusiasms.

When we turn to look at the similarities in the subject matter between different mosaics, a number of patterns emerge. One of the most striking is the exceptional popularity of Bacchus and Venus. Since many of the surviving mosaics decorated a triclinium where themes of conviviality and mild eroticism would have been appropriate, it is perhaps not unexpected to find the realms of wine and love evoked in this way. The two deities were shown together in different parts of the mosaic in room A at Frampton (*colour plate 6*). Its layout was suitable for a dining room as there was room to place couches around the bust of Venus without obscuring any of the figures. Diners in this position would have been able to view the goddess of love and the god of wine from this position.

The Bacchic cantharus can be spotted in many mosaics, not just those depicting the god. In some cases, the vessel is small and might have been included just to fill a space. In other cases, however, it is so large that it must have had particular significance. The examples in the Bacchus mosaics of Leadenhall Street and Old Broad Street in London (*colour plates 20* and *21*), for instance, are matched by the prominence of those with the Cupid on a dolphin at Fishbourne (*45*) and Orpheus at Littlecote Park and Whatley (*colour plate 2* and *31*), to name just a few, while in the Brantingham mosaic, large and somewhat ungainly canthari decorate the spaces between the central bust and the water nymphs.

In these latter pavements, where Bacchus himself is not shown but where the canthari are exceptionally large, it is notable that another important theme of the mosaics is water. The most emphatic depiction of a cantharus, shown set apart in the apse of the room B mosaic at Frampton, was placed opposite the bust of Neptune in a mosaic whose border was awash with pairs of dolphins (*18*).

For the Romans, enjoyment of wine was a serious business. One scholar has counted 25 different names for drinking cups. They mixed their wine with water and frowned upon the drunken Gauls who imbibed wine neat and whom they educated into better ways (Ammianus Marcellinus XV, 12, 4). Some of the vessels shown in mosaics and described as 'canthari' for convenience might in fact have been craters, the much larger mixing vessels. Perhaps the sea beasts in the Fishbourne mosaic and the nymphs of the Brantingham pavement were incorporated to provide a visual link between water and wine (*45* and *21*). This link continues in the Orpheus pavements, where the stylised pool, shells and sea panthers at Littlecote Park, and the dolphin in the apse and marine creatures around the bust of Tyche at Whatley, all refer to water (*colour plate 2* and *31*).

The combination of dolphins and canthari was used in many mosaics. The Bradford on Avon and Downton pavements are two of the most attractive (*colour plates 1* and *17*). Given the legend that Bacchus turned the Tyrrhenian pirates into dolphins, whereupon they repented of their wrongdoing and became friendly to man, the association is as unsurprising as it is visually appealing. But it is also noticeable that some of the canthari are depicted spurting water. The dolphins mosaic from Verulamium is a case in point (*50*), while liquid seems to bubble up within two of the canthari in the Neptune mosaic from the same town (*64*). Shapes recorded as emerging from the canthari in the Whatley apse (*31*) could be regarded as foliage or might represent fountains.

Were the images of the dolphin and the cantharus used because they were both lucky symbols (and perhaps their power increased in combination), or were they alluding to the normal practice of mixing water with wine, a practice that may well have been carried out in many of the rooms with the mosaics? Although the link between water and wine is capable of being analysed in a practical way, the association of Orpheus with water is less easy to explain in such terms. In addition to the examples mentioned above, it is notable, for instance, that the Horkstow mosaic included a marine thiasos (*colour plate 11*), that Neptune and sea beasts were shown in the adjoining panel at Withington (*27*), and that naiads are included in the Great Pavement at Woodchester, a mosaic whose centrepiece apparently once had a depiction of fish (*25*).

Where marine mosaics are found in baths, the location alone provides ample explanation for the choice of theme. The scatter of marine creatures in the mosaic in the baths at Great Witcombe (*43*) is the most extensive catalogue of sea creatures still visible, despite its damaged and gloomy appearance today. Its mainly two-tone appearance in shades of blue/black and white enhances the marine feel. A particularly interesting feature is the mosaic 'mat' on one side, marking the threshold of the original doorway which coincides with the modern entrance to the room. The motif of a stylised gateway recalls the similar gateway in the border of the Seasons mosaic at Brading, although there it was located at the innermost end of the room (*16*). Both seem to have been special positions.

As well as water, there was a particular interest in the marking of time, especially the seasons, perhaps because the repetitive round was reassuring. 'If Winter comes, can Spring be far behind' is not only the sentiment expressed by Shelley in *Ode to the West Wind* but is one that encapsulates the promise of hope embodied in the unvarying way in which the seasons succeed one another. By analogy with the cycle of life, they hint at a renewal to come. The seasons mosaics were not necessarily directly concerned with salvation – they were, after all, only floors – but they strike a comforting note in a world fraught with anxiety. They indicate that the universe is ordered and predictable, and this gives confidence that man's role in it is not a mere caprice. The seasons affect life on a daily basis, too, as they dictate when to plant crops and when to reap the produce. It is no surprise that they and similar themes were overwhelmingly popular throughout the Roman world, particularly in those areas such as North Africa and Britain that were renowned for supplying grain to other parts of the empire.

So far, we have seen that the imagery of some mosaics bore only a superficial significance, while the Roman viewer of others might have teased out a more complex message. Where the mosaics show deities and characters from myth, their backgrounds and relationships to one another would have been well known to the contemporary audience, thus adding an extra layer of meaning invisible to the eye.

For instance, Cadmus, who was shown slaying the serpent of Mars in mosaics at Brading, Frampton and Pitney (*16, 5* and *15*), enjoyed a shared significance with Aeneas, who appeared at Frampton grasping the golden bough as his passport to the underworld and at Low Ham dallying with Dido (*5* and *13*). Both were foreigners who travelled abroad to found a city: Thebes in the case of Cadmus, and Rome in the case of Aeneas.

Venus, the mother of Aeneas, was regarded as the legendary ancestress of the Roman race. Mars had a similar role as, in most legends, he was regarded as the father of Romulus and Remus. He and Venus were the parents of Harmonia, who became Cadmus' wife.

Aeneas was a prime example of a hero who, after the distractions of Dido, went on to fulfil his destiny. In a similar vein, Achilles felt himself unable to resist casting off his woman's disguise and joining the Trojan war.

Aeneas was one of a select number of characters who were permitted to visit the underworld and to return. Others who did so included Orpheus and Hercules. They had managed to evade the clutches of death and were therefore figures of hope and reincarnation. Salvation was also at the heart of the myths of Ganymede and Ariadne, mortals who were respectively carried away by Jupiter and Bacchus.

General links of this nature and family connections can be discerned between the characters in mosaics with multiple figure scenes. Were they deliberate? To explore such territory is to enter uncertain realms. The whole topic of whether a programmatic reading can be applied to Roman art is fraught with controversy.

It takes us away from a strict evaluation of the evidence itself, requiring the evidence to be viewed as part of a wider picture. Inevitably, personal preferences and prejudices come into play. Some scholars eschew any speculation, while others espouse a detailed reading with enthusiasm. The problem becomes even more acute when a mosaic is fragmentary or where characters lack distinctive attributes, giving rise to understandable concerns as to how reliable an identification of them can ever be.

While it is important not to massage the evidence to fit a given interpretation, if several component parts naturally fall within a certain theme, it is perhaps permissible to see whether the remaining images are consistent with it. If so, is this merely coincidence, or is it the result of deliberate contrivance on the part of the designer? Often caution suggests coincidence. If the number of coincidences starts to mount up, however, there comes a point when it looks a less than satisfactory interpretation, and we can perhaps venture to suggest an element of deliberation on the part of the designer.

A case in point is the Seasons mosaic at Brading (*9* and *16*). Two of the couples in the eastern part are complete (the lower part of figure *16*). Ceres and Triptolemus, with their attributes of corn and plough, are so distinctive that their identity has never been in doubt. The figures now identified as Attis with a water nymph are not wholly unambiguous and have only been established by comparison with representations of Attis elsewhere. The third scene is slightly damaged but the missing parts are not crucial and the identification of Lycurgus attacking Ambrosia is secure. The fourth panel is incomplete and no distinctive attribute survives to show us the identity of this couple. One approach is that adopted in chapter 2, namely to evaluate the various figures who might be represented by a naked male chasing a female, and to see whether this narrows the number of possibilities. In the case of the Brading couple, arguably it does, and suggested identifications of Apollo and Daphne seem reasonable. We are still left, however, with an identity based on likelihood rather than certainty.

When we look at the eastern part of the Seasons mosaic as a whole, leaving the tentative Apollo and Daphne to one side for the moment, we see that the other three scenes refer to major cults – those of Ceres, Cybele and Bacchus – and that those cults have particular associations with specific seasons: spring, winter and autumn. One view is to regard these factors as purely coincidental. There were, after all, many deities from which the designer or the mosaicist could make his or her choice, and festivals to the gods often took place at more than one season. Are the apparent links illusory?

When we add the fourth couple into the equation, does it reinforce or weaken the theory? Apollo is another deity, and his cult was particularly associated with summer. If the fourth couple are indeed Apollo and Daphne, and if the couples were all intended to allude to a season, the theory works. It also receives support from the other images in this part of the mosaic. The head of Medusa appears in the centre, and we know that Medusa appears in the centre of Seasons mosaics at Bignor (*33*) and York, so she was evidently regarded as a suitable companion. The desire to invoke her power to avert evil throughout the year is readily understandable. Winds were also appropriate with seasons, as attested in classical literature and shown in the Grand Mosaic at Pitney (*colour plate 7*). Their appearance at Brading is complementary to a seasonal theme.

An analysis of the Brading mosaic reveals other links, perhaps coincidences or perhaps the result of careful design. One pair of panels located opposite each another refers to grain (Ceres and Triptolemus) and grapes (Lycurgus and Ambrosia); staple commodities in the Roman diet. If the interpretation of Attis and Apollo is applied to the other pair of panels, they both show water nymphs. As water is vital for growth, the presence of water nymphs – images with allusions to water – is unsurprising.

In addition, the stories of both couples involved trees, although the trees are not shown in the mosaic. According to Ovid, Attis was turned into a pine tree after he castrated himself (*Metamorphoses* X, 103-105), while Daphne was famously turned into the laurel.

We might also note that there are similarities between adjoining pairs. In two of the couples, the male (Lycurgus and Apollo) is giving unwanted attention to the female, who is metamorphosed into a vine (Ambrosia) and a tree (Daphne) respectively. In the other two couples, the male is passive and receives help from the female: Ceres gives corn to Triptolemus, and the water nymph represents the reeds that provided the safe haven for Attis when he was abandoned after his birth.

It is more difficult to subject the four scenes in the western part of the Brading mosaic (the upper part of figure *16*) to the same sort of analysis given that one is almost entirely missing and two others are fragmentary. We can note, however, that Perseus and Cadmus were both monster-slayers and that each of these scenes shows a pool.

It has long been noted that the Seasons mosaic at Brading alludes to the sea (in the form of the marine panel at its eastern end), the earth (in the form of the 'seasonal' couples), and the sky (in the form of the astronomer and, arguably, the Tropai and the allusions to the constellations).

Similar allusions to water, earth and sky can perhaps be discerned in another Seasons mosaic, this time the much earlier example from Dyer Street, Cirencester (*34*). Fruits of the earth were recalled by Bacchus who was present in one panel. Hunting is represented by Actaeon, and hunting itself recalls another product of the earth, namely the living creatures that were 'harvested' in the hunt. If the central figure was the winged horse Pegasus, as seems likely, we have a creature of the air who also possessed spring-making talents. Pegasus has displaced Medusa who appears here in a minor compartment, but Pegasus was closely connected with Medusa as he was her offspring. The link between Medusa and the seasons seen in mosaics elsewhere is still evident.

There are other connections between the images of this mosaic. Silenus appears opposite the panel with the now lost Bacchus and was a member of his entourage.

It seems likely from the evidence of other mosaics that Diana was shown opposite Actaeon, but as the compartment was entirely lost we cannot know. If Diana was paired with Actaeon, the mosaic would contrast a god and one of his supporters with a goddess and a figure who had infamously offended her.

The difficulty with this analysis is that the putative Diana is entirely missing and the identification of Pegasus rests solely on the existence of part of the forelegs. Given the uncertainties, some scholars would shun such a discussion altogether, but to do so would remove one of the great pleasures of enjoying the mosaics and trying to unravel their meaning.

Similar speculations can be extended to the Grand Mosaic at Pitney, where Cupids in the guise of seasons decorated the mosaic in the inner part of the triclinium, while Bacchus was the central figure in the mosaic in the outer part (*colour plate 7*). Like the Brading pavement, the Pitney example featured winds and four couples. Two figures appear to have been misplaced (Mercury and Paris). If their positions are reversed, the pairings would be Neptune and Amymone, Paris and Venus, Mercury and Syrinx, and Phaedra and Hippolytus.

Venus and Phaedra, shown opposite one another in the mosaic, represent two opposing views of love. Paris prized it above earthly power and riches, and was rewarded by Venus with Helen's hand. Hippolytus shunned love altogether, and his abstinence prompted the scorned Venus to inflame Phaedra with her illicit passion. It is notable that although one protagonist avidly espoused love while the other actively avoided it, the stories of both ended unhappily: in Paris' death in the Trojan war set in train by the abduction of Helen, and in Hippolytus' death at his father's instigation following Phaedra's false accusation. In compositional terms, Paris and Phaedra are both seated and hold their left hands to their heads in a gesture that indicates they are pondering a difficult problem, while the assurance of Venus is contrasted with the diffidence of Hippolytus. The message seems to be about the perils and pains of love and to demonstrate that they cannot be avoided.

On the other hand, the remaining couples emphasise the benefits brought by the gods to mankind. Neptune's love affair with Amymone concerned the ending of a drought and the provision of water. The gift bestowed by Mercury was in the form of music. Syrinx, the personification of the instrument he invented, was shown opposite Amymone and was similar to her in composition. The rocks on which she rests her right hand recall the shape of Amymone's urn. Similarly, the two gods are each shown striding eagerly forwards.

There are subtle links between characters in the adjacent couples. Neptune sent the sea monster that frightened Hippolytus' horses and led to his death, while Mercury played a part in the judgement of Paris to whom he led the three goddesses. Did the designer of the Pitney mosaic have these links in mind? If we are able to pick out thematic connections, it is even more likely that the Roman viewer of a floor would have done so, but how do we tell whether this type of scheme was intended? And can we even be certain that we have identified the characters correctly? Such speculations are stimulating but lack proof. They appeal to the instinct rather than the intellect — but there needs to be room for both faculties to be used if we are to maximise our understanding of the material.

Neptune, Bacchus, Venus and winds also appeared together in the mosaic in room A at Frampton (*colour plate 6*). Bacchus and Venus were respectively shown in the centre of the two parts of this room. Aligned vertically with them were Cadmus and Aeneas. There are family connections linking all four figures: Cadmus was the grandfather of Bacchus, while Venus was the mother of Aeneas and also of Harmonia, Cadmus' wife. Bacchus and Venus were both important fertility deities. Cadmus and Aeneas both roamed the world before founding a city.

Bacchus was flanked by figures whose identity has not been unequivocally determined. If the arguments supported and advanced in this book are accepted, they were Neptune, shown in the act of creating a spring, and Jupiter, shown as the shower of gold with which he consummated his relationship with Danaë. The emphasis here is on springs and showers, both essential for fertility. The four winds in the corner panels reinforce the theme. They recall the inscription in the mosaic in room B at the same site, which referred to Neptune's domain 'stirred by the winds'. The adjacent part of the mosaic showed Venus, the fertility goddess par excellence, also in a watery setting.

In compositional terms, the figures surrounding Bacchus comprise two heroes (Cadmus and Aeneas), and arguably two gods (Neptune and Jupiter), arranged in pairs on opposite sides of the mosaic. Connections between pairs of adjoining panels are also readily apparent. Cadmus and Neptune were shown in the act of spearing, while the scenes with Aeneas and Jupiter both involved gold.

Bacchus and Venus were also shown in separate parts of the mosaic in room B at Frampton: Bacchus as the main subject of the anteroom and Venus as the subject of arguably at least three (and probably all four) of the small panels in the main part of the room (*18*). Like the mosaic in room A, the mosaic in room B displayed family connections. The head of Neptune in the border in front of the apse aligned with Bellerophon mounted on Pegasus: both Pegasus and Bellerophon were offspring of Neptune. Cupid, the figure in the border of another side of the room, was the son of Venus.

The three surviving panels with Venus show her addressing Paris in the critical scene in which she offered him the hand of Helen if he judged her the winner in the famous beauty contest, thereby provoking the Trojan war; mourning her dead lover, Adonis; and reprimanding Cupid. They allude, as did the scenes in the Pitney mosaic discussed above, to the perils and pains of love, and form a contrast with Bellerophon's successful domination of the Chimaera. It is easier to slay monsters than to succeed in love. Neptune's watery realm encompasses the whole of this part of the mosaic.

The subjects of the striking and colourful mosaic at Lullingstone, although from the same room, appear at first sight to be disconnected (*colour plate 3*). In the apse, Jupiter is shown in the guise of a bull speeding across the sea with Europa on his back. In the main part of the room, the seasons are placed around the central panel which depicts Bellerophon, mounted on Pegasus, slaying the Chimaera. Unlike the other depictions of Bellerophon in Romano-British mosaics, the Lullingstone scene is given a marine setting. An explanation has been advanced that the water is an allusion to Pegasus' spring-making properties, but perhaps the reason is much more obvious: the designer might have wished to show Bellerophon in a setting that matched that of the Jupiter panel.

The contrast between the two riders with their mounts could not be more dramatic: in one case, an amorous abduction; in the other, a hero slaying a monster. But Jupiter was renowned for bringing fertilising rain and for controlling the changes of the seasons, while the myth of Bellerophon also had seasonal connotations. Perhaps the scenes are not so different after all, and both allude to material prosperity and the seasons.

Perhaps the most difficult to understand of all the Romano-British mosaics with multiple figure scenes is the enigmatic pavement from Horkstow (*colour plate 11*). The Roman visitor would first have encountered the chariot race (*72*). Set firmly on the earth, the figures progress in an anticlockwise fashion. The next section embodies a reference to water in the form of the marine thiasos in which the medallions are placed (*12*). The radial design suggests turning, although the marine creatures swim in both directions. In the innermost part of the room, the final section contains another radial panel, again suggesting movement (*29*). The larger quadrupeds proceed in an anti clockwise direction, while the smaller ones bound the opposite way. The attractive suggestion has been made that the awning border near the centre of this section replicates a dome, as if we are looking upwards to the figure of Orpheus in the sky.

Whatever the exact identity of the figures in the mysterious medallions – if indeed they were ever intended to depict specific rather than generic characters – the Horkstow mosaic embraces the realms of earth, sea and sky. The sense of movement is often interpreted as an allegory for the course of life and the turning seasons of the year. Despite its singular imagery, the underlying concerns of the mosaic are similar to those of other, less recondite, floors.

Unlike the difficult and ambiguous figures in the Horkstow medallions, those in the Keynsham mosaic are now refreshingly clear: Achilles on Scyros, Europa and the bull, and Minerva looking at her reflection as she plays the flutes (*4, 11* and *66*). We do not know the other subjects because only this part of the mosaic was accessible: the rest lies under a road.

On the face of it, the three excavated scenes seem unconnected. The characters do not play any part in each other's stories, nor are they related to one another. But there is an underlying theme that links them together. They all feature transformations. These are not the serious metamorphoses of the types famously related by Ovid, where the changes undergone by the hapless characters were permanent and were often instigated at the whim of a deity.

Instead, the characters shown in the Keynsham mosaic have all effected the changes themselves: Achilles into the appearance of a girl, Jupiter into a bull, and Minerva into an undignified figure with inflated cheeks. In each case, the change is reversible through the actions of the person concerned.

The Keynsham panels can be read at one level as pleasing depictions of popular myths. At a slighter deeper level, a theme of light-hearted, impermanent changes can be discerned. Going a stage further, what is reassuring about these changes is that they are under the control of character in question. Change – of the weather, of the seasons, and of human life – and man's ability to control or influence such change, were central themes to many of the Romano-British mosaics. It is fascinating to see the different ways in which the designers reflected this universal concern.

Within the scope of this chapter and of this book, it has only been possible to highlight some of the most impressive mosaics and to touch upon what they might have meant to those who looked at them before us. Although Roman viewers will have been steeped in Roman culture and ways of thought to a degree that we cannot possibly hope to achieve, they will themselves have had different standards of education, status and understanding. The craftsman who created the mosaic might simply have followed instructions from the designer. The servant in a villa might only have appreciated the images as attractive pictures – if he or she had time to notice the floors at all. The patron, proud of his commission, might have been faced with less educated guests whose inability to read all the allusions in a scheme might have frustrated him – or caused him pleasure when he reflected on his ability to recognise a more involved reading.

To all of us, Romans and modern museum-goers alike, the mosaics have the capacity to tantalise, intrigue and baffle, as much as they please the eye. We can read into them as much or as little as we choose. In trying to interpret them, perhaps the most reliable route is to try to see what they meant to those who designed them. Images in a mosaic are a form of communication like any other, and it is reasonable to assume that the designer was attempting to communicate his or her ideas, whether simple and straightforward or complex and crammed with allusions. If we find the messages of some mosaics unclear or ambiguous, it is because we have yet to find the key, not that the key is non-existent.

It is fashionable to shy away from speculation, and understandable that we should be wary of uncertain identifications and the dangers of making too much of limited evidence. But we need to be open to the possibilities if we are to make progress, and to be prepared to debate alternatives, if the study of mosaics is to progress and if we are to maximise the help provided by the clues embedded in them. There is a great deal to enjoy, and even more to learn.

The figured mosaics from Roman Britain already tell us much about the life and thought of that time. In their original contexts, the images entertained and protected those who could appreciate them. It is a source of pleasure as well as a challenge to allow them to continue to do so now.

GLOSSARY

aegis	Breastplate worn by the goddess Minerva with the Gorgon's head in the centre.
alpha and omega	The first and last letters of the Greek alphabet.
atrium	The central room in a Roman house, usually lit by an opening in the roof.
bestiarius, bestiarii	Wild-beast fighter(s).
bidens	A hoe with two teeth.
biga, bigae	Chariot(s) drawn by two horses.
caduceus	Wand or herald's staff; an attribute of Mercury.
cantharus	Two-handled drinking cup, especially the vessel held by Bacchus; the handles are usually attached to the top and base of the cup.
chi-rho	The first two letters of the name of Christ in Greek, used as a monogram.
cithara	Stringed musical instrument similar to but larger than the lyre, usually played on public occasions (Greek: kithara).
cornucopia	The horn of plenty.
crater	Vessel used for mixing wine with water; like the cantharus, it had two handles but these were usually attached to the base.
diptych	A pair of wax writing tablets.
Gorgon	Female monster with hair of snakes, whose look would turn the viewer to stone; used as a powerful amulet. Of the three Gorgons, the most famous is Medusa.
guilloche	Ubiquitous border found in Roman mosaics in the form of intertwining strands like a plait; the number of strands can vary but is commonly two or three.
harpe	A type of curved sword, used by Perseus to cut off the head of Medusa.
kalathos	A tall, basket-shaped container (Latin: Calathus).
ligature	Two letters combined into one.

lunette	On mosaics, a semicircular panel.
lyre	Stringed musical instrument similar to but smaller than the cithara; in daily life, it was more commonly played than the cithara.
maenad	Female member of the Bacchic thiasos.
mappa	Cloth dropped by the presiding official at the circus to signal the start of the race.
meander	Labyrinth-like motif, named after the river in Asia Minor famous for its twists and turns.
metae	The turning posts in the Roman circus.
modius	A dry measure of the Romans and the vessel used for measuring this quantity.
mural crown	The type of headdress worn by a Tyche; it is decorated with crenellations.
naiad	A nymph of a river or spring.
naufragium	Literally 'shipwreck'; used to refer to a crash scene in a circus race.
Nereid	A sea-nymph, one of the daughters of Nereus.
nimbus	A halo of light around the head of a divinity.
officina, officinae	Workshop(s).
orans, orantes	Christian figure(s) praying with upraised arms.
orbiculus, orbiculi	Small circle(s); specifically a textile ornament.
panther	A generic word used to describe a large feline other than a lion or tiger, especially one associated with Bacchus. Often used synonymously with leopard. The panther is not a separate species as is frequently but mistakenly assumed.
patera, paterae	Shallow, saucer-shaped dish(es) used in libations.
pedum	A shepherd's crook.
pelta	A crescent-shaped motif derived from a type of shield of this name used by the Amazons.
Phrygian cap	A type of conical cap with its top turned forward. Worn by inhabitants of Phrygia in Asia Minor, and in Graeco-Roman art especially associated with Aeneas, Attis, Ganymede, Orpheus and Paris.
quadriga, quadrigae	Chariot(s) drawn by four horses.
retiarius	A type of gladiator armed with a net, trident and dagger; usually fought a secutor.
saltire	A design in the form of a St Andrew's cross.
sarculum	A wedge-shaped hoe.
satyr	Male member of the Bacchic thiasos.
secutor	A type of gladiator armed with helmet, sword and shield; usually fought a retiarius.
Sibyl	One of a number of women possessed with a spirit of divination, who gave prophetic utterances; the Cumaean Sibyl was one of the most famous.
situla	A bucket-shaped vessel.
spandrel	The roughly triangular-shaped area formed between a circle and its enclosing square.

spina	The barrier running lengthways down the centre of a Roman circus.
stephane	A type of headdress; especially worn by Diana.
stibadium	A semicircular dining couch.
syrinx	Pipe made from reeds of different lengths, commonly used by herdsmen and shepherds; 'Pan-pipes'.
thiasos	The entourage of a deity, usually used in relation to Bacchus or Neptune.
thyrsolonchus	A spear disguised as a Bacchic thyrsus.
thyrsus	A staff, often wreathed with ivy and vine leaves and topped with a pine-cone, carried by Bacchus and his attendants.
triclinium	A Roman dining room, so named from its arrangement of three couches.
Tyche	The Greek Fortuna; especially applied to the personification of a town.
venatio, venationes	A wild-beast hunt in the arena.
xenia	Gifts from a host to his guests, used in relation to mosaics to describe the depiction of edible items.

DEITIES DEPICTED IN ROMANO-BRITISH MOSAICS WITH THEIR GREEK ANTECEDENTS

GREEK NAME	ROMAN EQUIVALENT
Aphrodite	Venus
Apollo	Apollo
Ares	Mars
Artemis	Diana
Athene	Minerva
Demeter	Ceres
Dionysus	Bacchus
Eros	Cupid
Gaia or Ge	Tellus
Hera	Juno
Hermes	Mercury
Kronos	Saturn
Persephone	Proserpina
Poseidon	Neptune
Selene	Luna
Zeus	Jupiter

GAZETTEER OF SOME OF THE MAIN SITES AND MUSEUMS WHERE FIGURED MOSAICS CAN BE SEEN

★ indicates a site or museum with a notable figured mosaic or collection.
★★ indicates a site or museum with an outstanding collection of figured mosaics.
Geometric mosaics, whole or fragmentary, can also be seen at most of these sites.

Aldborough Roman Town, near Boroughbridge, North Yorkshire (English Heritage) – Lion mosaic (p.54–5); fragment of Muse with Helicon inscription (pp.61–3). www.english-heritage.org.uk

Roman Baths Museum, Bath, Somerset – Sea beasts (p.97). www.romanbaths.co.uk

★★ Bignor Roman Villa, West Sussex – Attractively situated at the foot of the South Downs, with mosaics of outstanding quality displayed in thatched huts that are themselves of historic interest. Ganymede and 'dancing girls' mosaic (pp.31 and 118); remains of Seasons mosaic including head of Winter (pp.18, 80 and 104); Venus mosaic with cupid-gladiators (pp.104, 106, 139–40 and 148); Medusa and Seasons mosaic (pp.80 and 95); Medusa mosaic in baths (p.94). www.bignorromanvilla.co.uk

★★ Brading Roman Villa, Isle of Wight – Internationally important pavements now displayed in modern visitor centre, including Bacchus mosaic (pp.114 and 150–51); Orpheus mosaic (pp.65 and 80); Seasons mosaic (pp.37, 42, 53, 54, 56, 82, 88–90, 95, 117 and 129–30). www.bradingromanvilla.org.uk

Bristol City Museum – Bear from Withington Orpheus mosaic (pp.69 and 71); reproduction of Thomas Marsh's tracing of the Newton St Loe Orpheus mosaic (pp.71–2). www.bristol-city.gov.uk/museums

Caerleon Roman Fortress Baths, Caerleon, Gwent (Cadw) – Fragment depicting thyrsolonchus (p.116).
www.cadw.wales.gov.uk

National Roman Legion Museum, Caerleon, Gwent – Labyrinth mosaic (p.56).
www.nmgw.ac.uk

★ Chedworth Roman Villa, Gloucestershire (The National Trust) – Set in a beautiful rural location. Seasons mosaic (pp.35-7, 82, 85, 96, 117, 118, and 133–4); Bird and cantharus mosaic (p.103).
www.nationaltrust.org.uk

★★ Corinium Museum, Cirencester, Gloucestershire – Superb museum with major collection including Barton Farm Orpheus mosaic (pp.65-7); Hunting dogs mosaic (pp.96, 129 and 133-34); Seasons mosaic (pp.82, 96 and 117); Hare mosaic (pp.103-04); Venus mosaic from Kingscote (p.140); fragments from Admiral's Walk mosaic including dolphin (p.102).
www.cotswold.gov.uk

★ Colchester Castle Museum, Essex – Sea beasts mosaic; Wrestling Cupids mosaic (pp.41 and 104); fragments of radial mosaic with figures and inscriptions (p.92).
www.colchestermuseums.org.uk

Wiltshire Heritage Museum, Devizes, Wiltshire – Cherhill hunting dog fragment (p.152).
www.wiltshireheritage.org.uk

Colliton Park Town House, Dorchester, Dorset – Fragmentary remains of Seasons mosaic (p.85).
www.romantownhouse.org

★ Dorset County Museum, Dorchester, Dorset – Neptune mosaic from Fordington High Street (p.126); Neptune roundel from Hemsworth (p.126); large fragment with sea beasts from Dewlish (pp.97 and 121); Durngate Street mosaic with snakes and canthari (pp.102-03).
www.dorsetcountymuseum.org

Royal Albert Memorial Museum, Exeter, Devon – Small fragments from legionary emblem showing Pegasus and a capricorn (p.59).
www.exeter.gov.uk

★★ Fishbourne Roman Palace, near Chichester, West Sussex – Extensive and attractive site with reconstructed Roman garden. Its major collection includes the Cupid on dolphin mosaic (pp.18 and 121); Medusa mosaic (p.94); three mosaics with dolphins and fish or shells (p.97); mosaic with bird (p.22). Fishbourne also has an outstanding collection of early geometric mosaics.
www.sussexpast.co.uk

Great Witcombe Roman Villa, near Gloucester (English Heritage) – Sea beasts mosaic (p.97). Note that the mosaic is in a locked room and that access needs to be arranged in advance with English Heritage.
www.english-heritage.org.uk

** Hull and East Riding Museum, Hull – Important and well displayed collection including the Tyche or Muses mosaic from Brantingham (pp.63-4); substantial fragments from the large Horkstow mosaic including the chariot race panel (pp.45-7, 72-3, 84-5, 121, 130 and 146-7); Venus mosaic from Rudston (pp.92, 122, 130, 141 and 148-50); Neptune mosaic from Rudston (p.125); Victorious charioteer mosaic from Rudston (pp.83, 104 and 148).
www.hullcc.gov.uk

Leeds City Museum – Wolf and twins mosaic from Aldborough (p.58).
www.leeds.gov.uk/citymuseum

★ Jewry Wall Museum, Leicester – Panel showing Cyparissus and the stag (p.38); Peacock mosaic (p.106).
www.leicestermuseums.ac.uk

The Collection, Lincoln – Bust of Season (?) (p.135). Note that at the time of writing the museum is closed but is due to reopen in new premises.
www.lincolnshire.gov.uk

★ Littlecote Park, near Hungerford, Berkshire – Restored Orpheus mosaic in the grounds of Littlecote House Hotel (pp.31, 73, 90, 91, 102, 110-11, 132 and 137).
www.warnerleisurehotels.co.uk/hotels/Littlecote-house-hotel

★ British Museum, London – Venus mosaic from Hemsworth (p.141); bust with Chi-Rho from the Hinton St Mary mosaic (p.60); much-restored panel of Bacchus from Leadenhall Street, London (p.112); remains of Bacchus mosaic from Thruxton (pp.82, 108 and 112); Neptune panel from the Withington Orpheus mosaic (p.125). Note that the Peacock panel from Fenchurch Street, London, the remainder of the Hinton St Mary mosaic, and a number of fragments depicting animals and birds from the Withington Orpheus mosaic are held in the British Museum's store.
www.thebritishmuseum.ac.uk

Museum of London, London – Shell mosaic from Bucklersbury(p.143); fragment with female head from Finch Lane; fragment with sea beast from Birchin Lane.
www.museumoflondon.org.uk

★ Lullingstone Roman Villa, Kent (English Heritage) – Large mosaic depicting Europa and the bull plus Seasons with Bellerophon and the Chimaera (pp.29-31, 50, 82 and 106).
www.english-heritage.org.uk

Newport Museum, Gwent – Much-restored Seasons mosaic from Caerwent (pp.87-8, 91 and 115).
www.newport.gov.uk

Museum of Reading, Reading, Berkshire – Small panel with the head of a season from Silchester (p.84). The Museum of Reading also has geometric mosaics from Silchester on display and the remains of the Winds mosaic are in store.
www.museumofreading.org.uk

Salisbury and South Wiltshire Museum, Salisbury, Wiltshire – Dolphins mosaic from Downton (p.101).
www.salisburymuseum.org.uk

Scunthorpe Council Offices, Scunthorpe, Lincolnshire – Much-restored 'Ceres' mosaic from Winterton (p.132-33).
www.northlincs.gov.uk

North Lincolnshire Museum, Scunthorpe, Lincolnshire – Restored Fortuna mosaic from Winterton (p.135).
www.northlincs.gov.uk

Sherborne Castle, Sherborne, Dorset – Apollo and Marsyas mosaic from Lenthay Green (laid in the old dairy, now the tea-room) (p.110).
www.sherbornecastle.com

★ Somerset County Museum, Taunton, Somerset – Dido and Aeneas mosaic from Low Ham (pp.47-9); restored fragment depicting hunters from East Coker (p.153).
www.somerset.gov.uk/museums

★ Verulamium Museum, St Albans, Hertfordshire – Neptune mosaic (p.127); Lion and stag mosaic (p.151); Shell mosaic (p.143); Dolphins mosaic. (p.101).
www.stalbansmuseums.org.uk

City Museum, Winchester, Hampshire – Large fragment with dolphin (pp.100-101); Sparsholt mosaic with scallop shells (p.100).
www.winchester.gov.uk

The Oxfordshire Museum, Woodstock, Oxfordshire – Embroidery of the Bacchus mosaic from Stonesfield (pp.113 and 129).
www.oxfordshire.gov.uk

Museum of South Somerset, Yeovil, Somerset – Dolphins mosaic from Ilchester Mead (p.100).
www.southsomerset.gov.uk

★ Yorkshire Museum, York – Fragment with 'female head' (Bacchus?) (p.114); Sea bull; Seasons mosaic (pp.82-3 and 95); Medusa mosaic from Dalton Parlours (p.94). Note that the last two mosaics are mounted on a staircase and are easily missed as they do not lie on the normal route through the museum.
www.yorkshiremuseum.org.uk

FURTHER READING

Peter Johnson, *Romano-British Mosaics* (Shire Archaeology, 2002) is an inexpensive introduction to the subject. Roger Ling, *Ancient Mosaics* (British Museum Press, 1998) and Katherine M.D. Dunbabin, *Mosaics of the Greek and Roman World* (Cambridge University Press, 1999) are standard texts with brief discussions of mosaics from Roman Britain. A concise history of ancient mosaics is given in the chapter by David Smith in Martin Henig (ed.), *A Handbook of Roman Art* (Phaidon, 1983). Susan Woodford, *Images of Myths in Classical Antiquity* (Cambridge University Press, 2003) is an excellent introduction to iconography suitable for the general reader as well as the specialist.

Anne Rainey, *Mosaics in Roman Britain. A Gazetteer* (David & Charles, 1973) lists and briefly describes all the mosaics, figured and geometric, known to the author at the time. Roger J.A. Wilson, *A Guide to the Roman Remains in Britain* (Constable, Fourth edition 2002) is an invaluable travelling companion written by an author with an interest in mosaics. David S. Neal and Stephen R. Cosh, *Roman Mosaics of Britain, Volume I, Northern Britain* (Illuminata Publishers for the Society of Antiquaries of London, 2002) constitutes the first volume of a detailed, lavishly illustrated corpus of Romano-British mosaics. It has been followed by two other volumes: Stephen R. Cosh and David S. Neal, *Roman Mosaics of Britain, Volume II, South-West Britain* (Illuminata Publishers for the Society of Antiquaries of London, 2005), and David S. Neal and Stephen R. Cosh, *Roman Mosaics of Britain, Volume III, South-East Britain* (The Society of Antiquaries of London, 2009). Publication of the fourth and final volume is anticipated shortly.

Two standard texts by J.M.C. Toynbee include sections on mosaics and remain useful although they are no longer up to date: *Art in Roman Britain* (Phaidon Press for the Society for the Promotion of Roman Studies, 1962) and *Art in Britain under the Romans* (Oxford University Press, 1964).

D.J. Smith, 'The Mosaic Pavements' in A.L.F. Rivet (ed.), *The Roman Villa in Britain* (Routledge & Kegan Paul, 1969), 71-125, is still the main starting point and is particularly useful for its detailed bibliography of villas with mosaics. Another important work by the same author is 'Mythological Figures and Scenes in Romano-British Mosaics' in Julian Munby and Martin Henig (eds), *Roman Life and Art in Britain* (British Archaeological Reports 41 (i), 1977), 105-193.

Roger Ling, 'Mosaics in Roman Britain: Discoveries and Research since 1945', *Britannia* XXVIII (1997), 259-295, not only summarises developments in mosaic studies but also provides a detailed bibliography.

Mosaics are extensively discussed in Martin Henig's many publications, notably *Religion in Roman Britain* (Batsford, 1984); 'Late Roman Mosaics in Britain: Myth and Meaning', *Mosaic* 13 (1986), 13-20; 'Religion and Mosaics in Britain', *Mosaic* 16 (1989), 6-9; *The Art of Roman Britain* (Batsford, 1995); and *The Heirs of King Verica* (Tempus, 2002). Martin Henig and Anthony King (eds), *Pagan Gods and Shrines of the Roman Empire* (Oxford University Committee for Archaeology Monograph No. 8, 1986) contains papers discussing themes on mosaics by E.W. Black ('Christian and Pagan hopes of salvation in Romano-British mosaics') and by Martin Henig ('*Ita intellexit numine inductus tuo*: some personal interpretations of deity in Roman religion').

The most important volumes by the Royal Commission on Historical Monuments (England) for figured mosaics are: *London. Vol. III Roman London* (HMSO, 1928), *The City of York. Vol. I Eburacum. Roman York* (HMSO, 1962), *The County of Dorset* II.3 (South-East) and III.1 (Central) (HMSO, 1970) and *Iron Age & Romano-British Monuments in the Gloucestershire Cotswolds* (HMSO, 1976).

Coverage of mosaics in the *Victoria History of the Counties of England* is not comprehensive and varies in quality.

R.G. Collingwood and R.P. Wright, *The Roman Inscriptions of Britain Vol. II, Fascicule 4* (Alan Sutton, 1992), has a section on mosaics (*RIB* 2448).

Some Romano-British mosaics are listed in *Lexicon Iconographicum Mythologiae Classicae* (Artemis Verlag, Zurich, Munich and Dusseldorf, 1981-1997) under the name of the mythological character portrayed, but a substantial number are not included. J. Lancha, *Mosaïque et culture dans l'occident romain (Ier-Ve s.)* (L'Erma di Bretschneider, Rome, 1997), contains a section on some of the Romano-British mosaics (pp 281-291).

Important antiquarian works in addition to those listed below under individual sites include Sir Richard Colt Hoare, *The Ancient History of Wiltshire, Vol. II, Part II, Roman Aera* (London, 1819-21), 111-126 featuring Littlecote, Pit Meads, Rudge and others; Samuel Lysons, *Reliquiae Britannico-Romanae* I-III (London, 1813-1817) featuring Bignor, Cirencester, Frampton, Horkstow, Littlecote, Withington and Woodchester; and Thomas Morgan, *Romano-British Mosaic Pavements* (London, 1886), covering most of the mosaics then known. William Fowler's engravings of mosaics cover figured pavements from Horkstow, Leicester, Littlecote, Stonesfield, Winterton and York. Most are collected together in *Engravings of the Principal Mosaic Pavements* (Winterton, 1804). The rarer Royal Folio of *Engravings of Mosaic Pavements, Stained Glass, &c.* (1796-1829) is the most comprehensive collection.

Romano-British figured mosaics are discussed in:

A.A. Barrett, 'Knowledge of the Literary Classics in Roman Britain', *Britannia* IX (1978), 307-313

S.R. Cosh, 'Mosaics and Wine', *Mosaic* 30 (2003), 7-11

S.R. Cosh, 'John Lickman (1774-1844)', *Mosaic* 31 (2004), 6-11

Bob Croft (ed.), *Roman Mosaics in Somerset* (Somerset County Council Heritage Service, 2009)

R.P. Hinks, *Catalogue of the Greek Etruscan and Roman Paintings and Mosaics in the British Museum* (British Museum, 1933). (See also Catherine Johns, 'Mosaics from Roman Britain in the British Museum', *Mosaic* 14 (1987), 8-9).

Janet Huskinson, 'Some Pagan Mythological Figures and their Significance in Early Christian Art', *Papers of the British School at Rome* XLII (1974), 68-97

Janet Huskinson, 'Floor Mosaics from Yorkshire' in Boris Ford (ed.), *The Cambridge Cultural History of Britain, Vol. 1, Early Britain* (Cambridge University Press, 1992), 83-86

Roger Ling, 'Further Thoughts on Fourth-Century Mosaics', *Britannia* XII (1981), 292-293

Roger Ling, 'Brading, Brantingham and York: a New Look at Some Fourth-Century Mosaics', *Britannia* XXII (1991), 147-157

Roger Ling, 'Roman Mosaics in Fourth-Century Britain. Classical values in a disintegrating world', *Apollo* CXLIV No. 413 (July 1996), 16-22

Roger Ling, 'Inscriptions on Romano-British Mosaics', *Mosaic* 30 (2003), 14-16

Roger Ling, 'Three Inscriptions on Romano-British Mosaics', in Thomas Ganschow and Matthias Steinhart, *Otium. Festschrift für Volker Michael Strocka* (Remshalden, 2005), 219–222

Roger Ling, 'Inscriptions on Romano-British Mosaics and Wall-Paintings', *Britannia* XXXVIII (2007), 63–91

Thomas Morgan, 'Romano-British Mosaic Pavements', *Journal of the British Archaeological Association* XXXVIII (1882), 291-308

David S. Neal, 'Observations on the Mosaic from Micklegate Bar, York, and the Wolf and Twins Mosaic, Aldborough, N.Yorks.', *Mosaic* 9 (1983), 2-4. (See also Roger Ling, 'Venison and the Wolf Again', *Mosaic* 10 (1984), 17-19).

C. Roach Smith, 'On Roman Tessellated Pavements', *Archaeologia Cantiana* XV (1883), 127-141

D.J. Smith, 'Roman Mosaics in Britain: a Synthesis' in Raffaella Farioli Campanati (ed.), *III Colloquio Internazionale sul Mosaico Antico* II (Edizioni del Girasole, Ravenna, 1984), 357-380

D.J. Smith, *Roman Mosaics at Hull* (Third edition, revised by Martin Foreman, Hull Museums and Art Gallery, 2005)

Reinhard Stupperich, 'A Reconsideration of some Fourth-Century British Mosaics', *Britannia* XI (1980), 289-301

R.J.A. Wilson, 'Two Romano-British Inscriptions Reconsidered', *Mosaic* 31 (2004), 18-22

R.J.A. Wilson, 'Aspects of Iconography in Romano-British Mosaics: the Rudston "Aquatic" Scene and the Brading Astronomer Revisited', *Britannia* XXXVII (2006), 295–336

Patricia Witts, 'Mythological Scenes on Romano-British Mosaics' in Mongi Ennaïfer and Alain Rebourg (eds), *La Mosaïque Gréco-Romaine VII* 2 (Institut National du Patrimoine, Tunis, 1999), 615-622

Patricia Witts, 'Universal Messages. Iconographic similarity between the mosaics of Antioch and Britain', *Mosaic* 28 (2001), 13-17

Patricia Witts, 'Some Unsung Birds of Sussex', *Mosaic* 30 (2003), 17-21

Patricia Witts, 'Nymphs and Shepherds? A re-evaluation of scenes in mosaics from Brading, Frampton and Pitney', *Mosaic* 33 (2006), 17–20

Patricia Witts, 'Gods, Goddesses and Romano-British mosaics: a floor pantheon', *Minerva* Vol. 18, No. 1 (January/February 2007), 25–27

Patricia Witts, '"Excavating" in Archives', *Mosaic* 34 (2007), 14–21

Patricia Witts, *A Guide to the Mosaics in the Corinium Museum* (Cotswold District Council, 2009)

Patricia Witts, 'Mosaic Studies and Souvenirs', in *Proceedings of the XI International AIEMA Mosaic Symposium* (forthcoming)

The Bulletin of the Association for Roman Archaeology Issue 11 (August 2001) is devoted to Romano-British mosaics

Books and articles relating to specific sites include:

Aldborough

Stephen Johnson and David S. Neal, 'The Re-excavation and Study of the Helicon mosaic, Aldborough Roman Town', *Yorkshire Archaeological Journal* 74 (2002), 113-134

Henry Ecroyd Smith, *Reliquiae Isurianae* (London, 1852)

Patricia Witts, 'The Motif below the Muses at Aldborough and its Significance', *Yorkshire Archaeological Society Roman Antiquities Section Bulletin* No. 11 (1994), 10-11

Patricia Witts, 'Hercules at Aldborough? The Lion Mosaic', *Yorkshire Archaeological Society Roman Antiquities Section Bulletin* No. 12 (1995), 17-18

Patricia Witts, 'The Aldborough Wolf and Twins Mosaic: Roman or Victorian?', *Yorkshire Archaeological Society Roman Antiquities Section Bulletin* No. 13 (1996), 18-21

Bath

Stephen Clews, 'A Sea Beasts Mosaic from Aquae Sulis', *Mosaic* 23 (1996), 10-11

Bignor

Stephen R. Cosh, 'Alas poor Terentius, I knew him well! The Bignor inscription reconsidered', *Mosaic* 28 (2001), 4-7

Peter Johnson, 'The Mosaics of Bignor Villa, England: a Gallo-Roman Connection' in Raffaella Farioli Campanati (ed.), *III Colloquio Internazionale sul Mosaico Antico* II (Edizioni del Girasole, Ravenna, 1984), 405-410

Samuel Lysons, 'Account of the Remains of a Roman Villa, discovered at Bignor, in Sussex, in the Years 1811, 1812, 1813, 1814, and 1815', *Archaeologia* XVIII (1817), 203-221

Samuel Lysons, 'Account of further Discoveries of the Remains of a Roman Villa at Bignor in Sussex', *Archaeologia* XIX (1821), 176-177

Bradford on Avon

Mark Corney, *The Roman Villa at Bradford on Avon. The Investigations of 2002* (Ex Libris Press, 2003)

Brading

Anthony Beeson, 'Perseus and Andromeda as lovers. A mosaic panel from Brading and its origins', *Mosaic* 17 (1990), 13-19

Anthony Beeson, 'Achilles on Vectis. A new interpretation of a mosaic panel from Brading, with notes on other Romano-British representations of the subject in mosaic', *Mosaic* 24 (1997), 13-16

Stephen R. Cosh, 'In Praise of the Thrush', *Mosaic* 33 (2006), 14–16

Roger Ling, 'The Iconography of the Brading Mosaics', *Mosaic* 18 (1991), 14-20

John E. Price and F.G. Hilton Price, *A Description of the Remains of Roman Buildings at Morton, near Brading, Isle of Wight* (London, 1881)

Patricia Witts, 'Interpreting the Brading "Abraxas" Mosaic', *Britannia* XXV (1994), 111-117

Patricia Witts, 'The Brading "Dome"', *Mosaic* 28 (2001), 18-19

Patricia Witts, 'The Seasons Mosaic at Brading: Cult, Culture or Calendar?', *Mosaic* 31 (2004), 23-31

Patricia Witts, 'Roman Mosaics at Brading villa', *Minerva* Vol.16, No. 1 (January/February 2005), 30-32

Bramdean

Patricia Witts, 'The Lost Mosaics of Bramdean', *Minerva* Vol.13, No. 6 (November/December 2002), 43-44

Patricia Witts, 'The Lost Mosaics of Bramdean: the Days of the Week and Hercules and Antaeus' in Hélène Morlier (ed.), *La Mosaïque Gréco-Romaine IX* (École Française de Rome, 2005), 235–245

Brantingham

Joan Liversidge, D.J. Smith and I.M. Stead, 'Brantingham Roman Villa: Discoveries in 1962', *Britannia* IV (1973), 84-106

Caerleon

George C. Boon, 'The Mosaic Pavement from Backhall Street, Caerleon', *Bulletin of the Board of Celtic Studies* 19 (1962), 348-354

Roger Ling, 'Mosaics for the Military: the evidence from Caerleon', *Mosaic* 35 (2008), 16–22

David S. Neal, 'The Mosaic from Backhall Street, Caerleon', *Mosaic* 33 (2006), 9–13

David Smith, 'The Labyrinth Mosaic at Caerleon', *Bulletin of the Board of Celtic Studies* 18 (1960), 304-310

J. David Zienkiewicz, *The Legionary Fortress Baths at Caerleon, I. The Buildings* (National Museum of Wales and Cadw, Cardiff, 1986), contains a discussion by George C. Boon of the Backhall Street mosaic.

Caerwent

T. Ashby, A.E. Hudd and A.T. Martin, 'Excavations at Caerwent, Monmouthshire, on the Site of the Romano-British City of *Venta Silurum* in 1901', *Archaeologia* LVIII (1902), 119-152, esp. 140-141

Ilona Jesnick, 'The Caerwent Seasons Mosaic – Perhaps an Orpheus?', *Mosaic* 17 (1990), 7-13

David S. Neal, 'The Caerwent "Seasons" Mosaic', *Mosaic* 32 (2005), 12–14

Chedworth

Philip Bethell, *Chedworth Roman Villa* (The National Trust, 2006)

Roger Goodburn, *The Roman Villa, Chedworth* (The National Trust, 1979)

Cherhill

Peter Johnson, 'The Hunting Dog mosaic of Cherhill, Wiltshire', *Mosaic* 12 (1985), 14-15

Cirencester

Anthony Beeson, 'A Possible Representation of Scylla from Cirencester', *Mosaic* 17 (1990), 19-23

Professor Buckman and C.H. Newmarch, *Illustrations of the Remains of Roman Art in Cirencester* (London, 1850)

Alan McWhirr, 'Cirencester Mosaics', *Mosaic* 4 (1981), 5-7

Alan McWhirr, 'The Dyer Street Orpheus Mosaic Again', *Mosaic* 5 (1981), 17

Alan McWhirr, *Houses in Roman Cirencester* (Cirencester Excavation Committee, 1986), contains reports by David Smith on the mosaics.

W.B. Yapp, 'The Birds of the Corinium Mosaics', *Mosaic* 6 (1982), 19-25

Colchester

Philip Crummy, *Excavations at Lion Walk, Balkerne Lane, and Middleborough, Colchester, Essex* (Colchester Archaeological Report 3, 1984), contains reports by David Neal and David Smith on the mosaics.

Dalton Parlours

Stephen R. Cosh, 'Some Thoughts on the Dalton Parlours Medusa Mosaic', *Mosaic* 32 (2005), 26-27

Stuart Wrathmell and Andrew Nicholson (eds), *Dalton Parlours – Iron Age Settlement and Roman Villa* (Yorkshire Archaeology 3, Wakefield, 1990) contains a report by Neil Cookson on the mosaics.

Dewlish

Stephen R. Cosh, 'A new look at the mosaic in Room 11, Dewlish, Dorset', *Mosaic* 27 (2000), 12-14

W.G. Putnam and Anne Rainey, 'Fourth Interim Report on Excavations at Dewlish Roman Villa, 1972', *Proceedings of the Dorset Natural History and Archaeological Society* 94 (1972), 81-86, contains a report on the apsidal mosaic in room 11.

W.G. Putnam and Anne Rainey, 'Sixth Interim Report on Excavations at Dewlish Roman Villa, 1974', *Proceedings of the Dorset Natural History and Archaeological Society* 96 (1974), 59-62, contains a report on the marine mosaic.

Dorchester (Colliton Park)

John Lowe, *The Roman Town House, Dorchester. Guidebook* (Dorset County Council, 2008)

Downton

P.A. Rahtz, 'A Roman Villa at Downton', *Wiltshire Archaeological and Natural History Magazine* 58 (1963), 303-341, contains a report by David Smith on the dolphins and cantharus mosaic.

Exeter

Paul T. Bidwell, *The Legionary Bath-House and Basilica and Forum at Exeter* (Exeter Archaeological Reports: Vol. I, 1979), contains a report by David Smith on the mosaic fragments.

Fishbourne

Barry Cunliffe, *Fishbourne Roman Palace* (Tempus, 1998), is the latest general account, including many illustrations of the mosaics. Barry Cunliffe, *Excavations at Fishbourne 1961-1969* (Reports of the Research Committee of the Society of Antiquaries of London

Nos XXVI and XXVII, 1971) is the standard work although its discussion of the mosaics is surprisingly brief given their extent and importance.

Frampton

Anthony A. Barrett, 'A Virgilian Scene from the Frampton Roman Villa, Dorset', *Antiquaries Journal* LVII (1977), 312-314

Anthony Beeson, 'The Frampton Trident Bearer', *Mosaic* 27 (2000), 4-7

Stephen R. Cosh, 'A possible Achilles at Frampton', *Mosaic* 23 (1996), 13-15

Martin Henig, 'James Engleheart's Drawing of a Mosaic at Frampton, 1794', *Proceedings of the Dorset Natural History and Archaeological Society* 106 (1984), 143-146

Roger Ling, 'The Bellerophon Mosaic at Frampton: Inscriptions and Programmatic Intent', *Mosaic* 34 (2007), 5-11

Dominic Perring, '"Gnosticism" in Fourth-Century Britain: the Frampton Mosaics Reconsidered', *Britannia* XXXIV (2003), 97-127

Great Witcombe

Samuel Lysons, 'Account of the Remains of a Roman Villa discovered in the Parish of Great Witcombe, in the County of Gloucester', *Archaeologia* XIX (1821), 178-183

Hemsworth

Anthony Beeson, 'A Terracotta Goddess from Agrigento and the Venus of Hemsworth', *Mosaic* 28 (2001), 20-21

G.H. Engleheart, 'The Roman Villa at Hemsworth', *Proceedings of the Dorset Natural History and Antiquarian Field Club* XXX (1909), 1-12

Hinton St Mary

Roy T. Eriksen, 'Syncretistic Symbolism and the Christian Roman Mosaic at Hinton St Mary: a closer reading', *Proceedings of the Dorset Natural History and Archaeological Society* 102 (1980), 43-48

Sam Moorhead, 'An Inspiration for the Hinton St Mary Head of Christ?', *British Museum Magazine* No. 36 (Spring 2000), 22-23

T. Sam N. Moorhead, 'The Hinton St Mary head of Christ and a coin of Magnetius [sic]', in Nina Crummy (ed.), *Image, Craft and the Classical World. Essays in honour of Donald Bailey and Catherine Johns* (Montagnac, 2005), 209-212

K.S. Painter, 'The Roman Site at Hinton St Mary, Dorset', *British Museum Quarterly* XXXII (1967-8), 15-31

Susan Pearce, 'The Hinton St Mary Mosaic Pavement: Christ or Emperor?', *Britannia* XXXIX (2008), 193-218

Richard Reece, 'A Date for Hinton St Mary?', *Mosaic* 2 (1980), 21-22

J.M.C. Toynbee, 'A new Roman Mosaic Pavement found in Dorset', *Journal of Roman Studies* LIV (1964), 7-14

J.M.C. Toynbee, 'The Christian Roman Mosaic, Hinton St Mary, Dorset', *Proceedings of the Dorset Natural History and Archaeological Society* 85 (1963), 116-121

Horkstow

Anthony Beeson, 'The Medallions Mosaic. A new interpretation of the "Painted Ceiling" panel from the Orpheus Hall at Horkstow', *Mosaic* 20 (1993), 7-17

Anthony Beeson, 'The Dipping of Achilles. More thoughts on the Horkstow Medallions Mosaic', *Mosaic* 26 (1999), 6-7

Ilchester Mead

L.C. Hayward, 'Ilchester Mead Roman Villa', *Somerset & Dorset Notes & Queries* XXX (1974), 1-9, contains a report by David Smith on the dolphin mosaic.

Keynsham

Arthur Bulleid and Dom Ethelbert Horne, 'The Roman House at Keynsham, Somerset', *Archaeologia* LXXV (1926), 109-138

Patricia Witts, 'Unearthing the Keynsham Mosaics – "Excavating" in Archives II', *Mosaic* 35 (2008), 5–15

Kingscote

E.J. Swain (ed.), *Excavations: The Chessalls, Kingscote – 1975-1977 Seasons* (Kingscote Archaeological Association, 1978), contains a report by David Smith on the mosaics.

Jane R. Timby, *Excavations at Kingscote and Wycombe, Gloucestershire* (Cotswold Archaeological Trust, 1998), contains a report by David Neal and Stephen Cosh on the mosaics.

Littlecote

J.M.C. Toynbee, 'Apollo, Beasts and Seasons: Some Thoughts on the Littlecote Mosaic', *Britannia* XII (1981), 1-5

Bryn Walters, 'The "Orpheus" mosaic in Littlecote Park, England' in Raffaella Farioli Campanati (ed.), *III Colloquio Internazionale sul Mosaico Antico* II (Edizioni del Girasole, Ravenna, 1984), 433-442

London

John Edward Price, *A Description of the Roman Tessellated Pavement found in Bucklersbury* (London, 1870)

Charles Roach Smith, *Illustrations of Roman London* (London, 1859)

Low Ham

C.A. Ralegh Radford, 'The Roman Villa at Low Ham', *Proceedings of the Somersetshire Archaeological and Natural History Society* XCII (1946), 25-28

C.A. Ralegh Radford, 'The Roman Villa at Low Ham', *Somerset and Dorset Notes and Queries* 25 (1947), 1-6

Lullingstone

G.W. Meates, *The Roman Villa at Lullingstone, Kent. Vol. I: The Site* (Monograph Series of the Kent Archaeological Society No. I, 1979), discusses the mosaics (pp 75-83).

Martin Henig, 'The Lullingstone Mosaic. Art, Religion and Letters in a Fourth Century Villa', *Mosaic* 24 (1997), 4-7

Lydney

William Hiley Bathurst, with C.W. King, *Roman Antiquities at Lydney Park, Gloucestershire* (London, 1879)

R.E.M. Wheeler and T.V. Wheeler, *Report on the Excavation of the Prehistoric, Roman, and Post-Roman Site in Lydney Park, Gloucestershire* (Oxford University Press for the Society of Antiquaries, 1932)

R.P. Wright, 'A Revised Restoration of the Inscription on the Mosaic Pavement found in the Temple at Lydney Park, Gloucestershire', *Britannia* XVI (1985), 248-249

Newton St Loe

Anthony Beeson, 'Orpheus Rising. The quest for the lost mosaics of Newton St Loe', *Minerva* Vol. 6, No. 2 (March/April 1995), 22-26

Anthony Beeson, 'The mosaics of Newton St Loe', *Mosaic* 22 (1995), 20-21

Anthony Beeson and Martin Henig, 'Orpheus and the Newton St Loe Mosaic Pavement in Bristol City Museum', in Laurence Keen (ed.), *'Almost the Richest City', Bristol in the Middle Ages*, The British Archaeological Association Conference Transactions XIX (1997), 1-8

Ilona Jesnick, 'Newton St Loe; Orpheus, Running Animals and the Hunt', *Mosaic* 20 (1993), 18-23

James Russell, 'The Roman Villa at Newton St Loe', *Bristol and Avon Archaeology* 9 (1992), 2-23

G.R. Stanton, 'The Newton St Loe Pavement', *Journal of Roman Studies* XXVI (1936), 43-46

Pitney

Sir Richard Colt Hoare, *The Pitney Pavement discovered by Samuel Hasell Esq. of Littleton, AD 1828, and Illustrated from his Notes* (Frome, 1831 and London, 1832)

Patricia Witts, 'The Lost Mythological Figures Mosaic from Pitney, Somerset', *Journal of the British Archaeological Association* CXLVIII (1995), 1-5

Rudston

David E. Johnston, 'The Rudston Venus: an interpretation', *Mosaic* 14 (1987), 11-17

David E. Johnston, 'The Rudston Venus: a postscript', *Mosaic* 15 (1988), 14-15

I.M. Stead, *Rudston Roman Villa* (Yorkshire Archaeological Society, 1980) contains a report by David Smith on the mosaics.

Patricia Witts, 'The Rudston Small Figures Mosaic', *Mosaic* 26 (1999), 4-5 (reprinted from *ERAS News*, the newsletter of the East Riding Archaeological Society, No. 42, March 1995, 7-11)

R.J.A. Wilson, 'The Rudston Venus Mosaic Revisited: a Spear-bearing Lion?', *Britannia* XXXIV (2003), 288-291

Silchester

Stephen R. Cosh, 'The Seasons Mosaic from Silchester and its architectural context', *Mosaic* 24 (1997), 8-12

Articles by W.H. St John Hope and George E. Fox in *Archaeologia* LV (1896), 215-256; LVI (1899), 229-250; LVII (1901), 229-256; and LVIII (1902), 17-36 refer to and illustrate the figured mosaics.

Stonesfield

Tom Freshwater, Jill Draper, Martin Henig and Sarah Hinds, 'From Stone to Textile: The Bacchus Mosaic at Stonesfield, Oxon., and the Stonesfield Embroidery', *Journal of the British Archaeological Association* 153 (2000), 1-29

Joseph M. Levine, 'The Stonesfield Pavement: Archeology in Augustan England', *Eighteenth-Century Studies* XI, No. 3 (1978), 340-361

M.V. Taylor, 'The Roman Tessellated Pavement at Stonesfield, Oxon.', *Oxoniensia* VI (1941), 1-8

Thruxton

Martin Henig and Grahame Soffe, 'The Thruxton Roman Villa and its Mosaic Pavement', *Journal of the British Archaeological Association* CXLVI (1993), 1-28

Verulamium

R.E.M. Wheeler and T.V. Wheeler, *Verulamium. A Belgic and two Roman Cities* (Reports of the Research Committee of the Society of Antiquaries of London, 1936), describes the excavations in the 1930s. Sheppard Frere, *Verulamium Excavations* Vols I and II (Reports of the Research Committee of the Society of Antiquaries of London Nos XXVIII and XLI, 1972 and 1983) are the standard volumes for the later excavations. Unfortunately there is no separate discussion of the mosaics, as there is for the painted wall-plaster, in Vol. III

Winchester

Stephen R. Cosh, 'The Mosaic from Little Minster Street, Winchester', *Mosaic* 15 (1988), 11-12

Winterton

I.M. Stead, *Excavations at Winterton Roman Villa 1958-1967* (DoE Archaeological Reports No. 9, HMSO, 1976), contains a report by David Smith on the mosaics.

David S. Neal, 'The Winterton Orpheus Mosaic: A Surprise', *Mosaic* 11 (1984), 1-2

Withington

Samuel Lysons, 'An Account of the Remains of several Roman Buildings and other Roman Antiquities discovered in the County of Gloucester', *Archaeologia* XVIII (1817), 112-125, includes a discussion of the Withington mosaics

Woodchester

Samuel Lysons, *An Account of Roman Antiquities discovered at Woodchester in the County of Gloucester* (London, 1797)

D.J. Smith, 'The Villa of Woodchester and its Mosaics', *Mosaic* 9 (1983), 4-7

York

David Brinklow, R.A. Hall, J.R. Magilton and Sara Donaghey, *Coney Street, Aldwark and Clementhorpe, Minor Sites, and Roman Roads* (Council for British Archaeology for the York Archaeological Trust, 1986), contains a report by David Smith on the Aldwark bust.

Stephen R. Cosh and David S. Neal, 'Further thoughts on the Micklegate Bar mosaic', *Mosaic* 23 (1996), 16-17

For thematic studies in which Romano-British mosaics are discussed, see:

Bacchus
Valerie J. Hutchinson, *Bacchus in Roman Britain: The Evidence for his Cult* (British Archaeological
    Reports British Series 151 (i) and (ii), 1986)
Patricia Witts, 'Bacchus on Romano-British Mosaics', *Mosaic* 22 (1995), 15-19

Birds
Stephen R. Cosh, 'Bird Spotting on Romano-British Mosaics, *Mosaic* 36 (2009), 10–17

Circus imagery
Katherine M.D. Dunbabin, 'The Victorious Charioteer on Mosaics and Related
    Monuments', *American Journal of Archaeology* 86 (1982), 65-89
John H. Humphrey, *Roman Circuses* (Batsford, 1986)

Dolphins
David E. Johnston, 'Dolphins in Romano-British Mosaics', *Mosaic* 14 (1987), 18-22

Europa
Odile Wattel-de Croizant, *Les mosaïques représentant le mythe d'Europe (Ier-VIe siècles)* (De
    Boccard, Paris, 1995)

Marsyas
Piers B. Rawson, *The Myth of Marsyas in the Roman Visual Arts. An Iconographic Study*
    (British Archaeological Reports International Series 347, 1987)

Orpheus
Anthony J. Beeson, 'Orpheus Rediscovered', *Minerva* Vol. 5, No. 3 (May/June 1994), 12-15

Ilona Jesnick, 'Animals in the Orpheus Mosaics', *Mosaic* 16 (1989), 9-13
Ilona Jesnick, 'The mannerist depiction in Orpheus mosaics', in Asociación Española del
    Mosaico, *VI Coloquio Internacional sobre Mosaico Antiguo* (Guadalajara, 1994), 333-342
Ilona Jesnick, *The Image of Orpheus in Roman Mosaic* (British Archaeological Reports
    International Series 671, 1997)
D.J. Smith, 'Orpheus Mosaics in Britain' in R. Ginouvès (ed.), *Mosaïque. Recueil d'Hommages
    à Henri Stern* (Editions Recherche sur les civilisations, Paris, 1983), 315-328

Pegasus
Anthony Beeson, 'Pegasus the Wonder Horse and his portrayal on Romano-British
    mosaics', *Mosaic* 23 (1996), 18-23

Seasons
Roger Ling, 'The Seasons in Romano-British Mosaic Pavements', *Britannia* XIV (1983), 13-22
Patricia Witts, 'Seasonal Animals in Romano-British Mosaics', in *Proceedings of the X International
    Colloquium of the International Association for the Study of Ancient Mosaics* (forthcoming)

Venus

Anthony Beeson, 'Venus and the fan', *Mosaic* 22 (1995), 4–14

Women

René Rodgers, 'Woman Underfoot in Life and Art: Female Representations in Fourth-Century Romano-British Mosaics', *Journal of European Archaeology* 3.1 (1995), 177–187

Iconographical aspects are also touched upon in:

Neil Cookson, *Romano-British Mosaics. A reassessment and critique of some notable stylistic affinities* (British Archaeological Reports British Series 135, 1984)
Neil Cookson, 'Mosaics: Myth, Meaning and "Aesthetics"', *Mosaic* 13 (1986), 20–23
Peter Johnson, 'Town Mosaics and Urban Officinae' in Stephen J. Greep (ed.), *Roman Towns: the Wheeler Inheritance* (CBA Research Report 93, 1993), 147–165
David E. Johnston, 'Some possible North African influences in Romano-British mosaics', in Peter Johnson, Roger Ling and David J. Smith (eds), *Fifth International Colloquium on Ancient Mosaics* I (Journal of Roman Archaeology Supplementary Series No. 9, 1994), 295–306

For discussions of the mosaics in their architectural context, see:

Stephen R. Cosh, 'Triconchal Rooms', *Mosaic* 27 (2000), 19–22
Stephen R. Cosh, 'Seasonal Dining Rooms in Romano-British Houses', *Britannia* XXXII (2001), 219–242
Stephen R. Cosh, 'Aquatic Apses', *Mosaic* 33 (2006), 4–8
Simon P. Ellis, 'Classical Reception Rooms in Romano-British Houses', *Britannia* XXVI (1995), 163–178
Dominic Perring, *The Roman House in Britain* (Routledge, 2002)
James Russell, 'The Keynsham Roman Villa and its Hexagonal Triclinia', *Bristol and Avon Archaeology* 4 (1985), 6–12
Sarah Scott, 'An Outline of a New Approach for the Interpretation of Romano-British Mosaics, and some Comments on the Possible Significance of the Orpheus Mosaics of Fourth-Century Roman Britain', *Journal of Theoretical Archaeology* 2 (1991), 29–35
Sarah Scott, 'A Theoretical Framework for the Study of Romano-British Villa Mosaics', in E. Scott (ed.), *Theoretical Roman Archaeology. Worldwide Archaeology Series* 4 (1993), 103–114
Sarah Scott, *Art and Society in Fourth-Century Britain. Villa Mosaics in Context* (Oxford University School of Archaeology Monograph No. 53, 2000)
Patricia Witts, 'Mosaics and Room Function: the Evidence from some Fourth-century Romano-British Villas', *Britannia* XXXI (2000), 291–324

For a wider perspective, Elaine K. Gazda (ed.), *Roman Art in the Private Sphere* (The University of Michigan Press, 1991), contains a number of interesting papers, including 'Signs of Privilege and Pleasure: Roman Domestic Mosaics' by Christine Kondoleon and 'Power, Architecture, and Décor: How the Late Roman Aristocrat Appeared to his Guests' by Simon P. Ellis.

For the design of the mosaics, see Robert Field, *Geometric Patterns from Roman Mosaics* (Tarquin Publications, 1988); David S. Neal, *Roman Mosaics in Britain. An Introduction to their Schemes and a Catalogue of Paintings* (Alan Sutton, 1981); and Susan Tebby, 'Geometric Mosaics of Roman Britain' in Peter Johnson, Roger Ling and David J. Smith (eds), *Fifth International Colloquium on Ancient Mosaics* I (Journal of Roman Archaeology Supplementary Series No. 9, 1994), 273-294

For how mosaics were made, Roger Ling (ed.), *Making Classical Art. Process and Practice* (Tempus, 2000) contains chapters on mosaics by Priscilla Henderson and Roger Ling, plus a chapter by Roger Ling on 'Working Practice' that covers mosaics. Donald Strong and David Brown (eds), *Roman Crafts* (Duckworth, 1976), contains chapters by Frank Sear on 'Wall and Vault Mosaics' and David S. Neal on 'Floor Mosaics'.

The myths illustrated on the mosaics are mentioned in countless texts, but particularly useful sources include Apollodorus, *Bibliotheca*; Hyginus, *Fabulae*; Nonnos, *Dionysiaca*; Ovid, *Amores;* Ovid, *Heroides*; Ovid, *Metamorphoses*; Philostratus, *Imagines*; and Virgil, *Aeneid*. Most are available in the Loeb Classical Library and some have been published by Penguin Classics. *The Myths of Hyginus* have been translated and edited by Mary Grant (University of Kansas Publications, Humanistic Studies, No. 43, Lawrence, 1960). For general background, Pierre Grimal, *The Dictionary of Classical Mythology* (Blackwell Reference, 1986), not only summarises the myths but contains a wealth of references to classical texts. Robert Graves, *The Greek Myths* 1 and 2 (Penguin, 1960), also contains copious references. A recent work is Simon Price and Emily Kearns (eds), *The Oxford Dictionary of Classical Myth and Religion* (Oxford University Press, 2003).

FURTHER RESOURCES

Dr David Smith has donated his archive to the Roman Research Trust. It is housed in the Institute of Classical Studies, London. See Geoffrey B. Waywell, 'The David J. Smith Mosaic Archive at the Institute of Classical Studies', *Mosaic* 26 (1999), 15. For a description of the archive and some of its highlights, see Patricia Witts, 'Romano-British Mosaics – Dr David Smith's Archive' in Daniel Paunier and Christophe Schmidt, *Actes du VIIIème Colloque International pour l'étude de la mosaïque antique et médiévale* Vol. II (Cahiers d'archéologie romande No. 86, Lausanne, 2001), 465-472. For a complete list of all David Smith's publications, including his pioneering work on 'schools', see Patricia Witts, 'Dr David Smith', *Mosaic* 25 (1998), 4-8.

ASPROM (The Association for the Study and Preservation of Roman Mosaics) publishes an annual journal, *Mosaic*, supplemented by newsletters. It also organises two symposia a year. Copies of most back issues of *Mosaic* can be obtained from the Honorary Secretary. (www. asprom.org)

ASPROM is the British branch of AIEMA (l'Association internationale pour l'étude de la mosaïque antique), which organises regular international colloquia. AIEMA periodically publishes extensive Bibliographies listing publications on all aspects of ancient mosaics. (45 rue d'Ulm, 75005 Paris, France. www.archeo.ens.fr/spip.php?rubrique136))

INDEX

References in bold relate to illustrations.

If you are interested in purchasing other books published by The History Press,
or in case you have difficulty finding any of our books in your local bookshop,
you can also place orders directly through our website

www.thehistorypress.co.uk